REWRITING THE CHICANO MOVEMENT

Rewriting the Chicano Movement

New Histories of Mexican American Activism
in the Civil Rights Era

Edited by Mario T. García
and Ellen McCracken

THE UNIVERSITY OF
ARIZONA PRESS
TUCSON

The University of Arizona Press
www.uapress.arizona.edu

ISBN-13: 978-0-8165-4261-1 (hardcover)
ISBN-13: 978-0-8165-4145-4 (paperback)

Cover design by Derek Thornton, Notch Design
Cover image: Protesters with banner march during the Marcha de la Reconquista in Sacramento
© Pedro Arias. Courtesy of the UCLA Chicano Studies Research Center.

Publication of this book is made possible in part by the proceeds of a permanent endowment created
with the assistance of a Challenge Grant from the National Endowment for the Humanities, a federal
agency.

Library of Congress Cataloging-in-Publication Data
Names: García, Mario T., editor. | McCracken, Ellen (Ellen Marie), editor.
Title: Rewriting the Chicano movement : new histories of Mexican American activism in the civil
    rights era / edited by Mario T. García and Ellen McCracken.
Description: Tucson : The University of Arizona Press, 2021. | Includes bibliographical references and
    index.
Identifiers: LCCN 2020046803 | ISBN 9780816542611 (hardcover) | ISBN 9780816541454 (paperback)
Subjects: LCSH: Chicano movement—History.
Classification: LCC E184.M5 R438 2021 | DDC 973/.046872—dc23
LC record available at https://lccn.loc.gov/2020046803

Printed in the United States of America
♾ This paper meets the requirements of ANSI/NISO Z39.48-1992 (Permanence of Paper).

For Luca Amado García

CONTENTS

ACKNOWLEDGMENTS

W E WANT to first thank all of the contributors to this volume for their support and patience in the project. We also want to thank all who participated in the 2018 Sal Castro Memorial Conference on the Emerging Historiography of the Chicano Movement, which laid the foundation for this book. Our gratitude further goes to the many sponsors of the conference held at the University of California, Santa Barbara.

We want to thank Kristen Buckles, who eagerly embraced the project of an edited volume based on some of the papers presented at the conference. Kristen is the epitome of a supportive and encouraging editor. It is a delight to work with her and her colleagues at the University of Arizona Press.

In addition, we want to thank the two anonymous reviewers of the book manuscript for their careful readings and helpful comments.

We also want to acknowledge the work of Yazmín Domínguez, student research assistant for the Sal Castro conferences, whose tireless work helped make the 2018 and 2020 conferences a success. We wish her the best in her future career.

REWRITING THE CHICANO MOVEMENT

INTRODUCTION

The Chicano Movement, Chicano History, and the New American Narrative

MARIO T. GARCÍA

I

"**C**HICANO POWER!** Chicano Power!"

This was the *grito*, or cry, of the Chicano Movement of the late 1960s and 1970s.

It was a call for Chicanos, or Mexican Americans, in the United States to assert their civil rights and ethnic and cultural identity, and for the empowerment of Chicano communities. It was a call by the then second largest minority in the country to receive recognition and respect. Today, of course, Chicanos and other Latinos make up the largest minority in the nation, with some sixty million people and about 20 percent of the total population. Some demographers believe that by 2050 one out of every three Americans will be Latino.[1]

The term "Chicano" has a long and interesting history. It may have been first used by Mexican immigrant workers as early as the 1920s, but its origins are not clear. It was possibly a version of *mexicano* but pronounced *chicano*, perhaps with an indigenous pronunciation. By the 1940s, the term became appropriated by second-generation Mexican Americans, especially the countercultural *pachucos* and zoot-suiters who saw Chicano as a countercultural and rebellious term. Pachucos and zoot-suiters were predominantly urban, in barrios or communities such as East Los Angeles and South El Paso. Pachucos in particular were young

Mexican Americans, both male and female (pachucas), who expressed their alienation from both Anglo-American culture and the Mexican culture of their immigrant parents by developing a street culture of their own. This included an argot, *caló*. Zoot-suiters got their name from wearing the elaborate zoot-suit first worn by young African Americans. Some pachucos were zoot-suiters, depending on whether they could afford to purchase the suit. Both pachucos and zoot-suiters called themselves Chicanos. Young Mexican Americans in the barrios who were neither pachucos nor zoot-suiters also referred to themselves as Chicanos after the 1940s.

In the 1960s, the term Chicano was discovered, or rediscovered, by a new generation—the Chicano Generation. This generation also saw itself as countercultural but in a politicized way. To be a Chicano in the 1960s and 1970s was to be an activist in the Chicano Movement.

The term Chicano is still used today, especially on campuses that have a Chicano Studies program or department, which helps to perpetuate the term even though newer generations of Mexican Americans use the term much less. In its place is the older term "Mexican American," first used by other second-generation U.S.-born Mexicans beginning in the 1930s, and since the 1980s newer terms such as "Hispanic" and "Latino." "Hispanic" originates from government and commercial interests, which desired an umbrella term for all people of Latin American ancestry, including Chicanos, to better market on a national level rather than to fringe markets. "Latino" was invented as a counter-term to "Hispanic" by some who felt that the latter term was too Euro-centric and did not suggest the more mixed ethnic and racial dimensions of Latin Americans. These terms have evolved to be more gender inclusive, such as "Chicana/o," "Chicanx," "Latina/o," and "Latinx."

The Chicano Movement, proudly utilizing the term "Chicano," advanced Latino political power in the country, which has become a reality. Latinos, as some assert, may hold the key to the White House. But this and other achievements have much of their roots in the Chicano Movement. The Chicano Movement was the largest and most expansive civil rights and community empowerment social movement by people of Mexican descent up to the 1960s and 1970s. It was a reaction to the continued poverty and discrimination faced by Mexican Americans and lack of opportunities equal to those of other Americans. The new Chicano Generation was first inspired by the courageous struggles of the farmworkers movement to achieve dignity and union recognition to better their material conditions. Led by César Chávez and Dolores

Huerta, the farmworkers after a five-year strike against the powerful grape growers in the Central Valley of California finally achieved a major victory in 1970 by pressuring the growers to recognize their union, the United Farm Workers (UFW).

With this inspiration, the Chicano Movement surfaced in urban areas, where the majority of Chicanos lived. The movement battled on many political fronts, such as attempting to overcome the legacy of segregated and inferior public schools in the barrios. Unable to convince school administrators to reform the schools, students took the issue into their own hands. In East Los Angeles this led to the "blowouts," or walkouts, by thousands of Chicano students in March of 1968. These students were strongly influenced by a committed and charismatic teacher, Sal Castro, and by key student leaders such as Paula Crisostomo, John Ortíz, Mita Cuarón, Freddy Resendez, Harry Gamboa, Cassandra Zacarias, Bobby Verdugo, and others.

Chicano students on college campuses also began to organize and laid the foundation for a strong and vibrant Chicano student movement. Students called for the recruitment of more Chicano students and for college administrations to relate to Chicano communities. Moreover, inspired by El Plan de Santa Barbara in 1969, which called for the establishment of Chicano Studies programs on the campuses, Chicano students pressured and protested throughout the Southwest for such programs. New departments and research centers are the direct result of the Chicano Movement.

The Chicano Movement also reacted to the U.S. war in Vietnam, especially because funding for social programs in the barrios linked to President Lyndon Johnson's War on Poverty, including job retraining, was being cut to pay for the war. Young Chicanos were also being disproportionately drafted into the military, sent to the war, and suffering high casualties. The Chicano Movement saw the U.S. intervention in Vietnam as an unnecessary and unjust war and protested against it. These protests were highlighted by the National Chicano Moratorium on August 29, 1970, in East Los Angeles when some twenty thousand, mostly Chicanos, protested against the war. The protest was organized by key leaders such as Rosalio Muñoz. Not willing to allow Chicanos to rule the streets of East Los Angeles for even one day, L.A. county sheriffs viciously and unjustly attacked the protestors, resulting in a riot and the killing of three Chicanos, including Ruben Salazar, the most prominent Mexican American journalist in the country. Despite the assault on the moratorium, Chicanos had strongly expressed their opposition to the war.

The Chicano Movement took on a variety of other issues, including police abuse, the plight of undocumented immigrants, the lack of support by the Catholic Church of its Mexican American parishioners, and the lack of Chicano representation in the mass media. Another significant manifestation was a Chicana feminist movement. Young Mexican American women had participated in large numbers in the Chicano Movement but faced sexism there. As a result, many Chicanas, while still pledging loyalty to the movement, began to develop as feminists and to organize as Chicana feminists, through conferences and their own publications. They pressured the movement to accept women as key leaders and to listen to Chicana voices.

One of the other major issues confronted by the Chicano Movement was the lack of effective political representation. For years the two-party system had neglected the Chicano communities. While most Mexican Americans since the 1930s had voted for the Democratic Party, that party had taken them for granted and given little in return, so Chicanos argued. One key movement leader, Rodolfo "Corky" Gonzales, considered the parties a two-headed monster. So Chicanos organized a third party, La Raza Unida Party (RUP). Initially and successfully organized in South Texas communities by key leaders such as José Ángel Gutiérrez, the RUP spread throughout the Southwest. In Denver, Corky Gonzales formed a chapter. In East Los Angeles, Raul Ruiz likewise helped to form chapters of the new party. While the RUP did not win many electoral victories, it placed much pressure on the two national parties to respond to Chicano issues. This was especially the case with the Democratic Party, which began to run Chicano candidates for various offices, initiating the ascendance of Chicanos and other Latinos within the party, an important part of contemporary Latino political power.

Through its confrontational politics, the Chicano Movement forced many reforms that benefitted not only Chicanos but other Latinos as well, such as Puerto Ricans, who had their own movement politics in solidarity with the Chicano Movement. The movement most notably forced educational reforms, including bilingual education and the development of Chicano studies. At the same time, it forced open the doors of institutions of higher education. Many more Chicanos attended college because of the movement. A number of colleges and universities today have been designated Hispanic Serving Institutions (HSI), which means that at least 26 percent of their undergraduate student population is Hispanic. This "browning" of American colleges and universities is one of the greatest achievements of the Chicano Movement. Increased college enrollments have also led to an expansion of the Chicano and Latino middle class, which has increased the number of Chicano/Latino professionals in education, law, medicine, and business. This expanded middle class has become involved in political and community leadership, which has increased Chicano/Latino voting and the number of Chicano/Latino elected officials. Moreover, the Chicano Movement's stress on cultural affirmation has resulted in the increased presence of Chicano/Latino culture and artists in the media, cinema, theater, and other cultural outlets.

II

These profound changes directly and indirectly attributable to the Chicano Movement have led to increased interest in the history of the Chicano Movement. It is not that historians neglected the movement in the post-movement period of the 1980s and 1990s. However, with some exceptions, historians focused on earlier periods in order to better understand the roots of the Chicano experience. This was understandable given the dearth of research in Chicano history as a whole. Moreover, the immediacy of the movement meant historical perspective was lacking.

As a result of this research, publications on Chicano history as a whole have exploded over the last fifty years. This research includes studies of the Spanish conquest of areas that became part of the United States, such as from Texas to California.[2] Others have focused on the Mexican experience after Mexican independence in 1821 and up to the time the United States forced a war on Mexico and conquered its northern frontier—El Norte.[3] The period following the American conquest of what became the American Southwest has also received attention.[4] However, historians have tended to study the twentieth century more, including mass Mexican immigration to the United States during the first three decades of the century. The Great Depression years have likewise received attention, as has World War II, when thousands of Mexican Americans went to war in support of the United States. Finally, the post–World War II era, especially the 1950s, is also beginning to receive attention.[5]

Some pioneering studies on the Chicano Movement also appeared during the last two decades of the twentieth century. These include works by Juan Gómez-Quiñones, Gerald Rosen, Carlos Muñoz, Richard Santillán, Christine Marín, Ignacio García, Ernesto Chávez, and Marguerite Marín. Gómez-Quiñones wrote on the Chicano student movement, as did Carlos Muñoz with a focus on Los Angeles. Gerald Rosen examined the ideology of the movement. One of the best works in this early literature was Ignacio García's history of La Raza Unida Party. Richard Santillán also focused on La Raza Unida Party. Ernesto Chávez and Marguerite Marín, like Muñoz, focused on Los Angeles as a key location by examining manifestations other than the student movement. Finally, Christine Marín wrote one of the first biographies of Corky Gonzales, a key movement leader in Denver.

These early studies are being significantly augmented in the new millennium. There has emerged a renaissance of Chicano Movement studies. Historians and other scholars, many of them younger professors or graduate students, are rediscovering the Chicano Movement. This new generation seems even more aware of how the movement impacted the lives of many Chicanos and other Latinos in the country. They recognize the movement as a seminal event in the long history of Mexican Americans. While they note that there were earlier civil rights and labor rights struggles, they recognize that the Chicano Movement was unprecedented in its size and impact. The Chicano Movement created the new Chicano and Chicana, and by extension the new Latino and Latina. Contemporary Latino political power is the direct result of the movement.

What distinguishes this new historiography is its focus on the diversity of the movement. Earlier views seemed to suggest that the movement was more monolithic and that the cultural nationalism of the movement was adhered to by most activists. Contemporary historians and other students of the movement see much more diversity in all movement aspects. For example, the movement is being studied in a variety of locations and spaces, not just the main centers of the movement such as California and Texas. Now movement history is being excavated in the Pacific Northwest, New Mexico, Arizona, and the Midwest. Also, greater attention is being paid to the role of women in the movement and their key contributions. Studies of new locations and different communities reveal how the movement manifested itself regionally and locally and how it was mobilized around community issues pertinent to that locale. In other words, the Chicano Movement was not only a national movement but a local one. Moreover, beginning with Jorge Mariscal's groundbreaking 2005 book, *Brown-Eyed Children of the Sun*, some scholars revealed how the cultural nationalism of the movement, Chicanismo, was not monolithic. Other ideological influences such as Third World consciousness, Marxism, and feminism also affected the mindset of Chicano activists, and we saw how the four could be combined. As a result of looking at the Chicano Movement in such a diverse way, this new literature is revisionist and critical. It is a rewriting of the Chicano Movement.

This new Chicano Movement history is also impacting our understanding of American history. This adds to the revisionist nature of the new Chicano Movement historiography. I turn to this revisionism in the next three sections.

III

The Chicano Movement is one of the most important periods in Chicano history. It challenged as never before the inferior status of people of Mexican descent within the United States. It challenged the status quo. It challenged the stereotype of Mexican Americans being lazy, passive, and sleepy people. This stereotype was in circulation by at least the mid-twentieth century. Packing boxes in southern California had labels that read: "Lazy Peon Avocados."[6] The image can be seen in film such as the 1942 *Tortilla Flat*, based on the John Steinbeck book. In the early 1950s, the Judy Canova radio show depicted Mexicans through the character of Pedro as a lazy and stupid Mexican.[7] American tourists in border cities such as Ciudad Juárez and Tijuana bought ashtrays and small statues in the form of a sleeping Mexican under a sombrero. In a speech in 1969, Corky Gonzales attacked this stereotype: "Chicanos still are seen as the lazy, sleepy Mexican wrapped in a serape. What they don't realize is that underneath that serape is a machinegun!"[8]

To counter such stereotypes, the movement pointed to Chicanos' long history of opposing racism and exploitation. It affirmed Chicanos' rich cultural heritage, including the Spanish language. It proposed a "new Chicano," a people of color because of their indigenous and mestizo, or mixed, heritage that they should be proud of. "Brown is beautiful," Chicanos proclaimed.

The movement also revised history by noting that Mexican Americans were not a traditional ethnic group resulting from immigration. Yes, many had crossed the border from Mexico, especially in the twentieth century, but this was not true of the first generation of Mexican Americans. That initial generation— the "conquered generation"—was a result of the U.S.-Mexico War of the 1840s, when the United States conquered Mexico's northern lands in a war of expansion. This first generation traced its ancestry to the initial Spanish colonies in that region and the mixing of Spaniards with indigenous people from Texas to California. This generation was already settled in what under U.S. rule became the Southwest. They were not immigrants but a settled population. As a later saying noted, "They did not come to the border, the border came to them." The Chicano Movement recognized and stressed the colonized nature of Chicanos in this history. Chicanos did not commence their experience within the United States as still another immigrant group, but rather as a colonized people. The Chicano Generation referred to this history and condition as "internal colonialism." Hence, the Chicano Movement also represented an anti-colonial struggle. Thus the Chicano Movement linked itself with Third World liberation and anti-colonial movements in Asia, Africa, and especially in Latin America, such as the Cuban Revolution of 1959 led by Fidel Castro and Che Guevara.[9]

As part of challenging the status quo, the Chicano Movement opposed the American capitalist system. It noted that Mexican Americans and Mexican immigrants since the turn of the twentieth century had been exploited as cheap labor in both rural and urban jobs. These were the "Mexican jobs" and "Mexican wages" that characterized the southwestern economy. Mexican workers contributed their blood, sweat, and tears in working for this country, but received very little of the fruits of their labor. Most did not achieve the American Dream.[10]

The Chicano Movement in its revisionist and oppositional interpretation of history stressed that Chicanos were fighting not only class oppression and ethnic and cultural discrimination, but also deep-seated racism. Earlier Mexican American civil rights struggles from the 1930s to the 1960s led by the Mexican American Generation used a "whiteness" strategy to argue that if people of Mexican descent were being recorded in the U.S. Census as "whites," then there was no basis for discrimination and segregation of Mexicans based on race.[11] The Chicano Generation eschewed such a strategy and noted that Mexicans had always been racialized in jobs, wages, housing, and education. The very term Mexican was racialized so that anything Mexican was considered by whites to be inferior. Chicanos emphasized this reality. They also argued that since they were a people of color, they not only needed to be proud of this but to combat racism as a people of color. The concept of racialization was an important recognition by the Chicano Movement and a way of challenging the mythic "melting pot." If there were such a pot, why had Mexicans and Black people, for example, not been melted? It was because of racialization, the movement argued.

Such racialization was nowhere more evident than in education. Since the beginning of mass Mexican immigration to the United States in the early twentieth century, American public schools were established in the barrios. They were referred to as "Mexican schools." These were segregated and inferior schools owing to decisions made by local school boards throughout the Southwest, including in California. They were inferior because they provided limited education with few resources and stressed vocational rather than academic education. Worst of all, teachers, predominantly Anglos, had low expectations of their Mexican American pupils, considering them to be racially inferior. The Chicano Movement took on the legacy of the Mexican schools in a variety of protests to bring attention to the inadequacies of such schools and how they constituted a racialized educational system.[12]

IV

The Chicano Movement, while focused on regaining a Chicano view of history, at the same time revised our views of American history. In doing so, it makes us reflect that the Chicano Movement and Chicano history is American history. It brings attention to the diversity of the American experience. For too long when the term "American" was used, what was important was not who was included but who was excluded. The Chicano Movement and Chicano history responded: "no más!"—no more! This is truer and even more important today based on the demographics and the growth of the Chicano/Latino population. It is even more important today when in California and other states the majority of our K–12 student population is increasingly becoming or already is Latino. How we conceptualize American history and how we teach it is important not only because of the changing nature of American society, but also because an inclusive American history is the academic and intellectual right thing to do. We cannot fully understand American history and culture if we do not take into account all ethnic groups. We are short-changing all of our students, both minority and non-minority, if we don't present and teach an inclusive history. For too long we have had a partial American history. We need the full American history that the Chicano Movement spawned in its conception of Chicano history and the field's implications for our understanding of American history.

The Chicano Movement helped to revise American history in several ways. One involved the basic question—what is the foundation of American history? Most of us have learned that the basis of this history is the thirteen original English colonies and their social and cultural evolution. Colonial religion, for example, is regarded as the origin of an American religious tradition. The same goes for finding the origins of American literature in colonial writings such as diaries and chronicles. The Chicano Movement–inspired history challenges all this. It stresses the Spanish-speaking origins of American history and culture. By the 1600s Spain had established colonies in what would become the United States. This included the future Florida and American Southwest. These Spanish settlements and Catholic missions are also part of American colonial history. They too represent the origins of American history. Franciscan missions are as much a part of the foundation of American religion as the Puritans of the Massachusetts Bay Colony. Spanish colonial diaries and chronicles are also part of the formation of American literature. The Chicano Movement reinserted a south-to-north perspective on the roots of American history.

How do Americans become Americans? We all know the standard answer: America is a nation of immigrants. That is largely but not fully true. American indigenous peoples were not immigrants; they were already here. Imported African slaves were hardly immigrants; they had no choice about coming to America. And then, as the Chicano Movement noted, the first generation of Mexican Americans were not immigrants either. They were already settled in the territories conquered by the United States in the 1840s. The Chicano Movement's rediscovery of the U.S.-Mexico War (1846–48) alerted Chicanos to the importance of this war to Chicano history. The presence of Mexicans in the United States had nothing to do with immigration but rather with Manifest Destiny, American expansionism, and conquest. The Mexican people living in this area became the Conquered Generation in Chicano history; the movement argued that later Mexican Americans, including immigrants, represented a permanent conquered population through the process of internal colonialism. This history reminds us that some groups, including the initial Mexican Americans, became Americans not through the classic immigration story but through conquest and colonization.

After the U.S. conquest, Mexican Americans, having lost much of their properties, and being subjected to American racism, might have become the forgotten Americans if nothing else had happened. What did happen was the beginning of mass immigration from Mexico beginning in the early twentieth century. This became the Immigrant Generation in Chicano history.[13] The Chicano Movement focused on Mexican immigrants, including those of the 1960s and 1970s, as the bearers and cultivators of "authentic" Chicano culture. While the authenticity can be questioned, because U.S.-born Mexican Americans can be said to possess their own "authentic" culture, still the movement romanticized immigrants because of their Spanish-speaking abilities and maintenance of

Mexican cultural traditions. What is important, however, is that the Chicano Movement and early Chicano historians rediscovered this initial mass movement from Mexico. This not only made immigration a central focus of Chicano history, but also began to suggest a revision of American immigrant history. Historians speak of the mass movement of immigrants in the early twentieth century from eastern and southern Europe as the "new immigrants." This designation is meant to differentiate the home countries of these immigrants from earlier locales such as the British Isles, Germany, Ireland, and northern Europe in the nineteenth century. But traditional historians do not integrate mass Mexican immigration into the concept of the "new immigrants," even though Mexican immigrants were entering the United States at the same time as those from Russia, Poland, Italy, and Greece. The Chicano Movement proposed a new imagining of American immigration as taking place not just via the Atlantic crossing, but in mass numbers northward from Mexico into the United States. This new immigration pattern continued into the twentieth century and on into the twenty-first, augmented by Central American migration.

The Chicano Movement, largely through the pioneering work of Carey McWilliams, who in 1948 wrote the first history of what he called the Spanish-speaking people of the United States, likewise discovered the effects of the Great Depression on Mexican Americans.[14] McWilliams may have been the first to discuss the large-scale deportation of Mexicans in the early 1930s under the Herbert Hoover administration. Some blamed Mexicans for the Depression and falsely claimed that they were taking jobs from "real Americans." As a result, the federal government in association with local governments rounded up and deported half a million people of Mexican descent across the border into Mexico. Some were part of a "repatriation" program, which sounds more acceptable than deportation. However, the results were the same. Mexicans were pressured to agree to leave the United States under threat of deportation. The majority, however, should not have been deported because they were U.S. citizens; they were the children of immigrants.[15] This was the largest deportation of any ethnic group in U.S. history to that time. The Chicano Movement promoted a reconsideration of the Great Depression years by introducing the topic of the mass deportation of Mexican Americans. It is unthinkable for historians today to exclude this history when discussing the Great Depression.

By the same token, and again influenced by McWilliams, the Chicano Movement through Chicano historians has brought attention to the role of Mexican Americans and other Latinos (such as Puerto Ricans) in World War

II. As many as half a million Latinos served in the U.S. military during the war, many in combat roles. Many never returned, and those who did were wounded physically or emotionally, usually both. This participation included Mexican American women, who served in various branches of the military. In recognition of their bravery, thirteen Latinos won the Congressional Medal of Honor during the war, the largest number proportionally of any American ethnic group. Until the movement and until Chicano historians brought this fact to public attention, most Americans, including historians, did not recognize the place of Chicanos and other Latinos in the Greatest Generation.[16]

One other area in which the history inspired by the Chicano Movement has helped in revising American history is civil rights. The history of civil rights has largely been a Black-white story. However, Chicano historians have uncovered multiple examples of early Mexican American civil rights struggles, involving organizations such as the League of United Latin American Citizens (LULAC), founded in the 1920s, and the American GI Forum organized after World War II. Prior to the Chicano Movement, Mexican Americans organized civil rights protests and movements against school segregation and discrimination in jobs, wages, restaurants, parks, swimming pools, housing, and even cemeteries. In addition, especially after World War II, Mexican Americans organized to gain effective political representation through increased voting and candidates. Of course, the Chicano Movement itself was a major civil rights movement. So American civil rights history is also a Brown-white history and even a Brown-Black history.[17]

V

In its search for Chicano history, the Chicano Movement spawned the first generation of professionally trained Chicano historians. The movement forced colleges and universities to expand and increase their enrollment of Chicano undergraduates and graduate students. A number entered into history programs and wrote dissertations on Chicano history. Because several acquired their PhDs in or around 1975, I refer to them as the Generation of 75 and more broadly as Chicano Movement–inspired historians. This includes myself, Richard Griswold del Castillo, Alberto Camarillo, Ignacio García, Ricardo Romo, Pedro Castillo, Arnoldo De León, and Gilbert G. González. Earlier pioneers of the Generation of 75 but also movement-inspired historians are Rodolfo Acuña,

Juan Gómez-Quiñones, and Feliciano Rivera. No Chicana historians received their PhDs at this time, but several would later, including Vicki Ruiz and Deena González. This pioneering cohort systematically began to research the different aspects of Chicano history noted above. They contextualized Chicano history, transforming memories and undocumented general knowledge into history by researching it, and most importantly, writing it and publishing it. History is not history until documented, written, and published. Otherwise, it fades as memories fade. By their association with the Chicano Movement, these were revisionist historians who challenged the status quo of American history. They paved the way for subsequent generations of historians to expand the horizons of Chicano history. Although they were generated by the movement, few if any of them focused on the Chicano Movement itself in their initial research. No doubt the movement was too close to them, and the greater need was to document pre-movement periods. And with some exceptions, historians in a second phase, of the last two decades of the twentieth century, also did not research much Chicano Movement history. But as research interests evolved, the ground was laid for a renaissance of studies of the Chicano Movement in the new millennium.

VI

The Chicano Movement was not monolithic. Chicano activists—the Chicano Generation—through the Chicano underground, movement press, and other expressions created an imagined community. However, the movement took place in geographic settings throughout the Southwest, Pacific Northwest, and in the Midwest. Communities expressed and organized the movement in their own ways. At the same time, larger manifestations brought activists together and helped to publicize the movement. The farmworkers' struggle led by such movement icons as César Chávez and Dolores Huerta in many ways launched the Chicano Movement. The grape strike of 1965 is often suggested as the start of the Chicano Movement. The farmworkers' struggle had its own momentum and goals; yet, through its creative use of Mexican ethnic symbols, such as the image of Our Lady of Guadalupe and what some identified as a version of the Mexican eagle on the union's banner, it caught the imagination of many young Chicanos in the cities. Many activists in the Chicano Movement first became involved in the movement through supporting the farmworkers and their grape and lettuce boycotts. These were their baptism into activism. Activists in the urban areas then pivoted to particular urban issues. Still, throughout the intense years of the movement, the farmworkers' struggle always remained a key and inspiring part.[18]

The Chicano student movement also became a key catalyst for the Chicano Movement. As more Chicano students, men and women, entered colleges and universities as a result of movement pressures and affirmative action, they found one another on the campuses. Chicano student organizations sprang up throughout the country. In the spring of 1969 at El Plan de Santa Barbara conference at the University of California, Santa Barbara, Chicano students issued the call for a unified student movement through a new umbrella organization to be called MEChA, or El Movimiento Estudiantil Chicano de Aztlán. Aztlán refers to the original homeland of the Aztecs, which Chicanos asserted was in the Southwest where most Chicanos lived and which they appropriated as their ancestral homeland. Student organizations made a variety of demands, such as the establishment of Chicano Studies departments and programs, student support systems, increased recruitment of Chicano students from the high schools, and the hiring of Chicano professors and administrators. They also supported the farmworkers' struggle through supporting the boycotts against nonunion labor grapes and lettuce. In addition, students became involved in the protests against the Vietnam War as well as the effort to build an independent Chicano political party, La Raza Unida Party. Chicano student activists formed a key part of the Chicano Generation, along with others who became involved in the movement as community activists, such as the Brown Berets.[19]

As part of the Chicano student movement, high school students in the East Los Angeles public schools organized a mass student strike to protest the legacy of the "Mexican schools" and the continued discriminatory conditions that Chicano students still encountered into the 1960s. Inspired by a charismatic and committed teacher, Sal Castro, the students demanded real education that would nurture critical thinking and not just accepting the status quo. They wanted more college-oriented classes and an end to the tracking system that pushed Chicano students into vocational education. They wanted to learn through their minds, not their hands. They insisted on a relevant education that would take into consideration their history and culture as Mexican Americans. They called for Chicano studies and more Mexican American teachers and counselors. They wanted to go to college.

When their efforts and requests were dismissed by school principals, school administrators, and by the school board, the students went on strike in the first week of March 1968. As many as twenty thousand participated, including not only those from the eastside schools, but also schools in other areas of Los Angeles supporting the Chicano students. The strike came to be referred to as the "blowouts," or walkouts. The strike forced the school board to begin negotiations with the students and community leaders to implement reforms. The blowouts initiated an urban Chicano Movement apart from the farmworkers' struggle and made educational justice a major early national protest issue. Students realized they had the power to bring about change, including their own change—a decolonization of the mind.[20]

The student movement especially at the college level led to the establishment of Chicano Studies departments and programs throughout the Southwest and later in other regions. As proposed by the historic El Plan de Santa Barbara in 1969, Chicano Studies was to be seen as a crucial part of the movement on the campuses. Chicano Studies was to link the campuses with the community. To achieve this, the curriculum of Chicano Studies had to be relevant to the community. It had to provide students with knowledge of the Chicano experience to allow them to extend their leadership into the communities. While teaching was emphasized in these programs, so was research. Chicano Studies was to produce new knowledge that would further empower the students and the community.[21] Born of the Chicano Movement, Chicano Studies has seen its greatest accomplishments in producing an immense amount of new knowledge through hundreds if not thousands of books, dissertations, articles, and conference papers on the Chicano experience. The greater challenge today is to integrate this new knowledge in all areas of the humanities and social sciences at the university level and critically into the K–12 curriculum.

One of the most significant manifestations of the Chicano Movement was the Chicano antiwar movement during the U.S. war in Vietnam. Chicanos were disproportionately being drafted into the military, and their casualty rate was also disproportionate to their population size. One study showed that while Chicanos represented 10 percent of the population of the five southwestern states including California, they represented 20 percent of the casualties in Vietnam from these states.[22] Many Chicano families were losing their sons in the war or seeing them return with physical and emotional wounds. In addition, federal programs in education, social services, and job retraining, for example, were being cut back in order to pay for the war. As a result, the Chicano Movement organized against the war. It began by supporting antidraft counseling, but Chicanos soon understood that the best way to end the draft was to end the war. Organized mass marches and rallies began to be held throughout the Southwest.

The antiwar movement further saw the need for a national protest. Taking place on August 29, 1970, in East Los Angeles, it was called a National Moratorium Against the War. Some twenty thousand people, mostly Chicanos, marched against the war, making it the largest protest during the Chicano Movement. The protest was also the largest antiwar protest by any American minority group, including African Americans. In some ways the moratorium represented the apex of the Chicano Movement, but it ended in tragedy. At the mass rally following the march, Los Angeles County Sheriff's deputies entered what is now Ruben Salazar Park and attacked the protestors, who included families and senior Mexican Americans, many of whom had lost loved ones in the war. The rally was destroyed because the police would not allow Chicanos for one day to rule the streets of East L.A. Only the police could do so. Hundreds of sheriffs attacked with billy clubs and shot tear gas projectiles into the crowd. Hundreds were arrested, many injured, and three were killed, including the most prominent Mexican American journalist of his time, Ruben Salazar. Despite this setback, Chicanos continued to oppose a war they considered unjust and unnecessary.[23]

Because Chicanos did not believe that their voices were being heard in Washington or in state capitols and even in local governments, they moved to organize an independent political party that came to be known as La Raza Unida Party (RUP). First successfully organized in small, predominantly Mexican American towns in South Texas such as Crystal City, the RUP movement soon spread throughout the Southwest as party candidates ran for local and state offices. Even if not successful in gaining offices, the RUP effort was important in challenging the dominant two-party system and promoting issues of concern to Chicanos. This effort at a third party was built on the belief that neither the Democratic Party nor the Republican Party cared about the Chicano communities; the parties took Chicano votes but never gave anything back. The RUP furthered the critical assessment of the American system by the Chicano Movement.[24]

Chicanas played major roles in the movement. Although women faced gender discrimination and sexism within the movement, they remained within it and asserted their leadership in many movement activities and struggles. Many women did not refer to themselves as feminists, but they still acted as Chicana feminists. While influenced by the white feminist movement, especially regarding equal rights for women, Chicanas expressed differences with white feminists. These differences came to be known as the triple oppression of Chicanas and other women of color. Triple oppression involved gender, race, and class discrimination. Chicanas were oppressed not only because of their gender but also because of their race as mestizas and their class positions as daughters of working-class families. The Chicana feminist movement saw women organizing their own conferences and rallies, their own organizations, and their own publications, but all within the Chicano Movement. This was their movement also. Hence the roots of contemporary Chicana feminism lie within the Chicano Movement.[25]

These key Chicano Movement manifestations included a major cultural component, which became known as the Chicano Renaissance. The term was first used by Felipe D. Ortego in a 1971 article.[26] The movement inspired many artists, poets, writers, and playwrights to apply their art in support of the movement. They became movement artists. They put aside the mistaken notion that art, at least good and great art, has to be apolitical. All art is political, Chicano artists asserted. It is political because it expresses a worldview within a historical context and is a reaction to that context. Hence, Chicanos made no apologies for being movement artists. Their art, including poster art, murals, poetry, novels, plays, and music, was all influenced by the movement and contributed to the consciousness of the movement.[27]

VII

By 2010 a significant amount of new research on the Chicano Movement was appearing, in publications and conference papers. Four decades after the main years of the movement, scholars, especially younger ones, were rediscovering the movement and its importance in Chicano history. A newer generation moved to explore what lay behind the mystique of the movement. Moreover, as many of the social and political issues addressed by the movement still seemed to exist, researchers sought the roots of these issues and how the movement had taken them on. Finally, the clear emergence of Latino political power in the country is reason for tracing the roots of this power. For these reasons and others, a new scholarship on the Chicano Movement appeared in the second decade of the new millennium.

As a result, I organized a conference on this emerging scholarship to be held at the University of California, Santa Barbara, my home campus. The conference, titled "Chicano Power! A Conference on the Emerging Historiography of the Chicano Movement," was held in February of 2012. Twenty-five participants presented papers on varied aspects of the movement. It was such a fruitful meeting that I decided to continue it in subsequent years with additional scholars. After the death of Sal Castro in 2013, I decided to call the conference the "Sal Castro Memorial Conference on the Emerging Historiography of the Chicano Movement." Because of Sal Castro's major contributions to the movement, especially his inspirational and organizational leadership in the 1968 school "blowouts," I felt that dedicating the conference to him was one way to keep alive his legacy. There have now been five such conferences, in 2012, 2014, 2016, 2018, and 2020. At each the range of presentations has been impressive, exploring varied locations of movement activity beyond key ones such as Los Angeles. Moreover, while some of this new research focuses on the key manifestations noted above, some are exploring aspects not usually highlighted, such as the relationship of the movement to undocumented Mexican immigrants and to organized labor.[28] In addition, some of this new research is expanding the time line of the movement beyond the mid-1970s, where most historians suggest the movement begins to decline, into the 1980s. While most presenters have been historians, some are researching the movement in other disciplines, such as literature, art history, anthropology, political science, and communications. Hence, each conference has had a certain interdisciplinary character. Presenters have come from beyond California and the Southwest, from the East, the Midwest, and the Pacific Northwest, which shows the greater geographic spread of Chicano Studies and those interested in it. Each conference has hosted about twenty-five presenters, including faculty and graduate students and even some undergraduates. There are no concurrent sessions at the conference, so everyone attends the same panels and has the opportunity to engage in the discussions. The conference takes place over two days, and its size allows a sense of community to develop among the participants. Most significant is the renewed attention to the Chicano Movement as a seminal moment in the Chicano experience.[29]

These characteristics were especially notable in the fourth conference in 2018. This was the most interdisciplinary one. It included, for example, several presentations on the Chicano Renaissance, especially the art, such as the mural movement during the Chicano Movement. The papers were unique in their thesis, research, and writing. As a result, we decided to bring together some of the papers in this volume. Papers were selected based on their quality and their significant insights about the movement. Some excellent presentations could not be included because they were part of books in progress or already committed to other publications.

VIII

The essays in *Rewriting the Chicano Movement* showcase some of the new scholarship on the Chicano Movement. This includes the search for new subjects in the movement beyond key historical fugues such as César Chávez, Dolores Huerta, Reies López Tijerina, Rodolfo "Corky" Gonzales, José Ángel Gutiérrez, and Sal Castro. In these essays additional movement leaders emerge. Moreover, they emerge in varied locations not often tied to the movement, such as in California's Central Valley, northern New Mexico, different parts of Texas, and the Midwest. The essays are by a combination of senior scholars and a new generation of young scholars. Above all, the essays acknowledge the centrality and lasting significance of the Chicano Movement to Chicanos and Latinos today. The essays include both those that reflect the more direct political struggles and manifestations of the movement and those that feature the cultural struggles through the Chicano Renaissance. We decided not to separate these two groupings, but rather to integrate them as a way of showing that all of these manifestations were part of one Chicano Movement.

To suggest a longer view of the Chicano Movement through historical precedents, Mario T. García's essay "Precursor of the Chicano Movement: Walkout! The 1936 El Paso School Strike" notes that even before the Chicano Movement, students in El Paso, Texas, used the tactic of a school strike and walkout to air their grievances about the public schools. The 1936 El Paso school strike involved middle-school Mexican American students who struck following the dismissal of their Anglo teacher, who, unlike many teachers in the "Mexican schools," believed that they were capable of receiving serious education. The school strike also revealed key student leadership, especially by young Mexican American women. Putting pressure on school officials and with support from their parents, the students won their five-day strike, and their teacher was reinstated. What is remarkable is that the El Paso strike took place decades before the better-known 1968 school blowouts in East Los Angeles. The El Paso walkout underlines that prior to the Chicano Movement, Mexican Americans—the Mexican American Generation—were already active in civil rights struggles, laying the groundwork and a context for the better-known Chicano Movement.

In her essay "Breaking Barriers for Inclusion: Chicanas Running for Public Office and the Chicana/o Civil Rights Movement in Texas," Tiffany Jasmin González reveals that throughout the state of Texas, Chicanas influenced by the movement vied for leadership in the electoral arena. Many were motivated by the growth of La Raza Unida Party (RUP) in Texas and ran for office under the banner of the RUP or were associated with it. They mostly campaigned for political offices in their home communities in order to assert an authentic form of representation that emanated from the grassroots rather than a leadership selected by the Anglo power structure. Of particular interest in this essay is the mention of Rosie Castro, a political activist in San Antonio, whose twin sons, Julián and Joaquin, influenced by their mother's activism, have gone on to become major political leaders themselves. Julián was elected mayor of San Antonio and later served in the cabinet of President Barack Obama. In 2019, he ran for president of the United States. Joaquin has served in the U.S. House of Representatives from the San Antonio area.

In "La Caravana de la Reconquista: The Brown Berets Contest Memories of Conquest," Omar Valerio-Jiménez presents an innovative discussion of the ideological role that the Brown Berets played in the Chicano Movement. Best known for their militancy in confronting police abuse and in the Chicano antiwar movement, the Berets also attempted to develop critical consciousness among Chicanos and even older Mexican Americans by attempting to revise the history of the Southwest. This is particularly evident in their Caravana de la Reconquista, their sojourn into the Southwest in late 1971 and early 1972. The Berets targeted historical monuments and locations that downplayed, dismissed, or negatively portrayed the Chicano role in history. This form of re-remembering was especially evident when they reached certain cities such as Tucson, Santa Fe, and Brownsville, where the Berets asserted the role of Mexicans in defending themselves against Anglos during and after the U.S.-Mexico War. Their presence there provided a Chicano version of history and in particular a history of racism toward Mexican Americans in the Southwest. It also showed the deep roots of Chicanos in the Southwest as part of the original settlements in the state. One aim of the Chicano Movement was to decolonize the "Mexican American mind" and to develop a new Chicano critical consciousness.

In "From Siqueiros to SPARC: The Historical and Ideological Roots of a Chicana Mural Movement," Juan Pablo Mercado examines the mural renaissance during the Chicano Movement from a longer historical perspective. He situates the work of Chicana muralist Judy Baca in the context of the work of the great Mexican muralist David Alfonso Siquieros, a major influence on the Chicano mural movement. Mercado focuses on the 1930s murals Siquieros did in Los Angeles. The critical and oppositional nature of Siquieros's murals provided the inspiration for Baca and other Chicano muralists to create socially minded murals that challenged the historical status quo as well as how Chicanos were represented or completely left out of history. SPARC is the Social and Public Art Resource Center in Venice, California, founded by Baca in 1976.

As earlier noted, the Chicano antiwar movement was one of the most important and powerful manifestations of the Chicano Movement. However, most attention has been on the antiwar efforts in Los Angeles, the site of the historic National Chicano Moratorium on August 29, 1970. In fact, there were myriad Chicano antiwar demonstrations in a number of other locations in the Southwest. One such site was Houston. The details of this important protest against the war in Vietnam are provided in Jesús Jesse Esparza's essay, "Chale con la Guerra: The Chicano Antiwar Movement in Houston, 1965–1975." Esparza shows that the antiwar movement in this Texas city had a particular history that included Chicano Vietnam veterans (*veteranos*), who provided a key and critical voice against the war. No other minority group had such a major antiwar movement.

Although Los Angeles was a major center of the Chicano Movement, the movement was organized in many locations throughout the Southwest and other regions. One that has not received as much attention is New Mexico. There is a false notion that Mexican Americans in that state who have identified as "Hispanos" did not embrace the term "Chicano" and did not participate in the movement. Some of the new studies of the movement challenge this mistaken view, including the essay by Ellen McCracken, "An Insider's Story of the Chicano Movement: Roque García of Santa Fe." McCracken focuses on the evolution of native New Mexican Roque García, who went from rural poverty to being a high school dropout in Santa Fe and an army veteran, and then in the late 1960s became a Chicano by becoming part of the Chicano Movement. He became active in the Chicano Movement initially and most importantly as a supporter of Reies López Tijerina and his land-grant movement to regain lands in what became New Mexico that Hispanos had lost after the U.S. conquest in the 1840s and afterward. In addition, García represented Santa Fe in the Poor People's Campaign in Washington, D.C., organized by Dr. Martin Luther King

Jr. in the summer of 1968. Back in Santa Fe, García became involved in community struggles to improve the Chicano westside barrio and to bring it effective political representation. McCracken's essay helps to incorporate New Mexico in the discussion of the Chicano Movement.

Veteran scholars Holly Barnet-Sanchez and Tim Drescher in their essay "Taking Chicanoa and Solidarity Murals Seriously" examine the lasting meanings of murals done in Estrada Courts and Ramona Gardens in eastern Los Angeles and in the Mission District in San Francisco during the Chicano Movement. According to the authors, these murals aimed to shape the ideology of the movement, Chicanismo, not just through the actual images but in the medium itself and how the murals were positioned. Here message and medium come together to influence awareness and consciousness.

The 1968 walkouts in the East Los Angeles schools are a pivotal moment in the Chicano Movement. They initiate the urban Chicano Movement, certainly in Los Angeles, and the beginning of a student movement in high schools as well as in colleges. Sal Castro, of course, is the most visible and noted figure of the walkouts. However, many of the students themselves emerged as leaders. One such leader was Mita Cuarón, who is the subject of Andrea Muñoz's essay, "Blowout! The Testimonio of Mita Cuarón and the 1968 East Los Angeles Walkouts." Based on oral history and utilizing the genre of the *testimonio*, or life story narrative, Muñoz explores Cuarón's background (she came from a politically active family), her key role in the blowouts, and her post-movement years. Through this testimonio, Muñoz highlights the leadership role of students in the walkouts and especially the key contributions of young female students such as Mita Cuarón.

In his essay "The Chicano Moving Image on Walls and Media Activism," Michael Anthony Turcios develops an innovative analysis of the visual strategy of motion in Chicano murals. Focusing on the art of Willie Herrón III, Gronk, and David Botello, he argues that the concept of the moving image is an important theoretical framework for studying the unconventional, yet important, historical role of Chicano murals during the movement. He analyzes the televisual and cinematic components of these key Chicano artists.

The Chicano student movement not only represented a new Chicano generation but was very significant in the politics of the movement both on and off campuses. In fact, the student movement was the most widespread part of the movement, because Chicanos began to attend colleges and universities in a critical mass throughout the Southwest and beyond. MEChA student organizations began to appear on most campuses, including those in the Central

Valley of California. Patrick Fontes studies the origins of the Chicano student organizations at Fresno State College in his essay "'We Were in a Foreign Land': The Chicano Movement in Fresno County." Fontes pays particular attention to the Chicano students' struggles to have a voice on campus and, in particular, one in the campus newspaper. This important struggle led to the formation of a Chicano student organization at Fresno State.

IX

Without doubt, there is a renaissance of research on the Chicano Movement. The Sal Castro Memorial conferences clearly reveal this. But this renaissance approaches the movement critically, in many ways rewriting the standard narrative. Hence it is revisionist historiography. This is particularly true of younger scholars, who are rediscovering the importance and vibrancy of the movement. This renewed interest is not a glorification of the movement, but a serious effort to critically understand the full dimensions of it. The movement achieved many reforms as well as empowered the Chicano community. However, there were also faults within the movement: for example, gender discrimination and authoritarian tendencies. The new historiography is well aware of these issues and explores them, but does not use a litmus test to judge the movement. Women battled gender discrimination, yet the Chicano Movement was also *their* movement and they were not going to abandon it. Moreover, a new generation of scholars concerned about continued anti-Latino and anti-immigrant sentiments, especially in the recent past, are also examining the movement to see how it organized around the critical issues in its time, and how these strategies might still be applicable today. Finally, the Chicano Movement as a historical movement may no longer exist, but its spirit lives on. The fight for social justice, for civil rights, for immigrant rights, and for human rights goes on. The Chicano Movement stands as a historical beacon for contemporary struggles and as a testimony that collective struggles can succeed. ¡Sí Se Puede!

NOTES

1.   See Matt Barreto and Gary M. Segura, *Latino America: How America's Most Dynamic Population Is Poised to Transform the Politics of the Nation* (New York: Public Affairs, 2014).

2.   See, for example, Ramón A. Gutiérrez, *When Jesus Came, the Corn Mothers Went Away: Marriage, Sexuality, and Power in New Mexico, 1500–1846* (Stanford, Calif.: Stanford University Press, 1991); Gilbert R. Cruz, *Let There Be Towns: Spanish Municipal Origins in the American Southwest, 1610–1810* (College Station: Texas A&M Press, 1988); Armando Alonso, *Tejano Legacy: Ranches and Settlers in South Texas, 1734–1900* (Albuquerque: University of New Mexico Press, 1998); Lisbeth Haas, *Conquests and Historical Identities in California, 1769–1936* (Berkeley: University of California Press, 1995); Gilberto Miguel Hinojosa, *A Borderlands Town in Transition: Laredo, 1755–1870* (College Station: Texas A&M Press, 1983); Douglas Monroy, *Thrown Among Strangers: The Making of Mexican Culture in Frontier California* (Berkeley: University of California Press, 1990); Gerald E. Poyo and Gilberto M. Hinojosa, eds., *Tejano Origins in Eighteenth-Century San Antonio* (Austin: University of Texas Press, 1990); Omar Valerio-Jiménez, *River of Hope: Forging Identity and Nation on the Rio Grande Borderlands* (Durham, N.C.: Duke University Press, 2013).

3.   See, for example, Andres Tijerina, *Tejanos and Texas Under the Mexican Flag, 1821–1836* (College Station: Texas A&M University Press, 1994); Timothy M. Matovina, *Tejano Religion and Ethnicity: San Antonio, 1821–1860* (Austin: University of Texas Press, 1995); David J. Weber, *The Mexican Frontier, 1821–1846: The American Southwest Under Mexico* (New Haven, Conn.: Yale University Press, 1982); Monroy, *Thrown Among Strangers.*

4.   Rodolfo Acuña, *Occupied America: The Chicano's Struggle for Liberation* (San Francisco: Canfield Press, 1972); David Montejano, *Anglos and Mexicans in the Making of Texas, 1836–1986* (Austin: University of Texas Press, 1987); Alberto Camarillo, *Chicanos in a Changing Society: From Mexican Pueblos to American Barrios in Santa Barbara and Southern California* (Cambridge, Mass.: Harvard University Press, 1979); Arnoldo De León, *The Tejano Community, 1836–1900* (Albuquerque: University of New Mexico Press, 1982); John R. Chávez, *The Lost Land: The Chicano Image of the Southwest* (Albuquerque: University of New Mexico Press, 1984); Richard Griswold del Castillo, *The Los Angeles Barrio, 1850–1890: A Social History* (Berkeley: University of California Press, 1979); Stephen J. Pitti, *The Devil in Silicon Valley: Northern California, Race, and Mexican Americans* (Princeton, N.J.: Princeton University Press, 2003); A. Gabriel Melendez, *So All Is Not Lost: The Politics of Print in Nuevomexicano Communities, 1834–1958* (Albuquerque: University of New Mexico Press, 1997); Robert R. Alvarez, *Familia: Migration and Adaptation in Baja and Alta California, 1800–1975* (Berkeley: University of California Press, 1987); and Sarah Deutsch, *No Separate Refuge: Culture, Class, and Gender on an Anglo-Hispanic Frontier in the American Southwest, 1880–1940* (New York: Oxford University Press, 1987).

5.   For examples of twentieth-century Chicano historiography, see the select following: Mario T. García, *Desert Immigrants: The Mexicans of El Paso, 1880–1920* (New Haven, Conn.: Yale University Press, 1981); Mario T. Garcia, *Mexican Americans: Leadership, Ideology, and Identity, 1930–1960* (New Haven, Conn.: Yale University

Press, 1989); Mario T. García, *The Chicano Generation: Testimonios of the Movement* (Berkeley: University of California Press, 2015); Vicki L. Ruiz, *Cannery Women, Cannery Lives: Mexican Women, Unionization, and the California Food Processing Industry, 1930–1950* (Albuquerque: University of New Mexico Press, 1987); Ricardo Romo, *East Los Angeles: History of a Barrio* (Austin: University of Texas Press, 1983); Edward J. Escobar, *Race, Police, and the Making of a Political Identity: Mexican Americans and the Los Angeles Police Department, 1900–1945* (Berkeley: University of California Press, 1995); Richard A. García, *Rise of the Mexican American Middle Class: San Antonio, 1929–1941* (College Station: Texas A&M University Press, 1991); David G. Gutiérrez, *Walls and Mirrors: Mexican Americans, Mexican Immigrants, and the Politics of Ethnicity* (Berkeley: University of California Press, 1995); Benjamin Márquez, *LULAC: The Evolution of a Mexican American Political Organization* (Austin: University of Texas Press, 1993); Cynthia E. Orozco, *No Mexicans, Women, or Dogs Allowed: The Rise of the Mexican American Civil Rights Movement* (Austin: University of Texas Press, 2009); Guadalupe San Miguel, *"Let All of Them Take Heed": Mexican Americans and the Campaign for Educational Equity in Texas, 1910–1981* (Austin: University of Texas Press, 1987); Zaragoza Vargas, *Labor Rights Are Civil Rights: Mexican American Workers in Twentieth-Century America* (Princeton, N.J.: Princeton University Press, 2005); Emilio Zamora, *The World of the Mexican Worker in Texas* (College Station: Texas A&M University Press, 1993); Carlos Kevin Blanton, *George I. Sánchez,: The Long Fight for Mexican American Integration* (New Haven, Conn.: Yale University Press, 2014); Neil Foley, *The White Scourge: Mexicans, Blacks, and Poor Whites in Texas Cotton Culture* (Austin: University of Texas Press, 1997); Gilbert G. González, *Chicano Education in the Era of Segregation* (Philadelphia: Balch Institution Press, 1990); George J. Sánchez, *Becoming Mexican American: Ethnicity, Culture, and Identity in Chicano Los Angeles, 1900–1945* (New York: Oxford University Press, 1993); Francisco E. Balderrama and Raymond Rodríguez, *Decade of Betrayal: Mexican Repatriation in the 1930s* (Albuquerque: University of New Mexico Press, 1995); Devra Weber, *Dark Sweat, White Gold: California Farm Workers, Cotton, and the New Deal* (Berkeley: University of California Press, 1996); Luis Alvarez, *The Power of the Zoot: Youth Culture and Resistance during World War II* (Berkeley: University of California Press, 2006); Maggie Rivas Rodríguez, ed., *Mexican Americans and World War II* (Austin: University of Texas Press, 2005); Matt García, *A World of Its Own: Race, Labor, and Citrus in the Making of Greater Los Angeles, 1900–1970* (Chapel Hill: University of North Carolina Press, 2001); Gloria E. Arredondo, *Mexican Chicago: Race, Identity, and Nation, 1916–39* (Urbana: University of Illinois Press, 2008); Natalia Molina, *Fit to Be Citizens: Public Health and Race in Los Angeles, 1879–1939* (Berkeley: University of California Press, 2006); Juan R. García, *Mexicans in the Midwest, 1900–1932* (Tucson: University of Arizona Press, 1996); Catherine S. Ramirez, *The Women in the Zoot Suit: Gender, Nationalism, and the Cultural Politics of Memory* (Durham, N.C.: Duke University Press, 2009).

6.   PowerPoint image used in my Introduction to Chicano Studies class. Also, google "Lazy Peon avocados labels" for image.

7. See García, *Mexican Americans*, 215.

8. Personal memory of attending that event.

9. See Acuña, *Occupied America*, which utilized the concept of internal colonialism. An important and influential proponent of internal colonialism was Robert Blauner, *Racial Oppression in America* (New York: Harper & Row, 1972).

10. See, for example, García, *Desert Immigrants*, and Camarillo, *Chicanos in a Changing Society*.

11. See García, *Mexican Americans*.

12. See González, *Chicano Education*; San Miguel, *"Let All of Them Take Heed"*; García, *Desert Immigrants*.

13. See, for example, García, *Desert Immigrants*; Camarillo, *Chicanos in a Changing Society*; Romo, *East Los Angeles*; Gabriela F. Arredondo, *Mexican Chicago: Race, Ethnicity, and Identity, 1916–39* (Chicago: University of Illinois Press, 2007); and Sánchez, *Becoming Mexican American*.

14. Carey McWilliams, *North from Mexico: The Spanish-Speaking People of the United States* (New York: Greenwood Press, 1949). See also McWilliams, Matt S. Meier, and Alma M. García, *North from Mexico: The Spanish-Speaking People of the United States*, 3rd ed. (Santa Barbara, Calif.: Praeger, 2016).

15. Abraham Hoffman, *Unwanted Mexican-Americans in the Great Depression: Repatriation Pressures, 1929–1939* (Tucson: University of Arizona Press, 1974); Balderrama and Rodríguez, *Decade of Betrayal*.

16. See Rivas-Ridríguez, *Mexican Americans and World War II*; Raul Morin, *Among the Valiant: Mexican Americans in World War II and Korea* (Alhambra, Calif.: Borden Publishing, 1966).

17. See, for example, García, *Mexican Americans*; Márquez, *LULAC*; Anthony Quiroz, *Claiming Citizenship: Mexican Americans in Victoria, Texas* (College Station: Texas A&M University Press, 2005).

18. The literature of the farmworkers' movement is voluminous, but, for example, see Richard Griswold del Castillo and Richard A. García, *César Chávez: A Triumph of Spirit* (Norman: University of Oklahoma Press, 1995); Miriam Pawel, *The Union of Their Dreams: Power, Hope, and Struggle in Cesar Chavez's Farm Workers Movement* (New York: Bloomsbury, 2009); Matt García, *From the Jaws of Victory: The Triumph and Tragedy of Cesar Chavez and the Farm Workers Movement* (Berkeley: University of California Press, 2012); Miriam Powell, *The Crusades of Cesar Chavez: A Biography* (New York: Bloomsbury, 2014); Mario T. García, *The Gospel of César Chávez: My Faith In Action* (Lanham, Md.: Sheed and Ward, 2007); Mario T. García, ed., *A Dolores Huerta Reader* (Albuquerque: University of New Mexico Press, 2008).

19. See Carlos Muñoz Jr., *Youth, Identity, Power: The Chicano Movement* (New York: Verso, 1989); Ernesto Chávez, *"Mi Raza Primero!": Nationalism, Identity, and Insurgency in the Chicano Movement in Los Angeles, 1966–1978* (Berkeley: University of California Press, 2002); Mario T. García, *The Chicano Generation: Testimonios of the Movement* (Oakland: University of California Press, 2015); David Montejano, *Quixote's Children: A Local History of the Chicano Movement, 1966–1981* (Austin: University of Texas Press, 2010).

20. See Mario T. García, *Blowout! Sal Castro and the Chicano Struggle for Educational Justice* (Chapel Hill: University of North Carolina Press, 2011).

21. See Chicano Coordinating Council on Higher Education, *El Plan de Santa Barbara: A Chicano Plan for Higher Education* (Oakland, Calif.: La Causa, 1969).

22. See section on Rosalio Muñoz in García, *Chicano Generation*.

23. See Lorena Oropeza, *Raza Si! Guerra No! Chicano Protest and Patriotism During the Vietnam War Era* (Berkeley: University of California Press, 2005); García, *Chicano Generation*.

24. Ignacio García, *United We Win: The Rise and Fall of La Raza Unida Party* (Tucson: Mexican American Studies and Research Center, University of Arizona, 1989); Armando Navarro, *La Raza Unida Party: A Chicano Challenge to the U.S. Two-Party Dictatorship* (Philadelphia: Temple University Press, 2000); Armando Navarro, *The Cristal Experiment: A Chicano Struggle for Community Control* (Madison: University of Wisconsin Press, 1998); José Ángel Gutiérrez, *The Making of a Chicano Militant: Lessons from Cristal* (Madison: University of Wisconsin Press, 1998).

25. Alma A. García, ed., *Chicana Feminist Thought: The Basic Historical Writings* (New York: Routledge, 1997); Maylei Blackwell, *Chicana Power! Contested Histories of Feminism in the Chicano Movement* (Austin: University of Texas Press, 2011); Dionne Espinoza, María Eugenia Cotera, and Maylei Blackwell, eds., *Chicana Movidas: New Narratives of Activism and Feminism in the Movement Era* (Austin: University of Texas Press, 2018).

26. See Felipe de Ortego de Gasca, "The Chicano Renaissance," *Journal of Social Casework*, May 1971.

27. Richard Griswold del Castillo, Teresa McKenna, and Yvonne Yarbro-Bejarano, eds., *Chicano Art: Resistance and Affirmation, 1965–1985* (Los Angeles: Wright Art Gallery, UCLA, 1991).

28. See Jimmy Patino, *Raza Si, Migra No: Chicano Movement Struggles for Immigrant Rights in San Diego* (Chapel Hill: University of North Carolina Press, 2017).

29. For examples of this new historiography, see Mario T. García, ed., *The Chicano Movement: Perspectives from the Twenty-First Century* (New York: Routledge, 2014). The essays included in this volume are based on some of the papers presented at the first conference in 2012. Other studies of the Chicano Movement not already referenced include: Jorge Mariscal, *Brown-Eyed Children of the Sun: Lessons from the Chicano Movement, 1968–1975* (Albuquerque: University of New Mexico Press, 2005); Juan Gómez-Quiñones and Irene Vásquez, *Making Aztlán: Ideology and Culture of the Chicana and Chicano Movement, 1966–1977* (Albuquerque: University of New Mexico Press, 2014); Marc Rodríguez, *Rethinking the Chicano Movement* (New York: Routledge, 2014); Lee Bebout, *Mythohistorical Interventions: The Chicano Movement and Its Legacies* (Minneapolis: University of Minnesota Press, 2011); Mario T. García, ed., *Chicano Liberation Theology: The Writings and Documents of Richard Cruz and Católicos Por La Raza* (Dubuque, Ia.: Kendall/Hunt, 2009); Max Krochmal, *Blue Texas: The Making of a Multiracial Democratic Coalition in the Civil Rights Era* (Chapel Hill: University of North Carolina Press, 2016).

1

PRECURSOR OF THE CHICANO MOVEMENT

Walkout! The 1936 El Paso School Strike

MARIO T. GARCÍA

O VER FIFTY years ago, between ten thousand and twenty thousand students, mostly Chicanos, staged the largest school strike in American history. These were the historic 1968 "blowouts," or walkouts, in Los Angeles. The walkouts predominantly affected the East Los Angeles high schools and middle schools. These protests were part of the Chicano Movement of the late 1960s and 1970s, the largest and most widespread civil rights and empowerment movement by people of Mexican descent in the United States. The protests in the first week of March 1968 were a reaction to a legacy of segregated and inferior education in the Mexican barrios of the Southwest and California. After the turn of the twentieth century, American public schools were established in the barrios when thousands of Mexican immigrants and political refugees crossed the U.S.-Mexico border, driven out of their home country by a lack of economic opportunities and the ravages of the Mexican Revolution of 1910. They were also pulled in by the need for cheap and manageable labor by employers on the U.S. side of the border. Railroads, agribusiness, mining operations, and urban industries welcomed this new infusion of predominantly unskilled labor for their operations. They hired these immigrant workers in "Mexican jobs," the lowliest job categories, and paid them "Mexican wages," the lowest wages in these industries. Class exploitation and racism or racialization combined to position or institutionalize Mexican immigrant labor in a permanent subaltern existence.

To add insult to injury, the children of these immigrants had to attend the infamous inferior "Mexican schools." The public schools never neglected Mexican American children. From day one, especially in urban areas, the public schools appeared in the barrios. But these were segregated schools, hence the term "Mexican schools," and because they were segregated, they were also inferior. These schools were characterized by a limited number of grade levels; limited physical space; overcrowded classrooms; underfunding; a tracking system that stressed vocational education rather than an academic one; and too many Anglo teachers who had low expectations of their Mexican American students. In addition, these schools expressed no appreciation for or sensitivity to Mexican culture and instead applied Americanization programs that among other things punished students for speaking Spanish on school grounds. The Mexican schools and what education they provided were certainly not a panacea to deal with poverty and lack of economic mobility within the barrios. Instead, they served the needs of employers for a continuation of Mexicans as cheap labor. Mexican American children would replace their immigrant parents in unskilled jobs, with perhaps some semiskilled ones as well. The children would learn English, which would allow them to better follow an employer's instructions, and learn enough about U.S. history and culture to be grateful for what they had and not challenge the status quo and the race/class system of the region. These Mexican schools were still operating in 1968 when courageous Mexican American students, now calling themselves Chicanos, and inspired by a charismatic and outspoken Chicano teacher, Sal Castro, dared to take on the legacy of the Mexican schools. They sought educational justice in the form of equal educational opportunities with Anglo students. The blowouts reveal Chicanos making history rather than just being victims of history.[1]

I

But the blowouts were not the first in Chicano history. During the period of what I term the Immigrant Generation in Chicano history, between 1900 and 1930, Mexican immigrant and refugee parents on occasion protested the inadequate conditions in the Mexican schools. The Immigrant Generation refers to the first mass wave of Mexican immigrants into the United States.

I call it the Immigrant Generation because at no later time will immigrants so totally dominate the Mexican experience in the United States, with the exception of northern New Mexico.[2] Protest, however, increased during the period of the Mexican American Generation between the 1930s and the Chicano Movement of the 1960s and 1970s. The Mexican American Generation are, for the most part, the children of the Immigrant Generation, or second-generation Mexican Americans. It is in this period that Mexican American civil rights leaders through new organizations such as the League of United Latin American Citizens (LULAC) and the American GI Forum challenged more directly educational injustice as represented by the Mexican schools that now included segregated and still inferior high schools. In some communities, activists demanded at a minimum the improvement of these schools in terms of physical facilities, including new schools to deal with severe overcrowding, and insisting that these schools be as adequately funded as the Anglo schools. In addition, these civil rights groups went to the courts for relief from school segregation. In 1946 Mexican Americans achieved a major breakthrough when in Orange County in southern California, Mexican American parents filed suit against the school district in federal court in the *Mendez v. Westminster* case. They claimed that the segregation of Mexican American children in the Mexican schools was a violation of California law that did not provide for such segregation, unlike that for blacks, Asians, and Native Americans. It was also a violation, they further claimed, of the Fourteenth Amendment of the U.S. Constitution in that such segregation violated the equal protection clause. The federal court agreed and called for the desegregation of the Orange County schools. Similar legal challenges would follow in Texas. The desegregation of the Mexican schools, however, was slow in coming, and in time, demographic changes, especially the increase in the Mexican population, would complicate desegregation efforts, for example, through busing. Still, the rule of law was clearly now on the side of Mexican Americans.[3]

II

The 1968 East L.A. blowouts are the best known of the walkouts; others would follow throughout the Southwest. However, the walkout in El Paso in 1936 needs to be acknowledged as an early milestone in this long road to educational justice. The 1936 Mexican American student walkouts did not have the larger implications of the later ones, but it is important to acknowledge it as a precursor.

III

The immediate cause of the 1936 walkout is strikingly similar to that of the 1968 walkout. Although the Chicano students in 1968 were prepared to strike if their demand for reforms were not adequately addressed by school officials, they did not have a fixed date for the protest. What triggered the walkouts was the principal at Wilson High School canceling the school play *Barefoot in the Park* on February 29, 1968, because he objected to what he believed was sexually explicit language. The Chicanos in the play reacted by spontaneously walking out of their classes and were joined by other students. This began the wider 1968 blowouts. Similarly, in the El Paso case the walkout occurred in part because of the cancellation of a school play that the Mexican American students in the low seventh grade had been rehearsing with their teacher, Miss Lillian Scott. However, the backdrop to both cancellations was the discriminatory policies in the Mexican schools. Not only did teachers have low expectations of the students, but they saw them as disciplinary problems and hence wished to strictly control them and punish them for any perceived indiscretions. Teachers who were perceived as too "soft" on the students could also pay a price. Mexican American students were seen as part of an unruly Mexican culture that needed to be eradicated in order for them to become good, law-abiding citizens and, indirectly, obedient future workers.[4]

In the El Paso case, the walkouts resulted from disciplinary action taken against some forty lower seventh grade Mexican American students at San Jacinto Elementary School, located at 1216 Olive Street in the southeastern part of the South El Paso barrio. The number of students in one classroom, forty, reveals the overcrowded conditions in the Mexican schools. South El Paso, also referred to as "El Segundo Barrio" by its predominantly Mexican-origin residents, was literally south of the tracks and south of the better-off Anglo-American neighborhoods. South El Paso, which also bordered the Rio Grande River, the boundary between El Paso and the Mexican city of Ciudad Juárez, served as the initial living quarters of arriving Mexican immigrants, especially during the early twentieth century. As an immigrant enclave, it was characterized by poverty and low-skilled Mexican immigrant workers. At the same time, the barrio was also an ethnic community where families came together for survival and adjustment to life in a new American society. Family units were the centerpiece of this adjustment, with community building augmented by Mexican Catholic churches as well as social and cultural organizations. As noted, the various American public schools scattered throughout the barrio were part of this new community.[5] San Jacinto School was named after the town in South Texas where a rebel Anglo Texan army defeated a Mexican army, which led to the independence of Texas in 1836.

The disciplinary action taken one hundred years later against some of the Mexican American students at San Jacinto—an echo of the 1836 defeat of the Mexican army—began when one of the teachers, Miss Elynor Boswell, believed that the students were misbehaving and acting "unruly." Miss Bowell kept them after school as a form of punishment and, in addition, ordered them to report early the next day for further disciplinary action. The after-school discipline occurred on Thursday, May 7. However, this action was challenged by Miss Scott, the homeroom teacher of the low seventh grade who also taught social sciences and geography. When she learned of the punishment, she confronted Miss Boswell and informed her that the students had their final rehearsal after school for their play *Texas Birds and Flowers*, in conjunction with the centennial celebration of Texan independence. They were to perform the play at school the next day not only for the San Jacinto teachers and administrators but for those of the other El Paso schools. The students had been practicing for some time and had done research on Texas birds and flowers. They also had designed their own costumes. and were finishing them. The play had to go on and they needed this one last rehearsal. Miss Scott did not contest that the students had misbehaved, but only requested that their punishment be postponed for the following week. Miss Boswell refused.[6] The students later explained to the *El Paso Herald-Post* that their so-called misbehavior had to do with their prolonged laughter at one of Miss Boswell's jokes. "Once Miss Boswell told us a joke and we didn't laugh," the pupils explained. "She scolded us, so the next time we laughed too long and she kept us after school." The students insisted that they had not misbehaved.[7]

Unable to get Miss Boswell to change her mind and allow the students to rehearse that afternoon after classes, Miss Scott decided to appeal to the principal, Miss Lillian Phillips. "I was certain that my principal would stand back of me in this situation," Scott stated, "because the play was not purely an entertainment proposition. It was the culmination of a six-week activity unit, one of the new curricular phases being tried out in the schools. Teachers from other schools were expected as observers."[8] Scott met with Phillips on either Thursday afternoon or Friday morning, May 8; however, the principal sided with Miss Boswell and told Scott that the students needed to be disciplined. Scott's students were already in their classroom finishing their costumes. However, the principal ordered Scott to go home instead of returning to her classroom. Phillips apparently gave no reason for this. Scott got angry and refused to go home and told the principal that she had done nothing wrong to be sent home. Phillips, in turn, informed the superintendent of schools of what she considered to be Scott's insubordination and informed Scott that she could take up her complaint with the superintendent's office. Mr. Lynn B. Davis, the assistant superintendent of schools and chair of the personnel committee of the school system, on receiving a call from Phillips about the incident, drove to the school and told Scott that her services were no longer needed. Scott had interpreted the principal's order for her to go home as her being fired from her teaching job. Davis confirmed this and also canceled the play.[9] "When [I] returned to the classroom," Scott told the *Herald-Post*, "the children asked me something about the costumes and I told them we were not going to have the play and to put the things away. Several began to cry. I did not dismiss the class." Scott added: "I realize today that I should have let the whole argument go by, given up the rehearsal and costume completion. But I naturally speak out. I was so certain of backing. I wanted to defend my rights. . . . I love those children at San Jacinto and I will hate to leave them."[10] Scott, who had been teaching in El Paso since 1921, told the press that she had few friends north of the tracks. "She has devoted her time and interest to pupils and their families in South El Paso," the *Herald-Post* reported.[11] Davis confirmed that Scott was being removed from San Jacinto and not reassigned to another school and that her contract would be reviewed by the school board. Scott told the press that she would not meet further with Davis since she believed that the decision to dismiss her was final.[12]

This series of events on Thursday afternoon and Friday morning created the conditions for the walkout. When Miss Scott's students learned from her that the play had been canceled and that she was being removed from the school, they spontaneously walked out and at first expressed their discontent in the hallways. Scott remained in her classroom the rest of that day but insisted that she did not dismiss the class, implying that her students had walked out on their own. The students stated that they would not return until Scott was reinstated.[13] The students clearly understood that some of their teachers did have high expectations of them and that some, like Miss Scott, genuinely loved to teach them and respected them and their families. Their support for their teacher indicates that despite the problems of the Mexican schools and their limiting the educational mobility of Mexican American students, some Anglo teachers in these schools believed in their students' ability to learn and progress.

After demonstrating in the hallways, the students went outside the school and demonstrated in support of Miss Scott. As they gathered, additional students from other classes joined the walkout and stayed there for some time. "We're trying to get the other kids in school to walk out," one student said.[14] A reporter who arrived at the scene noted that some one hundred students, both boys and girls, were involved. The *Herald-Post* referred to the demonstration as a "strike" by the students, who yelled out "We want Miss Scott!" Marshall Hail, who reported for the *Herald-Post*, was told by the students: "We're going to stay on strike until they give us back the teacher we love!" He further wrote: "Late yesterday the frenzied pupils surrounded the South Side school building and set up such a din that the whole neighborhood was attracted to the scene." During the demonstration, Miss Scott, according to Hail, sat in her classroom and refused to leave. "I won't be fired," she cried. "Her eyes were red with weeping," Hail observed, "and now and then she buried her dark head in her hands and sobbed bitterly." She refused to discuss the walkout. The students believed that their teacher had been imprisoned in her classroom and demanded her release. "They've locked her up," the students yelled. When Scott heard their shouts and looked out her second-floor window, the students saw her and, according to Hail, burst into tears, as did Miss Scott. Still convinced that Scott was being held against her will, some of the boys tried to batter down a rear door so she could escape. "Unable to get into the building," Hail observed, "some of the pupils found release for their anger by letting the air from tires of nearby automobiles." Moreover, when Miss Boswell, who had punished the students, came out of the building, the students booed her. "Down with Miss Boswell," they yelled. When asked by a reporter about the walkout, Principal Phillips declined to comment.[15]

Later that Friday afternoon, many of the striking students decided to carry their protests to the superintendent's office in downtown El Paso at the Vocational School building. They were led by Berta Díaz de León, one of the female walkout leaders. De León reminds one of key female leaders in the 1968 blowouts, such as Paula Crisóstomo and Mita Cuarón. The *Herald-Post* even compared de León to Joan of Arc: "Berta Diaz de Leon, dark-haired, bright-eyed

Low Seventh pupil, was the 'Joan of Arc' who led San Jacinto School pupils yesterday in a protest against the suspension of their teacher Miss Lillian Scott. The attractive little girl marched to the central school office in the Vocational School Bldg. at the head of her 40 Low Seventh classmates. 'We love Miss Scott and we want her back,' Berta proclaimed. 'She always treats us so nice.' 'You bet!' shouted out another student, Fernando Sotelo. 'We've got 200 students on strike,' he asserted, 'and we won't go back until Miss Scott comes back!'"[16]

At the school office, the students met with Dr. M. E. Broom, assistant school superintendent, who told them that they could still perform their play. However, this was countermanded by Superintendent Davis, who reiterated his cancellation of the play. The students also asked to speak to Miss Scott, but this request was denied by school officials. "They wouldn't let us speak to Miss Scott," one of the students, Carmen Avila, told a reporter.[17]

Rebuffed by school administrators, the students marched back to their school and continued their demonstration outside of the building, demanding that Scott be reinstated. Police were called, presumably by the principal, to disperse the protesting students. After the students left, the principal arranged for a special watchman to patrol the building to ensure that no students entered after school hours. Miss Scott, herself, had finally left later that day. The walkout received media attention by reporters from both the *Herald-Post* and the *El Paso Times*. In its Friday afternoon edition, the *Herald-Post* published a photo of the striking students and one of Berta Díaz de León.[18]

That afternoon the *Herald-Post* also printed a letter from one of the striking students, Carmen Avila, who wished to make it clear that the students had decided on their own to walk out in protest. "Miss Lillian Scott . . . was not responsible for the strike which we the pupils of San Jacinto School started," Avila wrote. "We love Miss Scott and we are trying to get her back as a teacher for our school." She denied that Scott had dismissed them from class. "I am only one of the many pupils that are on strike," Avila added, "and am writing this because I was a witness of the money spent, the time spent and the sacrifice that Miss Scott has done for us."[19]

The weekend arrived, but with rumors that many of the students would continue their strike on Monday. Undoubtedly, the students consulted with one another over the weekend and plotted their strategy for the following week. In the meantime, the administration announced that Miss Scott would not be dismissed from the school district, but, instead, would be transferred to Lincoln Park School in East El Paso. Her classes at San Jacinto would be taught

by Mrs. Helen Witholder from Lincoln Park. School board president Dr. E. J.
Cummins told the press: "We expect all students to return to their classes [on
Monday] and no further trouble is anticipated."[20] Moreover, *El Continental*, the
major Spanish-language newspaper in El Paso, provided its first coverage of the
walkout and gave the walkout its proper ethnic dimension by emphasizing that
all of the striking students, two hundred, were of Mexican origin.[21]

Monday morning the students' strategy became clear. They would not return
to school until Scott was reinstated. According to the *Herald-Post*, one hundred
striking students led by Berta Díaz de León arrived at San Jacinto at eight
o'clock that morning and, rather than go into the school as the administration
expected, instead protested in front of it. Police arrived when a reporter noted
that the students "demonstrated noisily." School board president Cummins and
Principal Phillips approached the students and pleaded with them to return to
classes. Most students refused; the few who obeyed were met with taunts and
jeers by the others, who called out, "We want Miss Scott." Cummins, when
asked by a reporter if the striking students would be punished, attempted to
defuse the issue by stating that no action would be taken against the students.
He stated: "I believe the worst of the strike is over. . . . The pupils will realize
they are harming themselves and will return to school." He suggested that the
majority of the students wanted to return, but "a few ringleaders are keeping
the issue hot."[22]

Intent on not returning to school, the students instead left the campus and
proceeded to march into the downtown business district. As they marched, they
encountered Cummins again on a street corner, where he pleaded with them to
return to their classes. "This is no way to act," he told them, no doubt surprised
by this defiance by Mexican American students whom he and other school
board members likely considered passive. The racialized stereotype of the "lazy,
sleeping Mexican" was being subverted by striking Chicano students, which is
why both in 1936 and 1968 school officials and Anglos in general were stunned
by the students' actions.

When Cummins told the students, "You ought to be ashamed of yourselves,"
they shouted back, "We want Miss Scott."

"The taxpayers spend a lot of money giving you an education," Cummins
responded, perhaps forgetting that the parents of the students were also taxpayers. "You ought to appreciate that."

"Will Miss Boswell stay at San Jacinto," one student, Hortensia González,
asked Cummins.

When Cummins said "yes," the students booed him. "Then we won't go back," they told the school board president. "We want Miss Scott. We don't like Miss Boswell."[23]

The students left Cummins and continued their protest march, or what the *Herald-Post* referred to as a "noisy parade," on the downtown sidewalks, no doubt startling business owners and others. The paper reported that seventy-five students participated in the march, although the newspaper patronizingly referred to them as "children." They carried banners that they had made over the weekend painted with red crayon, chalk, and ink, saying, "No Scott, No School." "One husky-lunged youngster," the *Herald-Post* noted, "carried the back of a writing tablet nailed to a stick, and inscribed—'Down with Miss Boswell.'" In addition, Berta Díaz de León waved her arms and led the students in a cheer, "Hurrah for Miss Scott!" As the students marched, police monitored them to make sure they did not spill over into the streets. According to the *Herald-Post*, the students "razzed" the police good naturedly, while the officers "answered the jibes cheerfully but told the children to 'keep moving.'"[24]

After demonstrating downtown, the students returned to the school, where they held another rally demanding that Miss Scott be reinstated. They also agreed to hold a meeting that afternoon at the home of Berta Díaz de León to discuss whether they would return to class on Tuesday or continue their strike.[25] Their reasons for going on strike were further conveyed on Monday afternoon when the *Herald-Post* published a front-page essay written by Vicente Mendoza, one of the strikers, entitled "Why We Love Miss Lillian Scott." Mendoza wrote:

> Miss Scott is a person who has given all her life to her job. That is to teach her children. She will get anybody to do as she says with few and kind words. She never whips a student until she has spoken to him about 10 times in a nice way, making him see the right thing because she has more patience with children than any mother has.
>
> She very seldom scolds a child and still you can go into her room and see everybody working as hard as they can, and if a pin drops it can be heard.
>
> Most of the teachers leave school a few minutes after 3 p.m. every day, while she gets home at 5 p.m. every day. She will spend her Sunday afternoon and evening until 10 p.m. working in the school, so she can make the room comfortable for her children.

Half of her salary is spent on us. She is always buying new books for us. She spends her money on picnics, hikes, balls, and all kinds of pretty things for us so that we will be happy and enjoy school.

There aren't many teachers like our dear Miss Scott and why should she be taken away from us? All of her students cried and walked out of the school. She didn't tell us anything about striking.

We were so mad and sad that we thought that was the only way to getting her back, because they won't even let us talk to her.

Oh, if we had known that we were to lose our teacher, we would have much rather taken 10 punishments than to see ourselves without her.

We hope our superintendent and our principal will see the matter over again and in the right way.

Because school will not mean much to us without our dear Miss Scott.[26]

IV

Although the Mexican American students took the initiative in the walkouts, their parents were also involved. After the children had made their decision to go on strike, the parents followed in support. The same occurred in the 1968 blowouts. In 1968, the parents helped to form the Educational Issues Coordinating Committee that negotiated the student demands for school reforms with school officials. In the El Paso case, some parents first showed their support by keeping their children from school on that Friday and Monday. On Monday, Principal Phillips told a reporter that sixty-four students were absent that day, including forty strikers and the rest for various excused reasons.[27] Likely the excused students included some deliberately kept at home by their parents. In addition, parents met Monday evening at the home of Francisco de León, the father of Berta, who lived at 106 Noble Street. Even those parents whose children were not striking agreed to keep their children at home. Secondly, they expressed concerns that school officials would retaliate against the walkout students. Mr. De León told a reporter that he would personally talk to Phillips about this concern. "I want to be sure that there will be no revengeful action taken against the students," he said. Thirdly, the parents agreed to sign and circulate a petition that called for Miss Scott to be reinstated at San Jacinto.[28]

Finally, they agreed to petition the school board to remove Phillips as principal because of her lack of support not only for the students, but for the parents. They charged that Phillips was "out of accord with all of us, parents of San Jacinto School children." In particular, the parents pointed out that Phillips had, for all practical purposes, disbanded the PTA, because she refused to meet with the parents in the evening. Apparently, the principal wanted the meetings in the afternoons, which conflicted with the work schedules of the working-class parents. The parents reported that Phillips had told them that she "had no time to lose with us at night in that respect." They noted that the previous principal, Mrs. Olga Pool Wilson, had met with the PTA in the evenings. In their petition, the parents requested the school board to reassign Mrs. Wilson as principal or someone else if not Wilson. The parents announced that they already had acquired 150 signatures in support of reinstating Scott and removing Phillips and expected at least a thousand signatures in total.[29]

In an editorial later that week, *El Continental* supported the parents and criticized school board president Cummins in particular for saying that he supported the concept of PTAs and yet had allowed Phillips to terminate the PTA at San Jacinto. The newspaper also observed that Mexican American children represented the majority of students in the El Paso schools and that the school district financially benefited from these numbers since state education funds were based on school enrollments. Yet at the same time, the newspaper noted, the southside schools were not receiving the majority of these funds, especially to upgrade facilities, which were in miserable condition. "It is time to do what is right and honorable and not on the basis of prejudice and politics," the paper concluded.[30]

V

With the students willing to extend the strike and with parents in support, school administrators blinked and agreed to carry out the following changes: (1) the school board and Principal Phillips reiterated that no punishment would be given to the striking students; (2) Miss Scott would return to San Jacinto the following fall and would be the homeroom teacher for the striking students; and (3) Phillips agreed to hold PTA meetings in the evenings to accommodate the parents.[31] In addition, students were encouraged to return to classes in a letter to them from Miss Scott. On Tuesday morning as students gathered at the school, Mr. Martin S. Rojas, one of the parents, read the letter that he had received from

Scott. "I appreciate more than I can tell the things you have tried to do for me," she wrote. "I want you boys and girls to do things in the best way—the peaceful way. The one thing I ask you to do for me and which will make me happier than anything else, is that you go back to school and show everyone what fine children you are." The students cheered.[32] While Scott's letter was important in helping to end the strike, the students had already made that decision when they met at Berta Díaz de León's home on Monday afternoon. They had by then learned of the concessions by school officials. This is how the *Herald-Post* described the meeting:

> Pretty, dark-eyed Berta Diaz de Leon, 12-year-old San Jacinto School student, ended the student strike with a short speech to striking students on the front porch of her home yesterday.
>
> Facing the group of howling, cheering students Berta raised her hand for silence.
>
> "All of you be quiet a minute," she commanded.
>
> The children obeyed.
>
> "Do you want to go back to school tomorrow?" she asked. "Now don't answer me yet. I want to say something.
>
> "Miss Phillips has told me that we can come back to school and she will not attempt any revenge for the strike.
>
> "Our parents have talked to Miss Scott and she says she is happy at Lincoln Park because school officials told her she could return to San Jacinto in September.
>
> "Miss Phillips says we are going to have a high seventh grade next fall and that Miss Scott would be the teacher.
>
> "Now, do you want to go back to school?
>
> Students looked at each other bashfully. One girl timidly said "yes."
>
> Another said she would go back to class. A boy shouted: "Let's go back."
>
> The children broke into cheering as one after another agreed to end the strike. They slapped each other on the back and laughed. The strike was over.[33]

The students affirmed their decision to return to school after they heard Miss Scott's letter the next day. In fact, when Principal Phillips appeared at the front door, she was given an ovation by the students. They walked into the building and went to their classroom. Still, a symbol of their struggle remained as a banner on top of the school flagpole. It read "We want Scott!"[34]

One parent, Mr. Rojas, who acted alone without the support of the other parents, circulated a resolution that urged the students to return to school and criticized their actions. The resolution stated that while the goals of the students to support their teacher were laudable, their tactics were misguided. It urged the students to return to their classes and allow their parents to take up the battle for them. The resolution had been prepared by liberal attorney W. H. Fryer, who had also met with the students and advised them to return to school.[35]

Although the students were pleased with the school concessions, they vowed to continue their effort to ensure that Miss Scott returned to San Jacinto. One student, Ida Peña, wrote a letter to the *Herald-Post* that appeared on the day the strike ended. She reiterated the love of the students for Scott and all of the support she gave them. Peña observed that even in the short run the students were going to suffer by being deprived of Scott's presence. "Now, not only Miss Scott is going to suffer," she wrote, "but so are we students which love her, just like a mother." Peña vowed that the students would keep demanding Scott's reinstatement even if in the end it was in vain. "We are asking the School Board as well as the people around our community to co-operate with us," she concluded, "and help win Miss Scott back to San Jacinto School."[36]

As for the parents, they criticized Mr. Rojas for siding with Principal Phillips, and those who had been meeting at the home of Mr. De León announced that they would continue their petition drive to make sure that Miss Scott was transferred back to San Jacinto and that Miss Phillips be removed as principal.[37] It is not clear how long the parents kept this movement alive, but they and their children had made it very clear that the Mexican American community would insist that the schools meet the needs of their community and be responsive to it. The 1936 strike ended, but it had made history—Chicano history.

VI

The 1936 El Paso walkout reflects larger issues concerning social justice and Mexicans throughout the border region and the Southwest. Mexicans were prized for one essential characteristic—cheap labor. Mexican immigrants were enticed across the border and contracted to work by the railroads, the mining industry, agribusiness, construction companies, and a myriad of other employers who hungered for this cheap labor source from Mexico that would bring them large profits. This relationship was established and institutionalized on a large scale in the early twentieth century. It continued throughout the century and exists even to this day. The public educational system, directly and indirectly, was organized in El Paso and elsewhere to reflect this relationship. To justify the exploitation of Mexican cheap labor, employers and others participated in the racialization of Mexicans, promoting the notion that to be Mexican was to be racially inferior—the sleepy, lazy, and passive Mexican. The public schools integrated this racialization. Mexican American students were seen as racially and mentally inferior to Anglo children and hence were provided with only limited and inferior education, with the intent, consciously or unconsciously, to augment the cheap labor force. Consequently, teachers had low expectations of their Mexican American students.

Although this essay does not analyze the particular pedagogical conditions in the San Jacinto School, its backdrop is the Mexican school syndrome. The walkouts revealed the patriarchal nature of the schools. Mexican American students were perceived to be undisciplined and disorderly and therefore had to be strictly monitored and controlled. To their credit, the students reacted to this by protesting when their play and their teacher were taken away from them. The 1936 student strike reflects a dialectic in the Mexican school structure. The schools could not control everything. For one, the figure of Miss Scott suggests that there were some teachers who had higher expectations of their students and who instead of approaching them as problems saw them as students with potential who needed love and encouragement. The students responded to this by their love and support for her. Hence, the dialectic includes the agency of the students themselves. They were not simply pawns in the schools. They desired an education and recognized those teachers who supported this and those who did not. Their strike and the changes that they achieved through this tactic empowered them and perhaps made them cognizant that they were not the problems; the schools were.

The 1936 walkouts show that the Mexican schools were early battlegrounds for later and more conflictive conditions. The strike further demonstrates that many Mexican parents were not passive about their children's education. They desired the best education for them and wanted to participate in that education by having community input into the schools. Education remains a battleground today. What we can take away from the historic 1936 strike is that Mexican Americans, Chicanos, and other Latinos have never been passive about educational opportunities, recognizing them as pathways out of poverty and marginalization. Knowing about the 1936 strike and other struggles for educational justice such as the 1968 blowouts is crucial in empowering us, our children, and students with the critical consciousness that educational justice can be achieved through nonviolent grassroots struggles—¡Sí Se Puede!

NOTES

1. See Mario T. García, *Desert Immigrants: The Mexicans of El Paso, 1880–1920* (New Haven, Conn.: Yale University Press, 1981) and Mario T. García and Sal Castro, *Blowout! Sal Castro and the Chicano Struggle for Educational Justice* (Chapel Hill: University of North Carolina Press, 2011).

2. For some sources on the Immigrant Generation, see García, *Desert Immigrants*; Alberto Camarillo, *Chicanos in a Changing Society: From Mexican Pueblos to American Barrios in Santa Barbara and Southern California* (Cambridge, Mass.: Harvard University Press, 1979); Ricardo Romo, *East Los Angeles: History of a Barrio* (Austin: University of Texas Press, 1983); George J. Sánchez, *Becoming Mexican American: Ethnicity, Culture, and Identity in Chicano Los Angeles, 1900–1945* (New York: Oxford University Press, 1993).

3. Mario T. García, *Mexican Americans: Leadership, Ideology, and Identity, 1930–1960* (New Haven, Conn.: Yale University Press, 1998); Charles M. Wollenberg, *All Deliberate Speed: Segregation and Exclusion in California Schools, 1855–1975* (Berkeley: University of California Press, 1976).

4. For the El Paso background, see García, *Desert Immigrants*, and Monica Perales, *Smeltertown: Making and Remembering a Southwest Border Community* (Chapel Hill: University of North Carolina Press, 2010).

5. See García, *Desert Immigrants*, 110–26.

6. *El Paso Herald-Post*, May 8, 1936, 1.

7. *El Paso Herald-Post*, May 9, 1936.

8. *El Paso Herald-Post*, May 9, 1936, 2.

9. *El Paso Herald-Post*, May 9, 1936, 1–2.

10. *El Paso Herald-Post*, May 9, 1936, 1–2.

11. *El Paso Herald-Post*, May 9, 1936, 1–2.

12. *El Paso Herald-Post*, May 9, 1936, 1–2.

13. *El Paso Herald-Post*, May 9, 1936, 1–2.

14. *El Paso Herald-Post*, May 8, 1936, 1.

15. *El Paso Herald-Post*, May 9, 1936. All quotations are from May 9.

16. *El Paso Herald-Post*, May 9, 1936.

17. *El Paso Herald-Post*, May 9, 1936.

18. *El Paso Herald-Post*, May 9, 1936.

19. *El Paso Herald-Post*, May 9, 1936, 1–2.

20. *El Paso Times*, May 11, 1936.

21. *El Continental*, May 10, 1936, 1.

22. *El Paso Herald-Post*, May 11, 1936.
23. *El Paso Herald-Post*, May 11, 1936.
24. *El Paso Herald-Post*, May 11, 1936.
25. *El Paso Herald-Post*, May 11, 1936.
26. *El Paso Herald-Post*, May 11, 1936.
27. *El Paso Herald-Post*, May 11, 1936.
28. *El Paso Herald-Post*, May 12, 1936.
29. *El Paso Herald-Post*, May 12, 1936; May 11, 1936; *El Paso Times*, May 12, 1936.
30. *El Continental*, May 15, 1936.
31. *El Paso Herald-Post*, May 12, 1936; *El Paso Times*, May 13, 1936, 2.
32. *El Paso Herald-Post*, May 12, 1936.
33. *El Paso Herald-Post*, May 12, 1936.
34. *El Paso Herald-Post*, May 12, 1936.
35. *El Paso Herald-Post*, May 12, 1936.
36. *El Paso Herald-Post*, May 12, 1936.
37. *El Paso Herald-Post*, May 14, 1936.

2

BREAKING BARRIERS FOR INCLUSION

Chicanas Running for Public Office and the Chicana/o Civil Rights Movement in Texas

TIFFANY JASMIN GONZÁLEZ

Every woman can influence the coming election with more than her vote. Women have all the skills necessary to conduct a neighborhood political campaign.
It's called grass roots politics. And grass roots politics is where elections are won and lost. Women can make a difference. Political issues affect the family and its future.
—EL FAMILIAR, SEPTEMBER 1980

PRESIDENT TRUMP'S 2016 election to office created a backlash of more women and people of color announcing their candidacy for seats at the local, state, and national level within the Democratic Party. Latinas are running for public office on the Democratic ticket as a way to bring about change and better represent the people in their districts in government.[1] For the 2018 midterm elections in Texas, former Dallas County sheriff Lupe Valdez campaigned for the Texas governor seat against Republican Greg Abbott; Sylvia Garcia of Houston ran for Texas's Twenty-Ninth Congressional District seat and won; former El Paso County judge Veronica Escobar replaced Representative Beto O'Rourke's in the Sixteenth Congressional District seat; Samantha Carrillo Fields of Lubbock ran for Texas House District 84 against John Frullo (Republican) but lost; and Celina Vasquez of Bryan won the election for the Justice of the Peace Precinct 4 seat.[2] This list is a glimpse of the political indention occurring across the nation—an increase in Latinas campaigning for public office in order to transform politics and public policy.

Although it might come as a surprise, Texas has a long history of Latinas running and winning seats to serve as public officials in government. The stories of Chicanas who ran for public office are without a doubt part of the historiographies of American politics and the Chicana/o Movement in the twentieth century. I make the case that one cannot study Texas politics, electoral politics in particular, without recognizing that Chicanas have also shaped politics, public policy, and the meaning of representation in government. I argue that Chicanas linked women's representation in government to the fight to transform Texas politics and to the social movements of the late twentieth century. It is within this historical context that I place the trajectory of Chicanas in electoral politics to detail the impact that both women and the civil rights movement had in Texas.

PUTTING THE CHICANA IN TEXAS POLITICS

Chicanas have long been "in the shadows," if not completely erased, from narratives of Texas politics and national histories of governmental and electoral politics.[3] Among the reasons Chicanas have been given cursory attention in histories of political leadership are that they engaged in grassroots and radical/progressive politics, challenged and also fought for inclusion in the U.S. two-party system, opposed sexism and patriarchy within El Movimiento, and the lack of research on institution-building that Chicanas conducted. Chicanas used their leadership and networking capabilities to advance their cause and simultaneously broaden the social movements of the time to address Chicana issues such as women's rights, multicultural education, racial and ethnic discrimination, reproductive justice, economic inequality, welfare rights, labor rights, and even the right for Chicana political representation in electoral politics. The strategies, or *movidas*, Chicanas developed allowed them to combat problems they and their communities experienced.[4] By getting to the root of American politics and by extension Chicano politics through feminist-driven methods, it becomes clear that Chicanas/Latinas are key constituents and politicians in American politics.

The field of Chicana/o history faces a "promising problem" because of the new questions and methodological tools that add to earlier writings to form a new Chicana/o history.[5] Writings on women in electoral politics are an addition to the work that "recognizes the increasing proliferation of identity, furthers the decentering of place, engages in a deeper critical reflection about the meaning of the field, and maintains a connection to the present and to social justice."[6] This chapter is part of the promise that advances the historical record of the Chicana/o experience in American history. When writing about Chicanas in government or political organizations, it is imperative to dig into government archives—city hall, presidential libraries, and the National Archives and Records Administration. These archives are gold mines for documents that outline the ways in which Latinas have worked in or influenced local, state, or federal politics. Just as historian Martha Cotera ardently argued, "A popular myth and often-used excuse for not producing curricula relevant to Mexican American women is that 'there is no literature available.'"[7] Over forty years later, her argument is a reminder that records on Chicanas exist despite archival politics.[8] More writings about Latinas and especially Chicanas and electoral politics complicate current understandings of American political history. To recover narratives about Chicanas in government or in political organizations, a historian must root through files in unconventional places to find the contributions women have made in shaping the past and present. In this essay, I explore the intergroup networks that Chicanas created to advance Chicana/o civil rights for the inclusion of Brown women in party politics in the 1970s. The multipartisan networks that the women established worked within solidarity politics that crossed racial, class, gender, and political lines. This political coalescence shaped the Texas Chicana political movement at the local, state, and national level for rights and power. I build on Cynthia Orozco's examination of Mexican American women's participation in the civil rights movement of the early twentieth century. Her study gives insight to the missed opportunity of creating a larger political movement when Mexican American men failed to recognize women as viable organizers who could vote.[9] Teresa Paloma Acosta and Ruthe Winegarten's *Las Tejanas: 300 Years of History* aptly demonstrates that Mexican-origin women's involvement as public officials "grew steadily in the last quarter of the twentieth century, evolving from their history of involvement in Tejano politics."[10] Scholars who have written on Texas politics and Mexican Americans have explored how race and class relations shaped state politics to become more diverse within the electorate.[11] This essay advances the historiographical conversations by illustrating the ways in which race, class, and gender inform decision-making processes to shape electoral politics as well.

In the 1970s, Chicanas influenced the Texas Democratic Party with the intergroup networks that they built. Chicanas' fight for representative justice rested on challenging racism, sexism, and classism, which had restricted them from having equal access to and wielding power in electoral politics. Their enfranchisement lay in gaining access to where public policy was made and politics occurred. Women advanced Chicana/o civil rights by recruiting other women to join feminist organizations and participate in party politics. The networks built illustrate the strategies and tactics that Chicanas relied on to promote feminism and party politics.[12]

In Texas, the white political machine dominated the Democratic Party, which resulted in platforms that did not always benefit Latina/os. In the 1970s, Chicanas/os in South Texas banded together to develop an alternative mechanism to combat racial discrimination and to create policy change at the local and state level. The formation of La Raza Unida Party (RUP), a third political party, sought Chicana/o self-determination through electoral politics and the expansion of civil rights to include Chicana/o issues. RUP challenged mainstream Texas politics across the state—from El Paso, Lubbock, San Angelo, Dallas/Fort Worth, Austin, Houston, and San Antonio to South Texas. Chicanas from RUP pushed for the recognition of the party at state and national political organizations. Chicanas built the political structure of RUP, as well as organized conferences, built voter power, maintained membership, campaigned, and created intergroup alliances.[13] The party provided Chicanas an opening to engage in party politics and organize more people across Texas.[14] Martha Cotera, an RUP cofounder, noted:

> The important people were the organizers, and the organizers were very often women. But they were not necessarily the ones running for office, and we needed them to run for office. We needed them because very often they had jobs that weren't threatened or they had no jobs. So they weren't threatened economically. They weren't vulnerable.[15]

Chicanas challenged gender discrimination and also enhanced women's consciousness about party politics and feminism.[16] To recruit more women into the political process, Chicanas formed Mujeres por la Raza, which focused on raising women's political consciousness to make them aware of their positionality in society, more active in the party, and run for public office within the party structure. In *Chicana Feminist Thought: The Basic Historical Writings*, edited by Alma M. García, Evey Chapa's "Mujeres por la Raza Unida (1974)" contends that women lacked the sophistication that was required by "confusing and misleading election laws and by the *movidas* [preplanned political moves] of the other two parties against our people."[17] Chicanas found ways to teach one another about the political process and work within their cultural knowledge to navigate Texas politics. Chicanas established social networks for the advancement of political autonomy, civil rights, and inclusion within electoral politics in Texas.

The women of RUP played a vital role in recruiting and empowering other women to engage in party politics. Virginia Muzquíz, Martha Cotera, Rosie Castro, Irma Mireles, María Elena Martínez, and Alma Canales were among the many Chicanas who ran for public office under the La Raza Unida Party ticket across the state of Texas.[18] In Crystal City, Texas, Muzquíz was well respected in the community because of her commitment to the political advancement of Chicana/os. She had worked with other women to sell poll taxes to Chicana/os and participated in the Political Association of Spanish-Speaking Organizations (PASSO) in Texas. In 1964, Muzquíz became the first Chicana to run for Texas state representative under the Democratic Party ticket for District 34, and the following year she ran for a seat on the Crystal City council with PASSO's assistance. Prior to RUP, it was not uncommon for Mexican-origin people to align themselves with the Democratic Party. In 1974, Muzquíz ran a successful campaign for Zavala County clerk under the RUP.[19]

Martha Cotera, a leading Chicana feminist and one of the cofounders of the RUP, ran for the State Board of Education in Congressional District 23 in 1972.[20] Aside from the RUP, Cotera participated in civic organizations such as the National Women's Political Caucus (NWPC), Texas Women's Political Caucus (TWPC), and Mexican American Business and Professional Women's Association (MBPWA). Often missing from writings about Chicanas in the Chicana/o Movement is their labor outside of organizational politics. Cotera's expertise in libraries and information services led her to work at the Texas State Library, the University of Texas at Austin, the Juárez-Lincoln Center (later Juárez-Lincoln University), and the Crystal City Memorial Library, and she later opened her own publishing business, Information Systems Development in Austin, Texas. Her expertise allowed her to address the lack of representation of Chicana/os and resolve a major problem in publishing. In 1976, Cotera published *Diosa y Hembra*, the first book to document Chicana feminist action from pre-Columbian times to the 1970s. She went on to publish *Feminism: The Chicana and Anglo Versions: A Historical Analysis* and *Profile on the Mexican American Woman*.[21] Cotera's feminist projects and her work in recovering

Chicana/o history as a librarian earned her a national reputation and the respect of many in political circles.

In San Antonio, Rosie Castro, a cofounder of San Antonio's RUP, ran for a seat on the San Antonio City Council in 1971. Although unsuccessful, she remained an activist and continued with RUP until the birth of her two sons, Julián and Joaquin Castro, in 1974. Castro's activism expanded to education, political reform, and better living conditions for the underserved in San Antonio. In an oral history conducted by José Ángel Gutiérrez, Castro reflected on one of the RUP's major impacts in Texas: "We opened up the process, made it more inclusive, we forced the public policy issues, and formed some resources that had never been before."[22] Castro's commitment to social justice and political activism was not in vain. Her sons have carried the torch of political engagement to create social and political change. In 2001, Julián Castro was elected to the San Antonio City Council, was mayor of San Antonio from 2009 to 2014, and then served as the U.S. Secretary of Housing and Urban Development under President Barack Obama from 2014 to 2017. In January 2019, Julián announced his run for the Democratic nomination for president of the United States. In 2013, Joaquin Castro was elected to serve in the U.S. House of Representatives for Texas's Twentieth Congressional District. Rosie Castro's activist legacy in the civil rights movement is embodied in the lives and political careers of her sons.

The work of Chicanas in the RUP created a pathway for more women to enter party politics in the 1970s. Their push for greater visibility in the RUP, party politics, and other feminist organizations, particularly later in the National Women's Political Caucus and the Texas Women's Political Caucus, enabled them to extend social influence across networks, share information with other women, and develop strategies to fight for civil rights. The intergroup networks that Chicanas established by participating in multipartisan organizations are another way of understanding the Chicana/o Movement.

NATIONAL WOMEN'S POLITICAL CAUCUS

In 1971, the National Women's Political Caucus was created, a multipartisan organization formed out of the frustration of liberal feminist women involved in the National Organization for Women (NOW).[23] The NWPC provided women an opportunity to participate in party politics within a national organization that championed women's rights, voting power, and women's representation in government. Betty Friedan, a member of NOW and cofounder of the NWPC, wrote:

> Women who have done the political housework in both parties, who have been ignored by the very men they have elected, know what we in the women's movement have learned when we've tried to get priority or money appropriated or even legislation enforced on issues like child care, abortion, or sex discrimination: what we need is political power ourselves.[24]

Betty Friedan gained a national reputation for her 1963 publication, *The Feminine Mystique*, where she argued that women, mainly white women, in the 1950s and 1960s lacked self-fulfillment and independent identities due to society projecting domesticity onto women after World War II.

Following the establishment of the NWPC, Texas women pushed for the formation of the Texas Women's Political Caucus (TWPC), a state-affiliated caucus that supported women running for political office through grassroots efforts. As Judith N. McArthur and Harold L. Smith wrote, "Functioning as the political arm of the women's movement, it [the TWPC] aimed to increase the number of women in elected and appointed offices and to work with both major parties to promote women's issues."[25] When the TWPC formed in Texas in 1971, only two women served in the state legislature, Senator Barbara Jordan (1966) and Representative Frances "Sissy" Farenthold (1968).[26] And no Chicanas at the time.

Considering that men dominated party politics, Chicanas faced several disadvantages in addition to racial and ethnic discrimination when running for public office—credibility, campaign funds, and networks. Perceived as unqualified, women struggled to gain credibility owing to societal perceptions. Family responsibilities and a lack of professional connections impeded their success in party politics. In addition, political parties overlooked women for public office, and some women lacked the confidence to take the plunge to run for office. To challenge the man's world of politics, women in the NWPC and in the subsequent affiliated state and local chapters shared networks, provided financial support, and taught campaign and fundraising skills to elevate women's self-confidence.

In November 1971, the TWPC held its first organizing conference in Austin, Texas. Liz Carpenter, cofounder of the NWPC and proponent of the Equal

Rights Amendment (ERA), gave the keynote address and urged the audience to recognize the political limitations that women faced within American politics: "It is time to end discrimination, and encourage women to run for the Legislature, the Senate, mayor, Congress, and local positions."[27] As a Texan, Carpenter was no stranger to the "good ol' boy" network in Texas politics. Her goal of promoting women to public office derived from her awareness of party politics and years of working in Washington, D.C. She had worked as President Lyndon Johnson's administrative assistant when he was vice president, and later acted as Lady Bird Johnson's press secretary when Johnson assumed the presidency.

The NWPC was among the earliest organizations that focused on increasing the number of women in government. In addition, the NWPC and TWPC were among the few multipartisan organizations that Chicanas participated in to advance their status in society and to enhance women's rights and political power for liberation. Many Chicanas in the RUP joined the TWPC as a way to push for political reform that included their needs as Chicanas, their rights as Brown women, and shape the mainstream women's movement.

In November 1971, the first TWPC state meeting focused on creating a future action plan via workshops: "Women's Priorities, Future Structure of the TWPC, Candidate Criteria, Political Procedures and Strategy, and Organizing on the Local Level."[28] Among the women assigned to lead a conference workshop was Alma Canales, who represented the RUP.[29] Chicanas presented a report to make the women of the caucus aware of their goal in entering the TWPC.

"Because racism is such a monumental obstacle for chicanos [*sic*] and other minorities in Texas, women of La Raza Unida cannot have the luxury of dealing exclusively with feminism and fighting male chauvinism," the report said. "Women struggling for women's rights know full well the burden of second-class citizenship and other injustices perpetuated by Texas political havoc."[30]

Owing to exclusion from the main party structure in Texas, Chicana participation in the caucus allowed them to make white women aware of their lack of representation because of sexism, racism, and classism. By funneling their civil rights activism within the caucus, Chicanas expanded their intergroup network. White women constituted the majority of membership in second-wave feminist organizations. The NWPC and TWPC would be no different. Chicanas knew that it was strategically vital for them to participate in organizations that had a cross-racial membership to create a broader awareness of their positionality in society.

"THE CHICANAS STIRRED UP A RUCKUS"

At the 1972 TWPC meeting in Mesquite, Texas, the caucus had adopted forty-six resolutions, which included the endorsement of state representative Frances "Sissy" Farenthold for governor as a Democrat and Alma Canales for lieutenant governor under the RUP.[31] Both Farenthold and Canales were eventually defeated. Although upset with Farenthold's lack of assistance to Canales when she ran for the lieutenant governor seat, Chicanas remained in the caucus and continued to strategize for greater political power. Much of the tension between Chicanas and the white women in the caucus such as Farenthold grew from the different cultural values and belief systems that shaped how they engaged in politics. For Chicanas, a system based on respect and honoring one's word informed their practice. Farenthold's lack of support to Canales was one of several betrayals Chicanas encountered while involved in the NWPC and TWPC.

In February 1973, the NWPC held its first convention in Houston, Texas, where the membership elected a chairperson, treasurer, and secretary to supervise the continued organizing efforts in the caucus. The new officers included Democrat Farenthold as chairperson and Republicans Audrey Rowe Colom (Black woman) and Bobbie Kilberg and Rhea Mojica Hammer of the RUP as vice-chairpersons. Upon Farenthold's election as chairperson, she pledged to bring change to society and help more women be elected to office across the nation.[32] Yet Chicana delegates from the RUP challenged Farenthold's commitment in helping them recruit more members. Farenthold responded, "Every group in this body has my commitment."[33] The newspapers reported that Chicanas "stirred up a ruckus with a controversial proposal they pushed through during a marathon business session which stretched from 7:00 p.m. Saturday until 3:35 a.m. Sunday."[34] In pressing for more visibility in the NWPC, Chicanas submitted resolutions that focused on Chicana issues and concerns. Among these was a call for the NWPC to endorse the RUP and for the third party's inclusion in "official and promotional material, which cited the Democratic and Republican parties."[35] The following resolutions focused on the establishment of the Chicana caucus to prioritize the Chicana experience, the endorsement of the National Chicana Welfare Rights Organization, and called for support of the Farah boycott and the United Farm Workers lettuce boycott, Chicana educational opportunities, and Chicana policy council members.[36] The Chicana resolutions demanded the NWPC take into account the unique struggles that Chicanas faced in society in the realms of labor, welfare, policy, and education, as well as made clear that if the caucus wanted a united front the leadership must include Chicana stances within its structure. The question of whether Farenthold or the NWPC supported Chicanas loomed large at the convention and thereafter.

Over a hundred Chicanas from across the country attended the first NWPC convention in Houston. Among the crowd were Rhea Mojica Hammer (Illinois), Alicia Escalante (California), Lupe Anguiano (Washington, D.C.), María Cárdenas, Martha Cotera, Evey Chapa, and Lydia Serra, as well as two white women, Jeanette Lizcano and Sally Andrade, who helped Chicanas maneuver discussions on the convention floor.[37] The women were leaders working to improve the Chicana/o community in their hometowns. Alicia Escalante's work involved the East Los Angeles Welfare Rights Organization (ELAWRO), an organization focused on seeing that welfare recipients were "treated with respect and dignity by the welfare administration."[38] Escalante and the ELAWRO advocated on behalf of Chicanas and Mexican single mothers for economic and social justice from a welfare system that discriminated against them.[39] At the NWPC convention Escalante made sure that attendees recognized that economic justice for Chicanas lay within the political realm. As a result, Chicanas called for the endorsement of the National Chicana Welfare Rights Organization by the NWPC. The cross-regional collaboration that the Chicanas established proved beneficial for building numerical power within the organization, forging networks for social and political capital, as well as advancing their goal of political representation in American politics.

After the NWPC convention in Houston, Chicanas in RUP remained hesitant, even questioned whether to stay within the TWPC. One of the reasons for the hesitation derived from Chicanas seeking autonomy in the NWPC, which the NWPC advisory committee had revoked after agreeing to the terms. At a Raza Unida convention in San Antonio, Texas, in December 1973, the women tabled a motion to stay or withdraw from the TWPC. A report from the San Antonio Raza Unida Party meeting documented the discussion:

> Another report was given by Marta Cotera who cited an incident of why it was not to our advantage to belong to the TWPC. She recalled to us the time when the TWPC women had endorsed Alma Canales, who was at the time running

for Lieutenant Governor, but in reality did little to help in Alma's campaign. She also talked about the time chicana's [*sic*] had asked for a separate Caucus during the NWPC in Houston of last year. This petition was passed and granted but with little or no effect on the NWPC and leaving us still at 1% at the bottom of the pyramid.[40]

The tensions that Chicanas experienced with the NWPC and TWPC centered on the patriarchal "liberal feminism" that white women espoused. Chicanas came into the caucus explaining that their intersectional disenfranchisement rested on sexism, racism, and classism. The triple oppression that Chicanas experienced led them to work for political reform in electoral politics by organizing in the RUP, the TWPC, and the NWPC. Instead of surrendering their efforts for the political development of women, some Chicanas stayed in the caucus as individual members because it gave them an advantage at the national level to distribute information. In 1974, the Chicana Caucus developed within the NWPC. In addition, other Chicanas of RUP channeled their energies to form the Mexican American Business and Professional Women's Association (MABPWA) in Austin in June 1974. In essence, Chicanas leveraged their power and continued to engage in radical politics under the guise of a different organizational identity, such as MABPWA in Austin.

Establishing MABPWA highlighted the women's financial power, in addition to their social and political power as business and professional women. MABPWA started as a Steering Committee, whose members had varying income levels and professions and represented different areas of Austin.[41] The formation of MABPWA strengthened the impact of Chicanas and Mexican American women in Austin. "The main purpose in this endeavor, however, was to bring about total improvement in the community."[42] The Steering Committee included Carlota Cardenas, Martha Cotera, Susana Elizondo, Anita Sylvia García, Ora Gloria, Marta de Luna, Amalia Rodríguez Mendoza, Hermelinda Rodríguez, Mary Helen Valdez, and Annabelle Valle. From March to June, the women met regularly to establish connections, develop a working relationship with one another, and build a more extensive network of Mexican American women from different parts of the city. On June 27, 1974, MABPWA held its Founders Meeting at the Sheraton Crest Inn in Austin. More than a hundred Chicanas attended, and Martha Cotera was elected as the organization's first president. Addressing the audience at the meeting was Pauline Martínez, who at the time worked as the U.S. Equal Employment Opportunity officer in San

Antonio, and belonged to the San Antonio chapter of MABPWA. The Austin Steering Committee invited her to the meeting to speak on the role of the business and professional Chicana in the community.[43] Martínez would later become the legislative officer of the TWPC and tasked with recruiting women to run for public office across the state.

Mexican American women joined MABPWA because they viewed it as an outlet for focusing on the development of women in the community. Lupe Morin, a former RUP member and an affiliate of MABPWA, recalled her reason for joining the organization:

> There were other Hispanic organizations but I was very disgruntled with organizations such as LULAC and G.I. FORUM because I went to a couple of their conferences during that period of time when I was at UT and they were very focused towards men. They wouldn't allow women to vote in the regular membership, they had auxiliaries. All of LULAC's officers were men. It was very dominated by the men folk and so I really didn't feel part of that. We were trying to find our own identity within ourselves.[44]

Over the next two years, MABPWA's goal of developing women in the community concentrated on encouraging and supporting Mexican-origin women to actively participate in public life through city boards and commissions, in city hall and state government. Not that much different from what many Chicanas had been doing in RUP or other feminist circles.

WOMEN IN PUBLIC LIFE

On November 9, 1975, the Lyndon B. Johnson Presidential Library and the LBJ School of Public Affairs at the University of Texas at Austin jointly sponsored a three-day conference to discuss how women were perceived in the media, government, and in overall society. The meeting resulted from the International Women's Year conference in Mexico earlier that year. With Texas having a large number of women active in public life, Liz Carpenter, the coordinator, and the conference committee believed that the meeting afforded a connection between grassroots, national, and international leaders.

The workshop and panel sessions included "Exploring the Gains and the Gaps of Women in the Power Structure in Texas," "Beating the Old Boy Game,"

"Don't Wait to Be Asked," and "The Gains and Gaps of the Rest of Us."[45] In the "The Gains and Gaps of the Rest of Us" workshop, Alicia Chacón, a Mexican American city clerk in El Paso, Texas, spoke of the effects of coalition-building on electoral politics.[46] In the midst of the Chicana/o Movement, Chacón made headway in local and state politics. She had been active in the Democratic Party, the TWPC, and local civic organizations. In 1974, she became the first woman to serve as a county official, signaling a transformation for women in government in El Paso. For Chacón, a change in representation signified that society's view toward women in public was evolving: "I definitely feel that my winning shows that the public is ready to accept women as serious candidates."[47] At the heart of creating change for Chicanas in Texas was grassroots politics and coalition-building. Chacón's involvement in electoral politics challenges the partial way Texas politics has been written.

At the Conference for Women in Public Life, Cotera spoke in the same workshop as Chacón and directed her testimony to the limitations that Chicanas faced in public life. Cotera started her speech by noting that she would not be limited to ten minutes and then went on to say:

> On a nationwide basis, Chicanas have no representative in the Women and Power Committee, no U.S. Senator, no U.S. representative, no federal judges, no high federal administrative position. At the state level in Texas, we have no state senator, no state representative, no judges, no mayors, one Chicana in a state commission.[48]

Chicanas still lagged behind white women in changing representation in government. The conference itself lacked Chicana representation. Things changed when Cotera and Pauline Martínez met Irma Rangel while discussing the lack of Mexican American women in politics at the Conference for Women in Public Life. When Rangel first met Cotera and Martínez, she had been working as an attorney in her hometown of Kingsville, Texas. Before becoming an attorney, Rangel had earned her bachelor's degree from Texas A&I University (now Texas A&M University–Kingsville) and taught in South Texas, California, and Venezuela. She published a guidebook for teaching elementary students to speak Spanish. Her passion for public service and improving her community led her to law school. In 1966, she enrolled in St. Mary's University School of Law in San Antonio, Texas, and graduated in 1969. Afterward, she worked as a law clerk for Judge Adrian Spears and then moved to Corpus Christi, Texas, to work as an assistant district attorney in 1971. Mexican American women lawyers faced hurdles to acceptance in the courtroom in Corpus Christi. Rangel experienced this when she became the first Mexican American woman assistant district attorney in the area. Two years later, Rangel returned to her hometown of Kingsville and became a partner at a law firm.

Rangel's involvement in party politics grew when her family and former professors urged her to run for Kleberg County Democratic Party chairperson in 1974. She won the election. Her activity in local politics gave her insight into the issues important to the Kleberg County constituency. When she attended the Conference for Women in Public Life, Martha Cotera and Pauline Martínez encouraged her to run for public office at the state level. Encouraging Rangel to run for office reflects the feminist agenda that Chicanas illustrated. Chicanas knew they had a stake in the future of Texas politics, and to have representation in government they had to support and empower one another. As Rangel remembered, "These same women were also members of the Texas Women's Political Caucus, that was the Mexican American caucus of the Texas Women's Political Caucus, and so Pauline came down from San Antonio and they kept on encouraging me to run, you know. And then I decided to discuss it with my mother and father, and they said, 'Well, you know, why not?' So, I went ahead and took the chance on running."[49] She would become a force to be reckoned with.

Rangel ran for Texas state representative because the incumbent in her district, Greg Montoya, was under federal investigation for paying private employees with state funds.[50] The investigation put him in a vulnerable position for reelection. Rangel campaigned at the grassroots level, going door-to-door in her district. Her campaign slogan, "Representation for a Change," declared that she would change the Kleberg County political climate.[51] She disrupted the gendered power dynamics and also changed policies to include the needs of all constituents—men, women, and children.[52]

The funding for Rangel's campaign came from different directions and amounted to nearly $9,800. The TWPC caucus members raised $1,750 toward Rangel's campaign. She also received support from migrant farmworkers, friends, family members, colleagues, and residents. Aside from the cost of her campaign, Rangel faced other difficulties. She had recently moved back to Kingsville and did not have many networks in the area. Rangel relied on her cultural values of family and *confianza* to campaign. Her parents and sister went to events with her. "They [Rangel's family] had always been loved and respected so I remember going to a Bingo and saying . . . 'I am Irma Rangel, you know, P.M.'s daughter *y la hermana de* [and the sister of] Minnie.' . . . [The people reacted with] 'oh, well, this is good,' and then they started applauding."[53] Rangel's family networks helped her. In addition, women migrant farmworkers volunteered time to Rangel's campaign before leaving to pick crops outside of Texas. In 1976, Rangel ran a successful campaign for a seat in the Texas State Legislature and became the first Mexican American woman elected to the House of Representatives. She remained in office until her passing in 2003.

Rangel challenged policies that often overlooked the needs of women and minorities in Texas. In many of her campaign speeches, she declared that she would focus on working "for better state-operated day care centers as well as welfare reform."[54] Her agenda centered on women's issues that had received little recognition in state politics and by those in office. Her most notable piece of legislation was House Bill 588, better known as the Top 10% Plan, which was passed in 1997. The legislation was a response to the 1996 *Hopwood v. State of Texas* decision, which barred universities from relying on race as a factor for admissions. Rangel and Senator Gonzalo Barrientos co-authored the Top 10% Plan legislation with the assistance of researchers (brain trust) from the University of Texas at Austin.[55] The Top 10% Plan required that all Texas public universities and colleges automatically admit students who graduated in the top 10 percent of their class. This law opened the door for minority students to top universities and colleges in the state of Texas. The Top 10% Plan also challenged legacy admissions in higher education, which gave preference to applicants who had family connections to a college or university. While in office, Rangel was a staunch proponent of higher education initiatives, the development of the College of Pharmacy at Texas A&M University–Kingsville, women's rights, social programs that aided poor single mothers, and the labor rights of the working class.[56]

"CARDENAS' REPUTATION RANKS HER IN POWER"

María Cárdenas, the first Chicana politician of San Angelo, Texas, also advanced women in electoral politics.[57] Cárdenas had been active in local politics and the RUP, and attended meetings that promoted Chicanas in political organizations, such as the Texas Women's Political Caucus. Cárdenas's contributions to the Chicana/o civil rights movement and Texas politics is another reason why Chicanas should be included in the histories of American politics. She was one of the many Chicanas who transformed the political system in the late twentieth century.

As a San Angelo resident, Cárdenas gained recognition for speaking out against racial and ethnic discrimination and political inequality in the area. She used San Angelo's newspaper to voice her opinions about politics and to debate residents about their views on issues. In one letter to the editor, she wrote that San Angelo students were learning negative racial stereotypes of Black and Chicano peers. "White children have been taught that Chicanos are dirty and have no ambition and some Blacks don't marry—but so are there whites, and that is a human failing and not because they are whites, Chicanos or Blacks."[58] The newspaper allowed her to build community and networks to advance her stances in San Angelo.

Cárdenas's activism stretched to the state level. At the 1971 RUP state convention in San Antonio, Cárdenas ran against Alma Canales for the state committeewoman position. Despite her loss, she continued to participate in the third party actively. In 1972, Mario Compeán, the state chairman for the RUP, named Cárdenas as Tom Green County voting delegate for the party.[59] She was also involved with Mujeres por la Raza. In a program for the 1973 Conferencia de Mujeres por la Raza Unida, Cárdenas was named as a workshop facilitator for the panel titled "Como Organizar en Pueblos Rurales/Semi-Rurales" alongside Elena Díaz and Diana Serna.[60]

Cárdenas's participation in the RUP, local politics, and the TWPC provided her support and the networks to bring about change within San Angelo. In 1975, Cárdenas launched a campaign to change San Angelo's electoral voting system from at-large representation to single-member districts. City council commissioners from at-large districts represented the whole town rather than individual neighborhoods. This led to inequity in resources and political power for minority districts. Single-member districts remedied the lack of representation at city hall, would mean districts were based on population numbers, and would require representatives to live in the district they sought to represent.

Cárdenas's campaign for single-member districts caught the attention of San Angelo residents, the community's Democratic Party, and the Mexican American Legal Defense and Educational Fund (MALDEF). She built networks with people who shared these concerns. The single-member district campaign created alliances that crossed race, class, and gender boundaries. On April 3, 1976, residents voted on a measure to restructure the electoral system. It passed by 1,358 votes and went into effect following the election of new single-member council representatives in 1978.[61]

In January 1978, Cárdenas announced her bid for the District 3 seat that encompassed the Rio Vista neighborhood district, a predominantly Latina/o neighborhood. On April 2, 1978, Cárdenas and Mary Burk (District 1) found themselves in a run-off against their opponents. On May 13, the *San Angelo-Standard Times* announced "Historic Single-Member District Election Seats Two Women."[62] Burk and Cárdenas both won their runoffs. Cárdenas served as District 3's council member from 1978 to 1983. While in office, Cárdenas pushed for improvements in her district, such as street paving, health care clinics, streetlight fixtures, and greater funding. In 1980, a survey named Cárdenas one of "the most powerful people in San Angelo."[63] Of the twenty-five to receive this recognition, she was the only woman. She also served as mayor pro tem during the 1982–83 term. Cárdenas left city politics when she lost her bid for the Tom Green County Commissioners Court Precinct 1 seat in 1983. However, she continued to contribute her political skills to local civic organizations until her passing in 1993.

In November 2001, the city of San Angelo dedicated a pedestrian bridge in the Rio Vista neighborhood in her honor. Near the bridge, a plaque reads: "Ms. Cardenas' inspiration and efforts helped make this bridge a reality. . . . The key to her success was her vision, sincere belief in the voice of the people, perseverance, and devotion to her cause that gained her the respect and admiration of many."[64]

CHICANAS IN POLITICS: REMEMBERING THEIR PLACE IN HISTORY

Chicanas have come a long way in electoral politics since the 1970s. In historicizing the work that women did to transform party politics, we move them from the sidelines to the center of the Chicana/o civil rights movement.[65] Chicanas engaged in grassroots activism to form intergroup networks that enabled them to collaborate with and empower other women to run for public office or assist their work in government capacities across regions. Stretching from the local to the state and to the national arena, these networks disrupted sexist, classist, and racist structures in party politics and political organizations. By working at the local level, Chicanas expanded the civil rights movement to a national scale. Having empowered themselves, their needs and concerns could no longer be dismissed. In contesting and attaining seats that men had held, they shaped public policy and politics. The fight for political representation in electoral politics carries beyond the Chicana/o Movement moment; Chicanas made a lasting impact for women to have the resources to run for public office.[66] Earlier generations of Latinas, especially Chicanas, laid the groundwork (through grassroots political activism) to disrupt electoral politics and government structures for representation and pave the way for the wave of Latinas to run for public office in the twenty-first century. If political parties took Latina power more seriously and communities encouraged and supported Latinas to participate in electoral politics, Latinas could remain a force to be reckoned with in American politics.

NOTES

1. I use the term Latina to refer to women of Latin American descent. Chicana is used to refer to women who used that identity during the Chicana/o Movement. I use the term Mexican American to refer to people of Mexican descent who did not clearly identify as Chicana/o during the civil rights movement or thereafter. I recognize the competing definitions of identity with Latina/os, especially with people of Mexican descent residing in the United States. I expand on this conversation in my dissertation, "Representation for a Change: Women in Government and the Chicana/o Civil Rights Movement in Texas."
2. The newspaper articles include: Christina Caron, "Lupe Valdez Prepares to Face Greg Abbot in Texas: 'This Election Is Not Going to Be Bought,'" *New York Times*, May 23, 2018; Abby Livingston and Julián Aguilar, "Texas Poised to Send Its First Two Latinas to Congress," *Texas Tribune*, March 6, 2018; "A Closer Look at Celina Vasquez, Candidate for Brazos County Justice of the Peace, Precinct 4," *Eagle*, February 4, 2018; Matt Dotray, "Democrat Samantha Fields Announces Campaign for Texas House 84," *Lubbock Avalanche-Journal*, September 13, 2017.
3. For a discussion of histories in the shadows, see Vicki L. Ruíz, *From Out of the Shadows: Mexican Women in Twentieth-Century America* (New York: Oxford University Press, 2008).
4. For more on Chicana *movidas*, see Dionne Epinoza, María Eugenia Cotera, and Maeylei Blackwell, *Chicana Movidas: New Narratives of Activism and Feminism in the Movement Era* (Austin: University of Texas Press, 2018), 11–15.
5. Carlos Blanton, ed., *A Promising Problem: The New Chicana/o History* (Austin: University of Texas Press, 2015), 1–19.
6. Blanton, *Promising Problem*, 19.
7. Martha P. Cotera, *Diosa y Hembra: The History and Heritage of Chicanas in the U.S.* (Austin: Information Systems Development, 1976), 1.

8.   Institutional archives (libraries, government institutions, centers, or organizations) collect, preserve, and showcase documents for historical preservation, which then shape the dissemination of knowledge and power structures. The act of collecting, preserving, and showcasing documents is political and dependent on institutional agendas. Documents on women of color are often missing from archives because of institutional agendas. To combat this archival marginalization, scholars are using digital humanities to collect, preserve, and showcase historical documents on Latinas. For more information on Chicana digital archival recovery projects, see María Cotera, "Chicana por mi Raza," http://chicanapormiraza.org/; Linda García Merchant, "Chicana Diasporic: A Nomadic Journey of the Activist Exiled," http://scalar.usc.edu/works/chicanadiasporic/chicana-diasporic-an-introduction?path=index.

9.   Cynthia Orozco, *No Mexicans, Women, or Dogs Allowed: The Rise of the Mexican American Civil Rights Movement* (Austin: University of Texas Press, 2009), 218.

10.   Ruthe L. Winegarten and Teresa Paloma Acosta, eds., *Las Tejanas: 300 Years of History* (Austin: University of Texas Press, 2003), 250.

11.   Max Krochmal, *Blue Texas: The Making of a Multiracial Democratic Coalition in the Civil Rights Era* (Chapel Hill: University of North Carolina Press, 2016); Ben Marquez, *Democratizing Texas Politics: Race, Identity, and Mexican American Empowerment, 1945–2002* (Austin: University of Texas Press, 2014).

12.   Alma Garcia, "The Development of a Chicana Feminist Discourse," *Gender and Society* 3, no 2 (1989): 217–38.

13.   Dionne Espinoza, "The Partido Belongs to Those Who Will Work for It: Chicana Organizing and Leadership in Texas Raza Unida Party, 1970–1980," *Aztlán: A Journal of Chicano Studies* 36, no. 1 (2011): 191–210.

14.   Emilio Zamora, "Raza Unida Women in Texas: Oral History, Pedagogy, and Historical Interpretation," *U.S. Latina and Latino Oral History Journal* 1 (2017): 29–46; Vicki Ruíz, *From Out of the Shadows: Mexican Women in Twentieth-Century America* (Oxford: Oxford University Press, 1998).

15.   F. Arturo Rosales, *Testimonio: A Documentary History of the Mexican American Struggle for Civil Rights* (Houston: Arte Publico Press, 2000), 391.

16.   Rosales, *Testimonio*, 392.

17.   Evey Chapa, "Mujeres por la Raza Unida (1974)," in *Chicana Feminist Thought: The Basic Historical Writings*, ed. Alma M. García (New York: Routledge, 1997), 178.

18.   I recognize that there were more Chicanas who ran for public office under La Raza Unida Party, but for the purpose of the paper, I have mentioned only the above.

19.   José Angel Gutiérrez, Michelle Meléndez, and Sonia Adriana Noyola, eds., *Chicanas in Charge: Texas Women in the Public Arena* (Lanham, Md.: AltaMira Press, 2007), 42–43.

20.   Letter exchange between Martha Cotera and Olga De Leon, September 1973, box 2, Correspondence—Complete 193 folder, Benson Latin American Collection, University of Texas at Austin.

21.   Elaine Ayala, "Mother-Daughter Research Spots Hispanic Heroines," *Austin American-Statesman*, September 1990, E1.

22.   Rosie Castro, interview by José Angel Gutiérrez, July 1, 1996, Tejano Voices Oral History Collection, University of Texas at Arlington, https://library.uta.edu/tejanovoices/xml/CMAS_123.xml.

23.   Newspaper clipping from *Jacksonville Press*, November 21, 1971, box 2K8, Texas Women's Political Caucus folder, Farenthold (Frances "Sissy" Tarlton) Papers, Dolph Briscoe Center for American History, University of Texas at Austin.

24.   Betty Friedan, *It Changed My Life: Writings on the Women's Movement* (New York: Random House, 1976), 171.

25.   Judith N. McArthur and Harold L. Smith, *Texas Through Women's Eyes: The Twentieth-Century Experience* (Austin: University of Texas Press, 2010), 224.

26.   McArthur and Smith, *Texas Through Women's Eyes*, 224. Historians have produced a rich body of literature on the history of Black women in electoral politics. See Martha S. Jones, *Vanguard: How Black Women Broke Barriers, Won the Vote, and Insisted on Equality for All* (New York: Basic Books, 2020); Mary-Elizabeth B. Murphy, *Jim Crow Capital: Women and Black Freedom Struggles in Washington, D.C., 1920–1945* (Chapel Hill: University of North Carolina Press, 2018); Ashley D. Farmer, *Remaking Black Power: How Black Women Transformed an Era* (Chapel Hill: University of North Carolina Press, 2017); Julie A. Gallagher, *Black Women and Politics in New York City* (Urbana: University of Illinois Press, 2012); Lisa G. Materson, *For the Freedom of Her Race: Black Women and Electoral Politics in Illinois, 1877–1932* (Chapel Hill: University of North Carolina Press, 2009); Mary Ellen Curtin, "Reaching for Power: Barbara C. Jordan and Liberals in the Texas Legislature, 1966–1972," *Southwestern Historical Quarterly* 108, no. 2 (October 2004): 210–31.

27.   Newspaper clipping, November 20, 1971, box 2K8, Texas Women's Political Caucus folder, Farenthold (Frances "Sissy" Tarlton) Papers, Dolph Briscoe Center for American History, University of Texas at Austin.

28.   *Jacksonville Progress*, November 22, 1971, box 2K8, Texas Women's Political Caucus folder, Farenthold (Frances "Sissy" Tarlton) Papers, Dolph Briscoe Center for American History, University of Texas at Austin

29.   Newspaper clipping from *San Angelo Standard-Times*, November 16, 1971, box 2K8, Texas Women's Political Caucus folder, Farenthold (Frances "Sissy" Tarlton) Papers, Dolph Briscoe Center for American History, University of Texas at Austin.

30.   Newspaper clipping, November 22, 1971, box 2K8, Texas Women's Political Caucus folder, Farenthold (Frances "Sissy" Tarlton) Papers, Dolph Briscoe Center for American History, University of Texas at Austin.

31.   "Some Walk Out During Women's Political Caucus," *Amarillo Globe-Times*, March 13, 1972.

32.   Newsletter I, Convention Report, February–March 1973, box 2008–088/7, Farenthold (Frances "Sissy" Tarlton) Papers, Dolph Briscoe Center for American History, University of Texas at Austin.

33. Peggy A. Simpson, "Women's Political Caucus More United Than Before," *Abilene Reporter News*, February 12, 1973, 4-C.
34. Simpson, "Women's Political Caucus."
35. "Chicana Caucus Resolutions," box 8, Organizational Activities—NWPC Chicana Caucus [1973] folder, Martha Cotera Papers, Benson Latin American Collection, University of Texas at Austin.
36. "Chicana Caucus Resolutions."
37. Cotera, *Diosa y Hembra*, 186.
38. Rosie C. Bermúdez, "Alicia Escalante, the Chicana Welfare Rights Organization, and the Chicano Movement," in *The Chicano Movement: Perspectives from the Twenty-First Century*, ed. Mario T. García (New York: Routledge, 2014), 95.
39. Bermúdez, "Alicia Escalante," 96–111.
40. "Workshop: Women's Political Caucus," box 5, folder 1, Mujeres por la Raza, 1973–1974, Raza Unida Party Records, 1969–1979, Benson Latin American Collection, University of Texas at Austin.
41. "Mexican American Business and Professional Women of Austin, History Document," box 1, folder 1, History, 1984–1993, Mexican American Business and Professional Women's Association, Austin History Center, Austin, Texas.
42. "Mexican American Business and Professional Women of Austin, History Document."
43. "Official Will Talk to Club," *Austin American-Statesman*, June 26, 1974.
44. Lupe Morin oral history, conducted by Amalia Rodríguez-Mendoza, AF–Biography, Morin, Lupe Files, Austin History Center, Austin, Texas.
45. "Conference on Women in Public Life," box 2, Correspondence Com. A-L (1976) CONT. [1970, 1975–77], Martha Cotera Papers, Benson Latin American Collection, University of Texas at Austin.
46. For histories on coalition-building, see Lauren Araiza, *To March for Others: The Black Freedom Struggle and the United Farm Workers* (Philadelphia: University of Pennsylvania Press, 2013); Allyson Powers Brantley, "'We're Givin' Up Our Beer for Sweeter Wine': Boycotting Coors Beer, Coalition-Building, and the Politics of Non-Consumption, 1957–1987" (PhD diss., Yale University, 2016), https://search.proquest.com/docview/1813628197; Krochmal, *Blue Texas*; Gordon Mantler, *Power to the Poor: Black-Brown Coalition and the Fight for Economic Justice, 1960–1974* (Chapel Hill: University of North Carolina Press, 2013).
47. Virginia Payette, "Take Top Roles in Political, Civic Work," *El Paso Herald-Post*, November 11, 1974.
48. Martha Cotera, *The Chicana Feminist* (Austin: Information Systems Development, 1977), 14.
49. Irma Rangel, interview by Karen McGee and José Ángel Gutiérrez, April 10, 1996, transcript, p. 10.
50. "Rep. Montoya Funds Probed," *Paris News*, December 5, 1974; "Rep. Greg Montoya Under Investigation," *Del Rio News Herald*, December 13, 1974.

51. Elizabeth W. Fernea and Marilyn P. Duncan, eds., *Texas Women in Politics* (Austin, Tex.: Women's Resources, 1977), 76.

52. "First Chicana Legislator," Ruthe Winegarten Papers, Dolph Briscoe Center for American History, University of Texas at Austin.

53. Cited in Sonia R. García, Valerie Martínez-Ebers, Irasema Coronado, Sharon A. Navarro, and Patricia A. Jaramillo, *Políticas: Latina Public Officials in Texas* (Austin: University of Texas Press, 2008), 39.

54. "Chicana Politico Favors More Day Care," *Austin American-Statesman*, October 24, 1976, B4.

55. David Montejano, "On Hopwood: The Continuing Challenge," in *Reflexiones: New Directions in Mexican American Studies* (Austin: Center for Mexican American Studies, 1997).

56. Nancy Baker Jones and Ruthe Winegarten, *Capitol Women: Texas Female Legislators, 1923–1999* (Austin: University of Texas Press, 2000), 204–6; Tiffany J. González and Nancy Baker Jones, "Irma Rangel," *Women in Texas History: A Project of the Ruthe Winegarten Memorial Foundation for Texas Women's History*, https://www.womenintexashistory.org/audio/irma-rangel/.

57. Le Killgore, "Cardenas' Reputation Ranks Her in Power," *San Angelo Standard-Times*, August 28, 1989, 1A.

58. "Must Learn from Young," *San Angelo Standard-Times*, September 9, 1971, Dr. Arnoldo De León Collection, West Texas Collection, Angelo State University, San Angelo, Texas.

59. Tiffany J. González, "Cárdenas, María Guevara," *Handbook of Texas Online*, https://tshaonline.org/handbook/online/articles/fcaeo.

60. "Conferencia de Mujeres por la Raza Unida," box 7, Raza Unida Party—Women, folder 9, Martha Cotera Papers, Benson Latin American Collection, University of Texas at Austin.

61. Norma Joe Williams, "SA Passes Single Member Plan," *San Angelo Standard-Times*, April 4, 1976.

62. Le Killgore, "Commission Voters Select Burk, Cardenas: Historic Single-Member District Election Seats Two Women," *San Angelo Standard-Times*, May 14, 1978, front page, Dr. Arnoldo De León Collection, West Texas Collection, Angelo State University. Quoted sentence taken from Tiffany J. González, "Pathways to Political Office: María Cárdenas and the Creation of Single Member Districts in San Angelo," *U.S. Latina and Latino Oral History Journal* 1 (2017): 98–116.

63. Killgore, "Cardenas' Reputation Ranks Her in Power."

64. González, "Cárdenas, María Guevara," https://tshaonline.org/handbook/online/articles/fcaeo.

65. For published works on the Chicana/o Movement, see Espinoza, Cotera, and Blackwell, eds., *Chicana Movidas*; García, ed., *Chicano Movement*; Jimmy Patiño, *¡Raza Si, Migra No!: Chicano Movement Struggles for Immigrants Rights in San Diego* (Chapel Hill: University of North Carolina Press, 2017); Mario T. García, *The Chicano Generation: Testimonios of the Movement* (Oakland: University of Califor-

nia Press, 2015); Felipe Hinojosa, "Medicina Si, Muerte No! Race, Public Health, and the 'Long War on Poverty' in Mathis, Texas, 1948–1971," *Western Historical Quarterly* 44 (Winter 2013): 437–58; Marc Simon Rodriguez, *The Tejano Diaspora: Mexican Americanism and Ethnic Politics in Texas and Wisconsin* (Chapel Hill: University of North Carolina Press, 2011); Maylei Blackwell, *¡Chicana Power! Contested Histories of Feminism in the Chicano Movement* (Austin: University of Texas Press, 2011); Mario T. García and Sal Castro, *Blowout! Sal Castro and the Chicano Struggle for Educational Justice* (Chapel Hill: University of North Carolina Press, 2011); David Montejano, *Quixote's Soldiers: A Local History of the Chicano Movement, 1966–1981* (Austin: University of Texas Press, 2010); Lorena Oropeza, *Raza Si! Guerra No! Chicano Protest and Patriotism During the Viet Nam Era* (Berkeley: University of California Press, 2005); Ernesto Chávez, *¡Mi Raza Primero! Nationalism, Identity, and Insurgency in the Chicano Movement in Los Angeles, 1966–1978* (Berkeley: University of California, 2002); Guadalupe San Miguel, *Brown, Not White: School Integration and the Chicano Movement in Houston* (College Station: Texas A&M University Press, 2001); Alma M. García, ed., *Chicana Feminist Thought: The Basic Historical Writings* (New York: Routledge, 1997); Ignacio M. García, *United We Win: The Rise and Fall of La Raza Unida Party* (Tucson: University of Arizona Press, 1989).

66. For a detailed analysis on the Chicano Movement moment debate, see David G. Gutiérrez, "Significant to Whom? Mexican Americans and the History of the American West," *Western Historical Quarterly* 24, no. 4 (November 1993): 527; Chávez, *¡Mi Raza Primero!*

3

LA CARAVANA DE LA RECONQUISTA

The Brown Berets Contest Memories of Conquest

OMAR VALERIO-JIMÉNEZ

N DECEMBER 1971, the Brown Berets arrived in Santa Fe, New Mexico, along their months-long march throughout the U.S. Southwest, called La Caravana de la Reconquista. From local residents, the Berets learned that General Stephen Kearny had raised the U.S. flag in the town's main plaza on August 22, 1846, and declared New Mexico to be part of the United States. Kearny, in charge of one of the military campaigns to take over Mexico's Far North, had led the U.S. army in capturing Las Vegas, New Mexico, months earlier at the beginning of the U.S.-Mexico War. One hundred and twenty-five years later, the Brown Berets purposely traced part of the path of Kearny's troops through New Mexico, held rallies to demand better living conditions and civil rights for Mexican Americans, and raised the Mexican flag at various plazas in the state. After the threats to, harassment of, and arrests of several march participants, one of the leaders of the Brown Berets reflected on the significance of Kearny's nineteenth-century actions. "It was never clearer to me that we were the descendants of the Mexican inhabitants who had lived under the United States occupation," David Sánchez wrote in his memoir, "descendants who continue to live as a subordinate population to a white society which continues to destroy our culture, our health, and our existence."[1]

This chapter will examine the multiple ways the Brown Berets contested memories of conquest during their 1971–72 march throughout the U.S.

Southwest. As they traveled from California across various states to Texas, the Berets collected, interpreted, and promoted collective memories. They visited various sites in the U.S. Southwest with ties to the U.S.-Mexico War, and invoked collective memories of the war and its aftermath to contest the nation's official history of the conflict. In addition to raising Mexico's flag at various stops along their march to commemorate Mexico's previous jurisdiction over the region, the Berets erected monuments to nineteenth-century Mexican rebels to remind local communities of their ancestors' resistance to the U.S. invasion. Rather than introducing democracy and civilization to the U.S. West, the war, according to the Berets, directly led to the dispossession of American Indians and Mexican Americans of their lands. This alternative view also addressed the war's legacies by tracing Mexican Americans' second-class citizenship to the broken promises of the Treaty of Guadalupe Hidalgo. The group's journey generated publicity for their cause, but also strategically reminded the nation that the U.S. Southwest was an American Indian and Chicano homeland. The Berets' symbolic "reconquest" of the region relied on reminding residents of the tragic consequences of the U.S. conquest, challenging the "conquered" mentality among some Mexican Americans, and asserting Chicanos' claim to the land and to U.S. citizenship. These Chicana/o civil rights activists strategically "remembered" the nineteenth-century conquest to raise awareness of Mexican Americans' contemporary poverty and disenfranchisement in the twentieth century.

GENESIS OF BROWN BERETS

The Brown Berets began organizing in the Los Angeles area in the late 1960s and achieved prominence through their participation in a series of events, including the East Los Angeles Walkouts, the Chicano Moratorium, a march from southern California to Sacramento, a months-long "caravan" throughout the Southwest, and the occupation of Catalina Island. Scholars have traced the origins of the Brown Berets to the Mexican-American Youth Leadership Conference, a meeting in April 1966 in Malibu, California, for high school student leaders to explore values, identity, and the label "Mexican American." Co-sponsored by the Los Angeles County Commission on Human Relations and the Wilshire Boulevard Temple's Camp Hess Kramer, the three-day conference included discussions of commonalities among the high school student leaders, with the goal of creating alliances to improve their schools and neighborhoods.

As their conversations extended beyond the conference, a group of six of the attendees, including David Sánchez, created Young Citizens for Community Action (YCCA) the following month.[2] This group sought to reform the local educational system through political action and electoral participation. The YCCA's first effective effort was to support the successful electoral campaign of Julian Nava to the Los Angeles school board. Several of these founding members eventually served on advisory boards for the Los Angeles mayor's office and the governor of California.[3]

Over the next few years, the YCCA evolved into the Brown Berets, a militant cultural nationalist organization that remained reformist despite its rhetoric. Various civil and religious organizations assisted the YCCA by providing training and encouragement to participate in neighborhood improvement and community participation projects. One of these groups, the Community Service Organization (CSO), introduced members to Richard Alatorre, who would become a state congressional aide and a state assembly member. Alatorre mentored the youth in community organizing and local politics. He also helped them meet farmworker leader César Chávez. As they gained political knowledge and met more Mexican American political and civic leaders, the members of the youth group began expressing more pride in their ethnicity, which led them to change the name of the organization to Young Chicanos for Community Action. With the support of Father John B. Luce, of the Episcopal Church of the Epiphany, the YCCA opened a coffeehouse, La Piranya, in East Los Angeles. La Piranya became a meeting place for local youth, and also a platform for talks by regional and national civil rights leaders such as Stokely Carmichael and Hubert "Rap" Brown of the Student Non-Violent Coordinating Committee, Reies López Tijerina of the Alianza Federal de Mercedes from New Mexico, and César Chávez of the United Farm Workers union. Such speakers increased the youths' politicization about issues beyond East Los Angeles and affecting other minority communities. The coffeehouse also hosted informational sessions on higher education to encourage local youth to attend college. Unfortunately, the meetings at La Piranya also drew the attention of the Los Angeles County Sheriff's Department, whose officers began harassing the coffeehouse customers. In response, the YCCA organized several protests in front of the East Los Angeles sheriff's station. These protests marked a shift in leadership and strategy for the YCCA, as several members discontinued their participation to concentrate on their college studies, and the YCCA became more confrontational under the leadership of David Sánchez. In January 1968,

Sánchez led the YCCA to change its name to the Brown Berets, and to adopt khaki-colored military garb and distinctive brown berets.[4] The Berets espoused a highly masculinist Chicano cultural nationalism and militant rhetoric against police harassment, and advocated for better schools. Despite their militant rhetoric, the Berets remained a reformist organization that identified both the U.S. Constitution and the Treaty of Guadalupe Hidalgo as laws that the United States needed to enforce.[5]

MARCHA DE LA RECONQUISTA

Frustrations with police harassment and the challenges of organizing a movement in the city led Chicano activists to plan a march from southern California to Sacramento, the state's capital. First, however, in response to the disproportionate Chicano casualties in the Vietnam War, Rosalio Muñoz, a recent UCLA graduate, and David Sánchez established the Chicano Moratorium Committee to plan a series of protests against the war. The protests culminated in the National Chicano Moratorium on August 29, 1970, which drew some twenty thousand to thirty thousand participants to Laguna Park in East Los Angeles, but was marred by police aggression, damaged buildings, and the deaths of several participants, including *Los Angeles Times* journalist Ruben Salazar, who had covered several Chicana/o Movement events.[6] Police harassment of the members of the Chicano Moratorium Committee increased in the aftermath of the August 29 march, while the committee began protesting police brutality in addition to opposing the war.[7] After the National Chicano Moratorium, the Chicano Moratorium Committee decided to launch La Marcha de la Reconquista (March of the Reconquest) in May 1971, to reach a larger audience and to gather information on broader problems confronting Chicano communities elsewhere in the state. This pilgrimage recalled the strategy used by the National Farm Workers Association in their 1966 march from Delano to Sacramento in support of striking workers.[8] Like the farmworkers, the Brown Berets sought to publicize their efforts among Chicano communities to build support for their cause, but also to help Chicanos in other towns fight for civil rights reforms. David Sánchez remembers fielding many telephone calls from activists throughout the nation and coordinating contact information prior to the march, but also feeling frustrated at the slow pace of organizing while dealing with the mass of paperwork. Along with other activists, he wanted to learn firsthand about problems facing Chicanos elsewhere in the state. The activists also wanted to escape the city, "with all its complexities and potential destructiveness." In particular, they wanted to take a break from the constant police harassment, undercover surveillance, and frequent arrests of activists. The Berets had been forced to close their headquarters because they could not afford the rent; so the march was also a way to make their headquarters "mobile" and escape the police pressure at the same time.[9]

The name given to the march recalled the mid-nineteenth-century conquest begun by the U.S.-Mexico War. The interpretation of the U.S.-Mexico War as a conflict that led to the conquest of Mexican Americans became widespread during the Chicano Movement in the late 1960s. The United States, many Chicana/o activists argued, had not enforced the Treaty of Guadalupe Hidalgo with respect to Mexican Americans' citizenship rights. A few years before La Marcha de la Reconquista, Reies López Tijerina had risen to national prominence with the Tierra Amarilla courthouse raid in New Mexico in June 1967. Tijerina had started La Alianza Federal de Pueblos Libres (the Federal Alliance of Free Towns), a land-grants organization, in 1963, with the goal of helping the Mexican American descendants of Spanish and Mexican land grantees reclaim their ancestors' property. In addition to characterizing the U.S.-Mexico War as a war of conquest, Tijerina had argued that the nation had not honored the Treaty of Guadalupe Hidalgo.[10] Through their public actions and interviews with the press, Tijerina's land-grant movement activists had exposed many Chicano Movement activists to the history of the war and the treaty. While details of the U.S.-Mexico War might not have been common knowledge among Mexican Americans, some had acquired a general understanding of the conflict. Through public school education, some activists discovered that the U.S. Southwest had been part of Mexico and sought more information in history books. According to David Sánchez, he first learned that California had been part of Mexico in the fifth grade. This knowledge led him to question Mexican Americans' role and status in the U.S. Southwest.[11] Other activists learned about the U.S.-Mexico War in university courses and from textbooks.[12] Central to these activists' understanding of the U.S.-Mexico War was the belief that the United States had failed to enforce the citizenship rights for Mexican Americans as stipulated in the Treaty of Guadalupe Hidalgo. An additional influence was Mexican immigrants, from whom activists learned an alternative version of the war. These immigrants viewed the conflict as it was presented in Mexico's history textbooks—that is, as an unprovoked and blatant act of aggression to acquire Mexico's land. For example, among the marchers in La Marcha de le Reconquista and La Caravana de la Reconquista were several young men who were recent Mexican immigrants.

The use of "reconquest" in the name of the marches also implied a historical agency for a Chicano community long subordinated throughout the U.S. Southwest. The term "reconquest" was consistent with the Brown Berets' belief that Mexican Americans' lands were "temporarily occupied."[13] But far from believing that Chicanos would retake control of the U.S. Southwest, the Berets used the term to refer to a state of awareness of rights and history.[14] While they considered the U.S.-Mexico War as a military conquest and Mexican Americans as a conquered people, many activists, including some of the Berets, asserted they did not have a conquered mentality or outlook. By declaring "reconquest" as their symbolic goal, these activists were presenting an alternative view of the war, and claiming a right to self-determination consistent with their embrace of cultural nationalism. Not surprisingly, several participants explained that one goal of La Marcha de la Reconquista was to "reconquer the rights and dignity of Chicanos," and to "reconquer [Chicanos'] rights to be treated like people, and not like second-class citizens."[15]

FIGURE 3.1. La Marcha de la Reconquista began in Calexico in March 1971 and traveled eight hundred miles to the state capitol in Sacramento. (Photo courtesy of UCLA's Chicano Studies Research Library, La Raza Collection.)

During the long march to Sacramento, activists learned about issues confronting Chicano communities along their route, but they also experienced several organizational and logistical problems during their three-month journey. Beginning at the U.S.-Mexico border town of Calexico, the activists were in high spirits, as a large crowd from both sides of the border cheered them on. Twenty-five activists demonstrated their ethnic pride by carrying a Mexican flag and beginning their march on May 5, 1971, a symbolic day commemorating the Mexican army's defeat of French imperial troops at the Battle of Puebla in 1862. Among the marchers were Brown Berets, supporters of the Chicano Moratorium Committee, members of the United Farm Workers union, and individual Chicanos from various parts of the nation.[16] Within a week, the marchers had covered sixty miles and were near the Salton Sea but had already confronted formidable obstacles, including the threats posed by speeding vehicles along the road, hot desert weather, and occasional hostility from local residents.[17] Practical logistical issues, such as securing food, water, and lodging for the marchers, as well as transportation for their supplies, became constant concerns. In the ensuing weeks, they would also face roadblocks set up by the Immigration and Naturalization Service (INS) and by local police departments. The core marchers often staged rallies at various towns along the route, and met with residents to learn about the challenges facing local communities. Joining the core group of marchers were residents, students, and farmworkers, who often traveled with the group for a few days. Although these reinforcements helped buoy the spirit and determination of the core group of marchers, some volunteers also created serious problems by encouraging drunkenness, drugs, and infighting among the participants.[18] Along the eight-hundred-mile march, the protesters promoted various issues in speeches at rallies and in interviews with news reporters. They sought to draw attention to the police brutality inflicted on Chicano communities, the farmworkers' struggle, Chicanos' claim to land, their ethnic pride, and their opposition to the policies of Ronald Reagan, the state's governor. When they arrived in Sacramento, the marchers held five days of rallies at various locations, including at Governor Reagan's house and on the capitol steps. By the last day of the march, they had added better education (and specifically more Chicano studies courses at universities), welfare rights, and prison reform to the list of issues they sought to highlight. Despite several formidable obstacles (including exhaustion, violent threats, and internal divisions) along their route, the protesters completed the grueling march to Sacramento to present their demands to the state government, and thus considered their primary goal accomplished.[19]

FIGURE 3.2. As the march passed through various communities along the route to Sacramento, local residents joined the Brown Berets and often shared with the marchers their community's concerns about civil rights issues. (Photo courtesy of UCLA's Chicano Studies Research Library, La Raza Collection.)

LA CARAVANA DE LA RECONQUISTA

The success of La Marcha de la Reconquista led the activists to plan another march to other states, which they called La Caravana de la Reconquista (Caravan of the Reconquest). This caravan began in southern California in fall 1971 and proceeded over the next year to Arizona, New Mexico, Colorado, and Texas, with a side trip to the Midwest. Like the California march, the months-long Caravana de la Reconquista attracted various students, activists, organizations, and local Brown Beret chapters, who helped increase the number of participants on weekends and in large cities. The core group of some twenty-five to thirty Brown Beret marchers would swell to one hundred or more when the participants in La Caravana entered large cities like Albuquerque and El Paso to participate in demonstrations.[20] Among the Brown Berets, there was a belief that the movement was dwindling and that the Chicano Moratorium Committee was in decline after the first march. These activists believed that continuing a march throughout the U.S. Southwest would help prolong the movement that pressed for issues important to the Chicano community.[21] The Brown Berets wanted to see the U.S. Southwest for themselves, map the region, and get to know activists in the region, where they planned to launch future organizing drives. The Marcha de la Reconquista had convinced the Brown Berets of the usefulness of mobile headquarters to avoid police harassment and surveillance; so despite the challenges, the group decided to extend the march across the Southwest. While various police departments and the FBI continued to harass the marchers during La Caravana, the police had their difficulties too because the Brown Berets were always on the move. Nevertheless, an FBI infiltrator briefly joined the marchers but left after the activists confronted him.[22] As they ventured outside of California, the Berets faced greater logistical challenges to coordinate a long-distance march. In response, they reached out to Brown Beret chapters in the states they visited to ask for food and water, as well as additional marchers.[23] As the group visited border states historically tied to Mexico, they capitalized on various opportunities to directly challenge public history about the U.S. Southwest, to learn about local issues, and to promote their message of cultural nationalism.[24]

CONTESTING THE HISTORY OF U.S. WESTWARD EXPANSION

As they traveled across the U.S. Southwest, the Berets often sought out local residents to learn about contemporary civil rights struggles and community issues. While visiting Tucson, Arizona, in November 1971, one of their local guides (Anna) explained community efforts to convert part of the city-run El Río Golf Course into a public park in Barrio El Río, a Chicano neighborhood.[25] After nine months of repeated demonstrations the city agreed to build a park, but it remained unnamed. The Chicano community wanted to name the park after Joaquín Murrieta, the nineteenth-century "social bandit" from California, so the Brown Berets decided to stage an unofficial christening ceremony for the park. They organized an "invasion," set up tents, took over a miniature children's "castle" in the middle of the park, and raised two flags (one for Mexico and one for the Berets) over the castle. The group then staged a march through various Tucson neighborhoods in order to announce a rally for the next day to name the park. As they had done similarly elsewhere along their Caravana de la Reconquista, the Brown Berets created a small monument to commemorate the park's name as "Parque Joaquín Murrieta." Prior to unveiling this monument, several speakers addressed the crowd, including one who spoke about the significance of Murrieta, California's gold rush, and the U.S. westward expansion. After characterizing the park's namesake as a great hero who "stole from the rich to give to the poor," the speaker claimed that Murrieta understood the severity of the destruction initiated by the European American westward movement. The speaker closed by summarizing European Americans' persecution of Mexicans during the gold rush and the environmental damage unleashed, and by affirming Murrieta's struggle for "our cultural survival."[26]

The visit to Tucson illustrated some of the ways the Brown Berets used collective memories to contest the official history of the American West and of Chicanos. Brown Beret leader David Sánchez recalled that the toy castle in the middle of the park intrigued the group and led them to organize the rally and unofficial christening. The castle was ten feet tall, built of sturdy concrete, and had authentic-looking gun sights. Sánchez remembered the group's fascination with the children's castle. "The park struck us as having been designed for battle and the fact that it needed a name intrigued us."[27] The military aspects of the children's castle in this unnamed park led the Brown Berets to recall collective memories of the nineteenth-century U.S. westward expansion as a military conquest. As they had done elsewhere along the march, the group raised the Mexican flag as a reminder that the park's land (and the territory of the state of Arizona) had formerly belonged to Mexico. While the Mexican flag served to trigger the collective memory of a pre-annexation period among some of the Mexican American residents of Tucson, it also angered the local police as well as residents who had no social or cultural connections to Mexico. Raising the Mexican flag also reminded residents that the Brown Berets' Caravana de la Reconquista was meant to highlight the Chicano community's grievances, many of which had begun with the U.S. conquest in the mid-nineteenth century. While the Berets surely knew that they could not physically reconquer the U.S. Southwest, the caravan did spread their message of symbolically reconquering the region by advancing efforts for Chicanos' self-determination and community control.

The Berets' symbolic "reconquest" of the region relied on challenging the official narrative of U.S. westward expansion, and reminding the region's residents of the tragic consequences of the U.S. conquest. One of the rally speakers, for example, inverted the American claims of "pacifying the wild west," calling that a justification for expansion onto lands claimed by Mexico and American Indian nations. "Today, this serves as a reminder," the speaker argued, "that the west was not wild until the expansion of the United States boundaries." By accusing the United States of making the west "wild," this speaker publicly contested the common narrative that the nation's westward expansion introduced progress to the region. This speaker also connected Murrieta to Mexican American resistance to the U.S. conquest. In this retelling of Murrieta's role in challenging American expansion, the social bandit's efforts were equated with the larger Mexican community's goals of protecting their land and culture. For Chicano activists, it seemed fitting that this park be named after a nineteenth-century Mexican American hero who had fought against American expansion. After all, the park was located in a Mexican American neighborhood and created through local community efforts in an area of the American West that had belonged to Mexico. Although the Berets' naming ceremony was unofficial and the monument was only temporary, the ceremony was consequential by fulfilling the community's wishes and pressuring city officials, who acquiesced to name the park after Joaquín Murrieta.[28] The unofficial naming ceremony, raising of the Mexican flag, and speeches denouncing U.S. westward expansion allowed the Brown Berets to effectively contest official public history of the American West and propagate an alternative memory of the war's tragic consequences for Mexican Americans. Moreover, their unofficial naming ceremony undoubtedly motivated some attendees and onlookers to read more about the nineteenth-century conquest of the U.S. Southwest.

As the Caravana de la Reconquista passed through Arizona, New Mexico, and Texas, the Brown Berets repeatedly experienced the transmission, contestation, and strategic use of collective memories of conquest. While visiting Silver City, New Mexico, the Brown Berets were forced to sleep in campsites after a local priest rescinded his initial offer to house them at the Catholic Youth Organization Center on discovering they were not students. The group split into three smaller units (two male and one female) in order to camp and train in different parts of Silver City. The Berets named the first unit the Nepomucenos squad after Juan Nepomuceno Cortina, the South Texas native who led a rebellion in 1859. The second squad was named Los Tigres after one of Pancho Villa's units during the Mexican Revolution in 1910. The third group, composed of Brown Beret women on the expedition, was named Las Juanitas squad after a Mexican woman whom California vigilantes hanged during the gold rush.[29] The symbolism of these monikers illustrates how the group used its understanding of the history of Texas, Mexico, and California to draw parallels between earlier struggles and their contemporary goals. The names also served to remind

FIGURE 3.3. La Marcha de la Reconquista attracted considerable media attention throughout the eight-hundred-mile route to Sacramento. (Photo courtesy of UCLA's Chicano Studies Research Library, La Raza Collection.)

group members and the public of an alternative history that was not taught in public schools. Finally, the monikers symbolized the Berets' understanding of the transnational history of resistance.

The appellations chosen for the three squads demonstrate how the Brown Berets harnessed collective memories of conquest and struggle for civil rights goals. The first two groups recall popular male rebels, one in Brownsville and the other in Mexico's northern states, who fought against injustice and for land reform, respectively. David Sánchez identified Cortina as a "famous Mexican general . . . who captured Brownsville, Texas[,] in 1859 to free twelve Chicano prisoners."[30] Although he does not acknowledge it in this description, Sánchez implicitly linked Cortina's efforts to fight criminalization by freeing Mexican American prisoners in 1859 with the Brown Berets' struggle to highlight the increasing incarceration of Chicano youth in the 1970s. The reference to a unit of Pancho Villa's soldiers highlights the importance of the Mexican Revolution and Mexican history to the Chicano movement, and it also demonstrates the transnational circulation of collective memories of struggle. The Berets' choice to name a squad after Pancho Villa's unit might have been an effort to link the contemporary land reform struggles in New Mexico with those of the Mexican

Revolution of the 1910s. The Berets undoubtedly also knew of Villa's 1916 cap-
ture of Columbus, New Mexico, which was about eighty-five miles south of
Silver City. Villa's daring capture of Columbus and ability to avoid General
John J. Pershing's troops increased his popularity among Mexicans and Mexican
Americans, who admired Villa's ingenuity and direct challenge to U.S. forces.
Finally, by choosing the name Las Juanitas for the all-female squad, the Berets
recalled a Mexican American woman who was hanged after she killed a white
miner in self-defense during an assault in the aftermath of the U.S. conquest.[31]
The squads' names demonstrate the Berets' desire to commemorate Mexican
and Mexican American heroes, and to offer a counter-history to the official
narrative of U.S. westward expansion. The names also helped remind the Berets
and their supporters in New Mexico of previous struggles against injustice, and
to promote the collective memories of these heroes among Mexican Americans,
who probably did not learn such history in their schools.

After a brief stop in Las Cruces, the Berets visited Mesilla, New Mexico,
on December 6, 1971, to highlight the failure of the United States to honor the
Gadsden Treaty of 1853. The treaty was signed in Mesilla, and completed the
U.S. purchase for the transfer from Mexico to the United States of some 29,600
square miles of land in present-day southern Arizona and southwestern New
Mexico. The Berets located the old town square, or Placita, where they believed
the Gadsden Treaty had been signed.[32] During their visit to the Placita, the
Berets met an elderly resident, Cruz Alvarez, who provided an alternative history of the Gadsden Purchase. According to Alvarez, Mexico initially refused to
sell the land designated as the Gadsden Purchase, but later acquiesced after the
United States threatened to use military force to obtain the land.[33] The exchange
with Alvarez served to disseminate a local resident's alternative collective conquest memory to the Berets. In turn, Sánchez wrote about this meeting and
propagated a collective memory of the Gadsden Treaty that countered the official U.S. narrative. Sánchez further explained that the United States had failed
to guarantee the civil rights of the Mexicans who remained in the territory
covered by the Gadsden Purchase. Like the Treaty of Guadalupe Hidalgo, the
Gadsden Treaty had guaranteed that Mexicans who remained in the ceded territories would receive full U.S. citizenship rights. The United States, the Berets
argued, had violated both treaties by failing to guarantee the civil rights of Mexican Americans. By using Mexican Americans' collective memories of the U.S.
conquest to illustrate the nation's failure to enforce nineteenth-century treaties,
the group also linked these legacies of conquest to the contemporary denial of

civil rights for Mexican Americans. Highlighting the "right to assemble" as one of the civil rights guaranteed to U.S. citizens, Sánchez offered several recent examples of the nation's violation of this right, including the police killings of *Los Angeles Times* reporter Ruben Salazar and two others during the Chicano Moratorium (August 29, 1970) and the police shootings of demonstrators in January 1971.[34] To underscore their right to assemble and their goal of reminding local residents of Mexico's prior claim to the land, the Berets camped out in the Placita and raised the Mexican flag on the town square's sixty-foot flagpole. Sánchez reflected on the Berets' choice by writing, "we felt proud that the Mexican flag was once again spreading its influence over these historical grounds." Their actions did not trigger an official response from the police, but some angry residents fired shots at the Berets. While no one was hurt, the violence directed at the Berets demonstrated that some local residents did not appreciate being reminded that the U.S. conquest had displaced a nation to which many local residents still held cultural and social ties.[35]

The Berets' efforts to symbolically reconquer the U.S. Southwest included challenging the narrative of a benign and uncontested U.S. conquest of New Mexico in the mid-nineteenth century. After visiting Las Cruces and Mesilla, La Caravana traveled north to Albuquerque, and then on to Santa Fe. As they entered Santa Fe in mid-December 1971, they learned from local residents that General Stephen Kearny had raised the U.S. flag over the city's main plaza in 1846 and declared the territory under U.S. control. This was another example of the transmission of collective war memories from local residents to the Berets. These residents warned the group of the hostility of local police. Undeterred, the group staged a march to the state capitol to demand "better living conditions" for Mexican Americans. The march led the police to arrest twenty-six Berets for supposedly violating a local ordinance prohibiting marches on the streets.[36] After gaining their release, the Berets continued along part of the route taken by Kearny as he led the forces of occupation into Mexico's Far North. Whenever they camped along the way, the Berets repeatedly raised the Mexican flag, which angered some local residents. Such a hostile reception to their peaceful protest undoubtedly influenced Sánchez's interpretation of the links between Kearney's invasion and the post-annexation consequences. From Santa Fe, the group continued to Las Vegas, New Mexico, where Kearny was believed to have begun his invasion of the U.S. Southwest. In his memoir of La Caravana, Sánchez provides some background on Kearny's nineteenth-century invasion of New Mexico, and the refusal of New Mexico's governor, Manuel Armijo, to resist the U.S. aggression. Sánchez includes a few details about the unofficial resistance from Mexicans and Pueblo Indians (and their subsequent massacre). His decision to include these details (which he gleaned from Rodolfo Acuña's *Occupied America*) demonstrates the emerging influence of Chicana/o history in shaping Mexican Americans' historical perspectives. It also illustrates how the collective memories of New Mexico residents combined with the counter-history offered by Acuña to shape an alternative history and memory of the U.S. conquest. General Kearny's forces had taken the U.S. Southwest by force, argued Sánchez, which began Mexican Americans' second-class citizenship. His conclusion about Kearny's significance clearly attributes Mexicans' initial subordination to the effects of the U.S. conquest and blames their continued subservience on the nation's failure to provide full civil rights.

The march continued to other southwestern states, with the Berets stopping at various locations to learn about community issues and to contest official public history. As the Berets traveled along the Rio Grande in South Texas, they learned new details about the U.S. provocation that initiated the U.S.-Mexico War in the vicinity of Brownsville. The Berets "learned that the southwest takeover started with the first Americans who began to lose their lives in violent clashes with Mexicans who resisted their invasion."[37] From local residents' collective memories, the Berets learned that the region's Mexicans had indeed resisted the nineteenth-century U.S. invasion. Such conquest memories underscore the view that the U.S. troop movement beyond the Nueces River was an invasion of Mexico's territory, and contradicted President Polk's infamous excuse for starting the war. Sánchez wrote: "The Americans were claiming the loss of American blood on American soil, but Mexico was claiming the loss of American blood on Mexican territory since the southwest was part of the Republic of Mexico." Sánchez concluded by identifying the Americans as "exploiters" and accusing the United States of forcibly taking the land from Mexico. While the Berets had a general understanding of the U.S.-Mexico War before embarking on their Caravana, their interactions with various Mexican American communities along their march led them to absorb local conquest memories. While such collective memories had been passed from one generation to another by family and neighbors, the Berets' visit to the region allowed local residents to inform these activists and spread such memories beyond their immediate community. Individual Berets surely shared this information on the war and the U.S. conquest with their family and friends back home, while others passed along this historical information to a wider audience through the

FIGURE 3.4. The Brown Berets' newspaper, *La Causa*, reported on the progress of La Caravana de la Reconquista, alerting readers throughout the U.S. Southwest of the route and dates when the marchers would arrive in their communities. (Photo courtesy of UCLA's Chicano Studies Research Library, David Sánchez Papers.)

Berets' newspaper, *La Causa*. Sánchez reached even more people by relaying this information in his book, published seven years after La Caravana. The Berets strategically used these newly acquired collective war memories to highlight the purpose of their trip—the symbolic "reconquest" of the U.S. Southwest by reshaping collective conquest memories for contemporary political purposes.

In addition to the Brown Berets learning about the U.S.-Mexico War, their visit to Brownsville gave them an opportunity to discover more about Juan Cortina from local residents, as well as to honor his legacy. Many Brownsville residents, the group was surprised to learn, had not heard of Cortina, a nineteenth-century resident who led a rebellion. This lack of knowledge of a famous Mexican American rebel illustrates the uneven dissemination of collective memories within a community.[38] It also confirms that the educational system failed to provide information about an important episode of resistance to American westward expansion. The Berets were pleased to meet an older woman, Teresa Canales, who shared her family's collective memories of Cortina. Canales claimed to be the sister of J. T. Canales (a local lawyer and politician), and a descendant of Cortina's family. She explained how Mexicans who became U.S. citizens after the war lost land because they lacked knowledge of U.S. laws, failed to pay property taxes, and relied on European American lawyers and real estate agents who defrauded them of property. Canales also described Cortina's 1859 shooting of a European American marshal to stop an incident of police brutality against a Mexican worker, and his raid on Brownsville. While explaining Cortina's role in the region, Canales described the U.S. government's failure to enforce the Treaty of Guadalupe Hidalgo to protect the property rights of Mexican Americans.[39] Given the Berets' criticism of the increasing incarceration of Chicano youth, their fascination with Cortina, who freed ethnic Mexican prisoners from Brownsville's jail, was expected. Before leaving the city, the Berets held a rally to dedicate a monument to Cortina for his role in fighting "for justice for the Mexicans living in the U.S."[40] As they had done elsewhere on their march throughout the Southwest, the Berets sought not only to correct the historical narrative about Mexican Americans, but also to create an alternative public history with their monuments to Mexican American heroes. Although temporary, the monuments served to commemorate Mexican American historical figures left out of the nation's official history.

By linking the long-term consequences of the U.S.-Mexico War to the continued subordination of Mexican Americans, the Berets strategically used conquest memories to advance their political agenda. They traced the origins of Chicanos' subordination to the aftermath of the U.S.-Mexico War, detailed problems facing the Chicano community, and challenged official public memories of the nation's westward expansion. To contest official memories of conquest, the Brown Berets created alternative monuments to Mexican Americans who had fought on Mexico's behalf during the U.S.-Mexico War or who defended Mexicans from European American attacks in the war's aftermath. They also attempted to raise the Mexican flag at war landmarks as a reminder of Mexico's former claim to the land. Ultimately, these and other Chicano activists combined collective memories of conquest with myths to construct a view of the U.S. Southwest as a Chicano homeland and to promote entitlement among Mexican Americans who had been politically and socially marginalized. As memory scholars remind us, the act of remembering is accompanied by the act of forgetting. While the official U.S. history remembered a "bloodless" conquest of the U.S. Southwest, it selectively forgot Mexican Americans' resistance during and after the war. The construction and dedication of monuments to Mexican American rebels like Joaquín Murrieta and Juan Cortina demonstrate the Brown Berets' attempt to create a counternarrative to the nation's public history and to propagate collective memories of these rebels as champions of civil rights. This activism illustrates the Berets' strategic use of conquest memories and the links between social and political uses of memory.[41] Each time activists recalled the war in their pamphlets, speeches, and/or media interviews, they reminded the nation of the long-term social consequences of the U.S.-Mexico War, the unfulfilled promises of the Treaty of Guadalupe Hidalgo, and the justifications for civil rights activism. Moreover, by recalling the war and the treaty's promises in their campaigns, activists reinforced and modified their communities' collective memories, thus transmitting conquest memories across several generations.

NOTES

1.   David Sánchez, *Expedition Through Aztlán* (La Puente, Calif.: Perspective, 1978), 99.
2.   Ernesto Chávez, *"¡Mi Raza Primero!" (My People First!): Nationalism, Identity, and Insurgency in the Chicano Movement in Los Angeles, 1966–1978* (Berkeley: University of California Press, 2002), 43.
3.   Chávez, *"¡Mi Raza Primero!,"* 43–44.
4.   David Sánchez, interview by Virginia Espino, oral history interview conducted by the UCLA Oral History Program, session 1, November 26, 2012.
5.   Chávez, *"¡Mi Raza Primero!,"* 56–60.

6.   Lorena Oropeza, *Raza Si! Guerra No! Chicano Protest and Patriotism During the Viet Nam War Era* (Berkeley: University of California Press, 2005), 145–47, 160–67; Chávez, *"¡Mi Raza Primero!,"* 65, 68–70; F. Arturo Rosales, *Chicano! The History of the Mexican American Civil Rights Movement* (Houston: Arte Público, 1996), 200–207.

7.   Chávez, *"¡Mi Raza Primero!,"* 72–77.

8.   Miriam Pawel, *The Crusades of Cesar Chavez: A Biography* (New York: Bloomsbury, 2014), 124–26.

9.   Oropeza, *Raza Si! Guerra No!*, 186; Sánchez, interview, session 4, December 20, 2012; Sánchez, *Expedition Through Aztlán*, 15–17.

10. Oropeza, *Raza Si! Guerra No!*, 69–72.

11. Sánchez, interview, session 1, November 26, 2012.

12. Manuel Gómez, interview by author, September 7, 2017.

13. Chávez, *"¡Mi Raza Primero!,"* 56.

14. Oropeza, *Raza Si! Guerra No!*, 186.

15. Jack Jones, "Chicanos March to 'Reconquer,'" *Los Angeles Times*, May 13, 1971; Jack Jones, "Chicanos 3-Month March to Capitol Reaches Salton Sea," *Los Angeles Times*, May 13, 1971; "Chicano March Ends in Near Skirmish," *Los Angeles Times*, August 8, 1971; Chávez, *"¡Mi Raza Primero!,"* 56.

16. Jones, "Chicanos March to 'Reconquer.'"

17. Jones, "Chicanos 3-Month March."

18. Sánchez, *Expedition Through Aztlán*, 18–51; on problems with alcohol and drugs during march, see pages 34, 41, 45, 49; Sánchez, interview, session 3, December 14, 2012.

19. "Chicano March Ends in Near-Skirmish"; "Protesters Call Reagan a 'European Wetback,'" *Los Angeles Times*, August 14, 1971; Sánchez, *Expedition Through Aztlán*, 51–54; Sánchez, interview, session 4, December 20, 2012. For an account of La Marcha de la Reconquista and some of the tension, see Rosalio Muñoz's testimonio in Mario T. García, *The Chicano Generation: Testimonios of the Movement* (Oakland: University of California Press, 2015), 211–319.

20. It is difficult to estimate the number of participants in a months-long march through several states because participants came and went for various reasons. Throughout La Caravana, local chapters of the Brown Berets would join the marchers before and after their city of residence. The Federal Bureau of Investigation provided some estimates on the core group of marchers, as the FBI had informants join the march at various times and also received reports from various local law-enforcement agencies. For example, the FBI estimated twenty-five to thirty Brown Berets marching into El Paso on July 7, 1972. See José Angel Gutiérrez Collection, MS 24, box 21, in the University of Texas at San Antonio's Special Collections Library, which contains redacted copies of the FBI reports about La Caravana. Folder 25 has reports on La Caravana as it passed through El Paso, San Antonio, and the Lower Rio Grande Valley.

21. Sánchez, interview, session 4, December 20, 2012; session 5, January 7, 2013.

22.   Sánchez, interview, session 5, January 7, 2013.

23.   Sánchez, interview, session 5, January 7, 2013.

24.   Chávez, *¡Mi Raza Primero!,*" 56.

25.   Gómez and Chilcott identify the golf course as El Río Golf Course, while Rosales identifies it as Del Rio Golf Course. Gómez and Chilcott also identify the neighborhood as Barrio El Río, and the adjacent neighborhoods (just south and southeast) as Barrio Manzo and Barrio Hollywood, respectively. See Angel Ignacio Gómez and John Henry Chilcott, *Outline of Mexican American Education* (Tucson, Ariz.: Impresora Sahuaro, 1973), 60–62; Rosales, *Chicano!,* 211.

26.   Sánchez, *Expedition Through Aztlán,* 73–76. Sánchez misspells the name of the park as "Joaquín Murietta."

27.   Sánchez, *Expedition Through Aztlán,* 74–75.

28.   Armando Navarro, *La Raza Unida Party: A Chicano Challenge to the U.S. Two-Party Dictatorship* (Philadelphia: Temple University Press, 2000), 208. This park came about through the grassroots efforts of the Chicano Leadership Coalition and the El Rio Coalition to create a neighborhood park out of the city-owned El Rio Golf Course, located in a barrio on the west side of Tucson. The intransigence of city officials and their disrespect for community activists helped fuel the creation of La Raza Unida Party in Tucson, according to activist Salomón Baldenegro.

29.   Sánchez, *Expedition Through Aztlán,* 83–86.

30.   Sánchez, *Expedition Through Aztlán,* 86. Cortina became a Mexican brigadier general in the 1870s, but was living in Texas and working on his family's extensive properties in 1859.

31.   According to literary scholar Maythee Rojas, the woman referred to as "Juanita" was in reality Josefa (Juvera) Loaiza. Rojas, "Re-Membering Josefa: Reading the Mexican Female Body in California Gold Rush Chronicles," *Women's Studies Quarterly* 35, no. 1/2 (Spring/Summer 2007): 127, 144.

32.   The Gadsden Treaty was signed in Mexico City. For more information on La Placita as a site of the Mexican American community celebrations, and the Mexican American women-led struggle against its redevelopment, see Lydia Otero, "La Placita Committee: Claiming Place and History," in *Memories and Migrations: Mapping Boricua and Chicana Histories,* ed. Vicki Ruiz and John R. Chávez (Urbana: University of Illinois Press, 2008), 44–70.

33.   Sánchez, *Expedition Through Aztlán,* 90. Sánchez identifies Alvarez as a colonel and as a former U.S. ambassador to Spain. According to an oral history interview, Alvarez was attached to the American embassy in Madrid, Spain, during World War I. Marie Carter and Cruz Richards Alvarez, *Cruz Richards Alvarez,* New Mexico, manuscript/mixed material, https://www.loc.gov/item/wpalh001139/, and http://lcweb2.loc.gov/mss/wpalh1/18/1813/18130506/18130506.pdf.

34.   Sánchez, *Expedition Through Aztlán,* 90–91.

35.   Sánchez, *Expedition Through Aztlán,* 91–93.

36.   "Berets March in Santa Fe," *Santa Fe New Mexican,* December 22, 1971. According to the *Santa Fe New Mexican,* police arrested twenty-three Brown Berets: "Brown

Berets Arrested Here," *Santa Fe New Mexican,* December 23, 1971; "Angeleños from Outer Space?," *El Grito del Norte* (Española, N.M.), February 18, 1972; *Valley Morning Star* (Harlingen, Tex.), December 22, 1971.

37. Sánchez, *Expedition Through Aztlán,* 155.
38. Alon Confino, "Collective Memory and Cultural History: Problems of Method," *American Historical Review* 102, no. 5 (December 1997): 1398–1400.
39. Sánchez, *Expedition Through Aztlán,* 156–57.
40. Sánchez, *Expedition Through Aztlán,* 158–59. Their monument might also have been a response to several historical markers about the U.S.-Mexico War that the group had seen on their visit to South Texas. After dedicating their monument to Cortina, the group visited the town of Santa Maria, where they read a historical marker with the following inscription: "This is the location where in April of 1848 [*sic*], the Mexican Cavalry killed 62 dragoons, perpetuating the Mexican-American War." Sánchez, *Expedition Through Aztlán,* 160. The historical marker focuses on the so-called Thornton Skirmish, which precipitated the war. It reads, "The spot where 'American blood was shed on American soil' April 25, 1846; here Captain Seth B. Thornton and 62 dragoons were attacked by Mexican troops." Contrary to the information on the marker, this spot was not on U.S. soil, but rather on El Rancho de Carricitos, owned by a Mexican rancher, and under Mexican jurisdiction. Omar S. Valerio-Jiménez, *River of Hope: Forging Identity and Nation in the Rio Grande Borderlands* (Durham, N.C.: Duke University Press, 2013), 134–35.
41. Confino, "Collective Memory and Cultural History," 1394.

4

FROM SIQUEIROS TO SPARC

The Historical and Ideological Roots of a Chicana Mural Movement

JUAN PABLO MERCADO

We proclaim that this being a moment of social transition from a decrepit to a new order, the creators of beauty must invest their greatest efforts in the aim of materializing an art valuable to the people, and our supreme objective in art, which is today mere individualist masturbation, is to create something of beauty for all, beauty enlightens and stirs to struggle.
—"MANIFESTO OF THE SYNDICATE OF TECHNICAL WORKERS, PAINTERS, AND SCULPTORS," *EL MACHETE*, JUNE 1924

I want to produce artwork that has meaning beyond simple decorative values. I hope to use public space to create public voice, and consciousness about the presence of people who are often the majority of the population but who may not be represented in any visual way. By telling their stories we are . . . visualizing the whole of the American story while creating sites of public memory.
—JUDY BACA, FROM "RICHMOND IDENTITIES: EXTRAORDINARY LIVES | ORDINARY PEOPLE"

THE CHICANA and Chicano art movement of the late 1960s and early 1970s expressed the political, social, and economic struggles of Chicanos and Chicanas in the United States and was unquestionably guided by the *muralistas* of the era. The work of Mexican activist and artist David Alfaro Siqueiros, from his epic six months in California in 1932 until his death in 1974, provided the foundations for that public artistic renaissance. I argue here that by assessing the early mural projects of Siqueiros while he was in exile in Los Angeles in 1932, we can trace back the historical and ideological origins of

Chicana and Chicano muralism. We will also see the deep-rooted link between Siqueiros and the activism and art of Judith F. Baca, and how she has pushed the mural movement forward through her work at the Social and Public Art Resource Center (SPARC).

Often the origins of the Chicana/o mural movement have been bestowed equally among Los Tres Grandes. For this study, one must ask, why emphasize Siqueiros and not Orozco or Rivera, or why not all three? While these are valid questions, and there is no doubt that the other two muralists produced extremely important art, neither Orozco nor Rivera was primarily involved in public art projects during this formative period in the early 1930s in California. Orozco painted in a dining hall at Pomona College, and Rivera painted at the Pacific Stock Exchange in San Francisco; those were spaces almost entirely reserved for the political, economic, and racial elite. For a myriad of reasons, though, the projects of Orozco (*Prometheus*, 1930) and Rivera (*The Allegory of California*, 1931) during this foundational period became a singular expression of their ideology. Since their work was accessible only to a select few, neither artist could develop the public or populist connection or accessibility that their work warranted. On the other hand, the development and application of Siqueiros's *América Tropical* in 1932 was able to convey a significant message, magnifying and disrupting a historical legacy of violence and imperialism in the most public of places, the Placita on Olvera Street. Siqueiros was responsible for the first major outdoor painting in Los Angeles created by a Mexican. Despite immediate efforts to destroy that public message, years later, in a moment of almost quixotic destiny, those images and that message revealed itself to an emerging generation of artists, activists, and radicals.

Just as in the aftermath of the Mexican Revolution, El Movimiento inspired a revival of muralism. And although the emerging form of Chicana/o muralism derived from Mexican muralism, it was distinct in many critical ways.[1] Here is precisely where the influence of Siqueiros on most all Chicana/o muralistas of El Movimiento can be understood and evaluated. For it was Siqueiros himself who declared: "My Friends, traditional fresco is dead!"[2] Siqueiros realized what many muralists of the sixties and seventies would also discover. "Mexican fresco ended up being mystical in its form, its colors, its composition, and its results. The new elements . . . had opened up a new world, an unsuspected aesthetic: trim, solid, electric, definite, concrete. It is the aesthetic of this epoch, it is the aesthetic of the developing new society."[3] Siqueiros had the foresight to accurately predict that Chicana/o muralistas would embrace this sort of new muralism and would go on to invent an acrylic painting method that Chicana/o artists would widely use in the future. Los Angeles would be the generative ground to accept and implement this new muralism, becoming the site of the largest concentration of Chicano murals in the United States, with estimates ranging from one thousand to fifteen hundred separate works painted between 1969 and 1993.[4] For these reasons, I argue that the roots of this artistic and political resurgence can be found in the revolutionary ideals and actions of David Alfaro Siqueiros.

INFLUENCE OF THE MEXICAN REVOLUTION

The Mexican Revolution of 1910 was the defining experience for Mexican muralists in the early twentieth century and beyond. This revolt was marked by violence and was motivated by a desire to delegitimize the regime of the dictator Porfirio Díaz. The "gains" of the Porfiriato came at the expense of most Mexican people, especially the poor and working class and indigenous people. Human needs were being frustrated by poor working and living conditions, corrupt political and business interests, and a lack of self-determination.[5] All of these factors led to a popular response, with many elements of a social revolutionary movement.[6]

While Mexican muralism certainly developed as a mode of advocacy and inspired political action in the period following the Mexican Revolution, at its essence it was an educative project that sought to teach the histories of Mexico to its people. These revised accounts of Mexican history would not privilege Europeans and regularly highlighted the struggles and uprisings of Mexicans against foreign interlopers as well as domestic autocrats.[7] Among the most significant artists of Mexico who worked to revise the history of their country from a revolutionary perspective was David Alfaro Siqueiros.

Siqueiros was born in Santa Rosalía (today Ciudad Camargo), Chihuahua, in 1896, and at a very young age was politicized by the mounting revolutionary fervor in Mexico. He attended the influential San Carlos Academy of Fine Arts in Mexico City, and as a teenager participated in the Great Strike of 1911, where students in the academy protested archaic and despotic methods of instruction. Although according to Siqueiros, "all I did then was to throw a few stones at things or at people, and little else."[8] After prolonged student protests, Antonio Rivas Mercado resigned his post as director of the academy, and Alfredo Ramos

Martínez was appointed new director. Shortly thereafter, Martínez developed a school at Santa Anita Ixtapalapa, one in a series of *escuelas al aire libre* (open air schools) in order to better appreciate the natural environment of Mexico. This was a crucial moment in the development of Siqueiros and his cohort of young artists because Martínez focused on Mexican art that would feature Mexican subject matter and not privilege European themes; Siqueiros would later note that it marked the beginning of a "new aesthetic."[9] This new aesthetic was imbued with the natural environment and popular culture of Mexico, and especially with its pre-Hispanic culture. This fact cannot be overstated: Siqueiros's training at the San Carlos Academy consciously rejected the philosophy that the subject matter and approach of true art was solely European in origin, an ideology that Siqueiros would later confirm during the Mexican Revolution.[10]

The pressures of revolution were too much to bear, and Siqueiros, in part inspired by the tales of his grandfather as a soldier, decided to enlist in the *ejercito* and fight for his convictions. Siqueiros attributes part of his artistic development to his experiences as a *carrancista* in the Mexican Revolution: "without that participation, it would not have been possible to have conceived or inspired much later."[11] Siqueiros went as far as to acknowledge that it was only after he had discovered the extraordinary architecture and culture of his country, an opportunity widely unthinkable for many young Mexicans, that he realized that Mexico had in fact an "amazing popular art—perhaps the most rich and varied of the whole world."[12] What he experienced as a soldier, coupled with the venture of traveling throughout the Mexican countryside, profoundly shaped Siqueiros and in his mind put to rest any notion of becoming an "apolitical bohemian, parasitic artist." Rather, he became a citizen artist committed to a revolutionary state.[13] His art had to represent something far beyond one-dimensional aesthetic values—it needed to support a national shift in political and historical consciousness.

His military service was not the only experience that shaped his ideas and artwork. Siqueiros was profoundly moved by the plight of working-class people throughout the globe, especially in the Western Hemisphere, and protested growing imperialist sentiments that aggressively targeted the international labor movement. As an example, during the first part of the twentieth century, Siqueiros opposed the U.S. economy becoming more and more entangled with global markets as part of an imperial project. This emergence gave rise to U.S. political and military intervention in the region. From President Theodore Roosevelt through President Woodrow Wilson, the United States constructed an idea

of liberal internationalism that rested on an ideology of economic and political progress. To guarantee this progress, the United States, and in particular
Woodrow Wilson, attacked both international and domestic threats to U.S.
imperialism. Prior to and during World War I, the United States engaged in a
series of military interventions in the Western Hemisphere—Mexico in 1914,
Haiti in 1915, and the Dominican Republic in 1916—all to promote "stability"
in the region along with protecting U.S. investments.[14] Siqueiros witnessed the
takeover of Vera Cruz in 1914 by U.S. forces, and the experience left an indelible
mark on the psyche of the budding artist, activist, and soldier.

INTERNATIONAL LABOR SOLIDARITY

During this period in the United States, political agitators like Eugene V.
Debs campaigned for drastic political and labor transformation. In the period
leading up to World War I, union membership rose rapidly by five million
workers in the United States. Additionally, during this period many small
rural farmers experienced deteriorating living and working conditions. These
circumstances—popular labor support and declining rural conditions—made
revolution in some way imaginable in the United Sates. Yet unlike in Mexico
and Russia, these working and living conditions were not enough to bring
about a "successful" social revolutionary movement, at least not one resulting
in a regime change that would radically remake society. Within this context,
we can connect international violence with an emerging fear of socialist antiwar movements in the United States. In particular, the response to revolts in
Mexico and Russia was severe repression in the United States. In 1917, President Wilson signed the Espionage Act, followed by both the Sedition Act
and the Immigration Act of 1918, resulting in the deportation of any alien who
opposed organized government. These repressive political tactics, combined
with progressive-era election reforms geared at appeasing political detractors,
worked to limit the radical movements in the United States, especially those
focused on labor.

By 1925, Siqueiros had moved to Guadalajara, Jalisco, where he was immersed
in the international labor movement and directly involved in organizing textile
workers and miners. In Mexico, the conditions for working-class folks in the
postrevolutionary period was toxic at best. First, workers had to deal with a
shattered infrastructure, a proscription of their labor rights, and destructive

transnational fiscal agreements. Second, dispossessed Mexicans who sought land reform had to deal with the prolonged violence that resulted from the secularization process sweeping the nation in the form of Cristeros.[15] Siqueiros was committed to forming unions independent of company-affiliated syndicates and believed that if workers could organize independently, they would be in a much better position to challenge oppressive working and living conditions.

Furthermore, Siqueiros also opposed "Yankee imperialism" and deleterious U.S. foreign policy.[16] In the period just after World War I, the United States, and more specifically Woodrow Wilson, sought to overturn many of the wartime regulations that had been implemented to secure the compliance of labor. President Wilson also sought to dismantle agencies that controlled industrial production and the labor market. This went hand in hand with widespread, officially sanctioned repression of political and social dissent. Massive labor strikes in the United States caused anxiety, stemming in part from the Mexican and Russian Revolutions. Siqueiros challenged this sort of global repression. For example, in 1927, he encouraged the Workers Confederation of Jalisco to implement a work stoppage in support of Nicola Sacco and Bartolomeo Vanzetti and against their looming executions, but also to demonstrate union power and solidarity.[17] The looming deaths of anarchists Sacco and Vanzetti represented a U.S. domestic policy that targeted immigrants, sought to check a supposed global radical conspiracy, and simultaneously gut civil liberties and labor rights. Siqueiros believed in direct action to protest growing imperialist attacks by the United States, as well as onerous labor conditions in Mexico. In the years to come, many of these themes would resonate significantly throughout his artwork, in a process that ultimately sought to transform the visual into social justice.

A MOVE TO GRINGO LAND

Siqueiros's effectiveness as a labor organizer coupled with his membership in the Mexican Communist Party (PCM) made him a prime target for police harassment, and predictably he found himself in prison for honoring his ideological views. By the early part of the 1930s, Siqueiros understood that if he wanted to continue to realize his political and artistic visions outside the walls of a prison cell, he would have to leave Mexico. With other major artists like

José Clemente Orozco and Diego Rivera stoking the mural movement in the United States, Siqueiros decided that he too must head north to gringo land and begin a new period in his life.[18]

Siqueiros arrived in the United States frayed from political and financial stresses in Mexico. Yet those experiences only strengthened his artistic resolve. In 1932, Siqueiros and his wife, Blanca, along with her son, arrived in Los Angeles with no money and few prospects for work. After connecting with fellow Mexican artist Luis Arenal, and with the backing of film director Josef von Sternberg, Siqueiros was able to organize a few exhibits of his paintings and prints for the local art community of Southern California. These relationships generated interest in his art and resulted in Siqueiros securing some income. After a series of smaller shows, Siqueiros held his first major exhibition in Los Angeles, which was well attended and proved very profitable. More importantly, however, it set the tone for his short-lived stay in the States. One evening during the exhibition "Siqueiros overheard [a] lady comment in a Southern accent that Mexicans must be sadistic to paint portraits of dead children."[19] While Siqueiros did concede that some of the content was very primitive, he also made it a point to underscore that it was "much more savage and brutal to lynch living Negroes."[20]

This searing commentary was roundly criticized in the local papers, yet it also made clear that Siqueiros would not hold back his ideological convictions. The art Siqueiros displayed illustrated how racial and class oppression had affected the lives of working-class peoples all across the Americas. I would argue that this is precisely when and where we see the Chicano/a mural movement emerging. Siqueiros called out the systemic racial oppression of U.S. hegemony in the Americas, and went further by pointing to the unfettered racial violence that concurrently plagued the United States. Indeed, the themes of labor rights, self-determination, and of course racial violence all figured prominently in the three murals Siqueiros created in Los Angeles in 1932.

In a remarkably prolific six-month period during 1932, Siqueiros completed three major projects in Los Angeles, including *Portrait of Mexico Today*, *Street Meeting*, and *América Tropical*. Siqueiros developed *Street Meeting* as his first mural in the United States when he was invited to teach fresco painting to a small group of artists at the Chouinard Art Academy. As Siqueiros experimented with different techniques, the advice of architects Richard Neutra and Summer Spaulding helped him settle on using white cement as the base for his painting on the exterior wall of the school. The choice of cement obliged

Siqueiros to use a quicker process to apply paint on the wall since the cement dried faster than traditional fresco. As Siqueiros was completely invested in developing and using modern techniques to paint, he viewed his experimentation as a necessary progression in his artistic evolution. New methods and techniques inspired him; he asserted that "a new society must have new material solutions."[21]

The content for *Street Meeting* was consistent with the political and artistic sentiments Siqueiros pledged to advance. On the exterior wall of the Chouinard Art Academy, Siqueiros composed a mural depicting a labor organizer talking with workers—presumably about advocating for their rights—and next to the organizer Siqueiros placed a black man and a white woman both holding children.[22] This image underscored two of the most pressing problems facing working-class peoples in the United States during this period. First, it challenged an oppressive anti-labor regime that had taken hold throughout the Americas. In the wake of a massive and unfounded deportation scheme by the U.S. government, hundreds of thousands of Mexican workers were being unfairly targeted. These events occurred against the backdrop of a larger attack on labor rights throughout the United States as a result of the Great Depression.

As for the interracial couple listening to a pro-worker speech, according to Siqueiros, "It occurred to me to paint black and whites together in Los Angeles. . . . [And] the result was that all the racist Americans were tremendously upset by the mural."[23] Siqueiros was referring to the intensification of racial violence throughout the United States. The fiercest manifestation of this violence came from the rebirth in the early 1920s of the Ku Klux Klan (KKK), who believed that the United States represented opportunity and freedom only for those of a particular religious and ethnic stock. Moreover, as KKK membership grew to more than five million members during the 1920s, its reach spread far beyond its Southern roots. The group expanded to the North and the West, and also expanded its attacks beyond blacks.

This new version of the Klan targeted Jews and Catholics, but also other groups like feminists, union leaders, and queer men; to the Klan, these groups threatened the racial purity and moral fiber of the country. Within these conditions, the powerful statement of *Street Meeting* was bound to cause controversy. In fact, the mural upset so many people that shortly after its debut, the school erected a wall to prevent viewing of the mural, and eventually *Street Meeting* was almost completely destroyed. Yet Siqueiros would not let this "fascist reaction" to his work dissuade him from advancing his critiques of Yankee imperialism.[24]

AMÉRICA TROPICAL

Partly because of the controversial nature of his themes, Siqueiros was commissioned by F. K. Ferenz, owner of the Plaza Arts Center, to paint a mural on the
wall of the Old Italian Hall overlooking the Placita on Olvera Street. While
Ferenz was clearly looking to cash in on the publicity a Siqueiros mural might
provide, he also attempted to hamstring Siqueiros by giving him the theme of
a tropical America. For Ferenz, a tropical America meant a continent of happy
gentlemen, surrounded by palm trees, squawking parrots, and where fruits fell
from the trees free for the masses—an exotic paradise. Instead, Siqueiros made
a powerful and dramatic critique of Yankee imperialism when he painted "a man
crucified, on a double cross and poised proudly over was the eagle of the U.S.
currency."[25] Because the mural depicted the struggles, harassment, and persecution of many men and women throughout the Americas, Siqueiros expected
a violent attack for dealing with these themes in such a public manner. The
mural also contained armed men of color, a public image that you still can't
paint in Los Angeles today. According to Siqueiros, "my mural was the mural
of a Mexican painter who had fought in the Mexican revolution . . . who knew
that his first duty before aesthetic concerns was to fulfill the expression of his
ideology."[26]

FIGURE 4.1. Roberto Berdecio, a close associate of Siqueiros during the
1930s, stands in front of *América Tropical* shortly after completion. (Mural:
© 2012 Artists Rights Society [ARS], New York/SOMAAP, Mexico City.
Photo: Getty Research Institute, Los Angeles.)

Although some critics found the themes insightful and politically salient, the highly anticipated mural was widely criticized in the media and almost immediately covered up. In a matter of weeks, the mural had caused so much political anxiety and tension that it was literally whitewashed. At the end of his six months' stay, Siqueiros's visa was not renewed by the U.S. government. During his brief sojourn in the states in 1932, two of his murals, *Street Meeting* and *América Tropical*, were almost completely destroyed, yet the ideological and historical impression that Siqueiros left would not as easily be erased.

The late 1960s and early 1970s were a time of revolutionary change in the United States and other parts of the world. The Chicana and Chicano Movement (CCM) was similar to many social movements of the era in that large groups of historically marginalized folks were assessing their relationship to white American society. They rejected cycles of poverty and lack of educational opportunities and demanded institutions that were more responsive to their particular cultural, political, and economic needs. Coincidentally, Siqueiros's *América Tropical* mural, whitewashed in 1932, had large chunks of the whitewash chip off and partly expose its imagery. The mural then came to represent, at least in the eyes of young Chicano and Chicana artists and activists, another glaring example of the inability of racist institutions to allow expressions of Chicano and Chicana experiences in the United States.[27] Accordingly, we should think of the CCM as a creative and revivalist surge that championed civil rights amid a larger set of social movements that fought for political recognition, an end to racial violence, and legal respect. More to the point, the CCM was a confluence of many significant struggles all aimed at social justice. The public art of David Alfaro Siqueiros helped to define and push that revivalist surge.

Clearly, *América Tropical* had a significant influence on the CCM and continues to influence contemporary Chicana/o artists and activists. But the mural did more than just establish a link between Chicanas/os in the United States and Mexicans; the CCM also had a profound effect on Siqueiros. From his earliest days, Siqueiros maintained a loyalty to and affinity for people of Mexican descent working and living in the United States, proclaiming, "I support the efforts of Mexicans living in the United States, it is of great importance to our own struggle."[28] The influence and commitment to solidarity is evident in the work of Siqueiros, who had been so moved by the efforts and actions of Chicana/o activists that he composed a drawing of Ruben Salazar, an iconic figure of the CCM. Salazar was a prominent Mexican American journalist in Los Angeles who was murdered during the Chicano Moratorium on August

FIGURE 4.2. David Alfaro Siqueiros with *Heroic Voice*, 1971. (Heritage Gallery records, 1944–2000. Archives of American Art, Smithsonian Institution.)

29, 1970. He was shot in the head with a ten-inch tear gas projectile after he and a companion sought refuge from police violence in the Silver Dollar Café.

Here we can trace the historical and ideological footing of the artistic expression of El Movimiento to the work of Siqueiros. For Siqueiros, art and activism were much more than a one-way relationship. Although he clearly shaped El Movimiento, both artistically and ideologically, he was also greatly influenced by the work of Chicana/o activists and artists. We can see throughout Siqueiros's murals that he infuses the themes of labor struggle, racial violence, and self-determination, all of which were central organizing principles of the civil rights struggles of Chicanas and Chicanos in the 1960s and 1970s. In short, Siqueiros and El Movimiento had developed a reciprocal relationship. Through his art, Siqueiros was able to distinctly communicate the tensions, struggles, power, and strength of a people when those people were in tumult and experiencing acute social changes. During this period, a young and promising Chicana artist attended the Taller Siqueiros workshop in Mexico to cultivate her mural art. Judith F. Baca would return from Mexico with a renewed sense of commitment and an indelible link to Siqueiros, his artistic approaches, and mural techniques.

MI ABUELITA

Prominent art historians have noted that muralism was the most important, widespread, and publicized facet of the Chicano art movement during the 1970s, and muralista Judy Baca was a fundamental part of that artistic renaissance.[29] Baca was born in Huntington Park in 1946 and was initially raised by her mother and grandmother in a small one-bedroom home in Watts before moving to Pacoima in the San Fernando Valley. From a very early age, Baca developed an "affinity for [her] grandmother," and together they forged a relationship that would set the aesthetic and spiritual underpinnings for Baca's life.[30] Baca recalls having formative conversations with her grandmother about where the focus of Baca's visions would be: "She would say, 'What did you dream?' . . . There was an exchanging of discussions very early . . . she paid very close attention to my dreams."[31] In turn, this creative and spiritual curiosity poignantly shaped Baca's worldview.

Baca's conception of the world was intimately tied to art. She would often accompany her grandmother to church and recalls "sitting in the pew and studying the imagery within the church."[32] She also remembers traveling to the central market with her grandmother, where she would see Simon Rodia working on the Watts Towers. As a young child, these profound experiences with her grandmother subtly and implicitly embedded a uniquely artistic consciousness that Baca later realized and pursued. Baca reflected: "the art was always the center of what I wanted to do and be."[33]

Yet pursuing a life as an artist was much more complex than Baca had anticipated. "When I stepped out of the university," she recalled, "I was perfectly equipped to do absolutely nothing."[34] Baca reflected that her grandmother had crossed the Rio Grande to come to the United States during the height of the Mexican Revolution, and here she was stepping into the world as an artist and there was also a revolution going on.[35] Like the Mexican Revolution, this social movement would be shaped and understood through the art that people generated in the era. During this formative period in her life, Baca struggled to conceptualize a way to work that allowed her to fulfill her most valued responsibilities as a woman, as a Chicana, and as an artist.

After becoming the first woman in her family to graduate college, Baca struggled to appreciate her role as an artist. In a story that Baca often recounts as central to understanding her trajectory into El Movimiento, she recalls a conversation with her grandmother regarding her artwork. "M'ija, what's it for?" her grandmother asked. Baca thought, "I don't know what it's for. I just spent all this time doing something, [and] I don't even know what it's for. . . . [For my grandmother] everything had its place in her world, you know. Everything had meaning and purpose." At this point, Baca realized that she had to use her particular skills as an artist to make connections with people that went far beyond self-gratification. Baca knew that her art needed to have *meaning and purpose*, and to "speak to the people [she] cared most about, [her] family and [her] community."[36] Baca sought to transmit the energies and changes of her community through her artistic projects.

The late 1960s and early 1970s provided fertile ground for movements of educational and artistic action. In 1970, Baca began teaching art in Boyle Heights through the Los Angeles Department of Recreation and Parks. Although she was not raised in East L.A., she did see many significant parallels between Pacoima and the barrios on the Eastside. She began to develop new strategies to work with young gang members, utilizing art education that underscored the interests and demands of the local communities. Baca eventually formed a crew of local youth dubbed Las Vistas Nuevas that incorporated the graffiti and tattoo culture that many of the youth venerated.[37] Las Vistas Nuevas developed their first mural project, *Mi Abuelita*, in the Hollenbeck Park bandshell.

The mural, depicting Baca's grandmother, was a direct commentary on the role of women in Mexican families, as well as an affirmation of the indigenous ancestry of Chicanos and Chicanas in the United States.[38] Moreover, because many of the young mural makers were from rival gangs, Baca had to coordinate a peaceful collaborative art project that reconciled many of the violent issues between these young adversaries. The mural also sent a message to people all across Los Angeles and around the United States as they struggled for social justice. By having Baca's *abuelita* as the central figure of the mural, demonstrating

FIGURE 4.3. Judith F. Baca, *Mi Abuelita*, © 1970. (Image courtesy of the SPARC Archives. sparcinla.org.)

compassion, strength, and agency, this public canvas disrupted deep-seated narratives of neo-coloniality, including patriarchy and racial violence.

After leading the mural program on the Eastside of Los Angeles for three years, Baca directed a successful proposal to the Los Angeles City Council that would become the first citywide mural program. Through the Citywide Mural Program, Baca and her team helped employ and train hundreds of young people all across Los Angeles, purchased materials for mural projects, and altogether helped to organize over four hundred mural projects in distinct communities bridging the city of Los Angeles. Despite the prodigious achievements of the program, the occupation of public space to include a public identity of subjugated peoples often resulted in censorship. Elected bureaucrats were not yet willing to reimagine the landscape of the city in such an explicit way. This led to a desire to form a different space of production that did not rely on a capitulation to city officials.[39]

In 1973, Baca sought to develop a mural in Estrada Courts, across the street from her first mural project, that recognized a profound contradiction within the Chicano Movement. The Estrada Courts murals, directed by Charles W. "Cat" Felix, promoted work that, according to Marcos Sanchez-Tranquilino, sought to "enhance or affirm gang turfs and their boundaries as unique or nondependent on each other for survival in a larger social context."[40] Baca had a close relationship with Felix, and she even introduced him to some contacts in the mayor's office; yet the mural that Baca envisioned—an explicit critique of the destructive and often-violent territorial claims by many Chicano youth— featured sharp criticism of some of the other Estrada Courts murals.[41] More- over, Baca's proposal for a mural centered on the experiences of women, and often those experiences were shaped by male militarism.[42]

Chicanas still faced extremely sexist and traditional ideas within El Movi- miento. Baca recalls that for many women, their role was to "get the coffee . . . the men were very powerful and very formidable."[43] Baca strove to find a way to do her work in a manner that did not have to follow the traditional sub- ordinated role of women. To complicate matters further, the mostly *veterano* muralist crew in Estrada Courts had initially pledged to avoid overtly political themes in exchange for resources and support from local politicians, merchants, and police.[44] The rejection of Baca's mural proposal should be viewed as a failed opportunity to open up the ranks of Chicano muralism to women. This moment is also a critical example of the internal contradiction to the radical equality El Movimiento sought to achieve. Patriarchy and sexism divided the most import- ant organizations and diffused some of the momentum of the movement. This contradiction resulted in the articulation of a new vision of this United States that included a more feminist ideal.

BACA, SPARC, AND *THE GREAT WALL OF LOS ANGELES*

Partly because of these rifts, Baca decided to operate full-time on the west side of Los Angeles, which came with its own issues. She lived in Venice, California, and even though she had been welcomed by the burgeoning feminist artis- tic scene there, she could not wholly reconcile with a movement that focused mostly on the desires and frustrations of middle-class white women.[45] Still, her participation in consciousness-raising circles shaped her ideology. For the first time in her life, Baca found a space to meet and share with professional women all concerned with advancing a feminist agenda. However, Baca never felt like she fully belonged among most of these women, whose ideas could be at odds with her own positionality. There was a fundamental lack of awareness of the experiences of women of color. This lack of recognition, or Achilles' heel as

Baca puts it, essentially held back the movement. A predominantly white group of women were attempting to define the issues of race for an entire group of women, and this would not allow for a truly inclusive perspective.[46]

Baca's struggles embodied a much broader national struggle over women's rights, reproductive rights, feminism, and movements for liberation. For example, the Combahee River Collective in Boston had formed in part to struggle against interlocking forms of oppression. It was impossible for these women to disaggregate their racial position from their class position and their sexuality. These struggles catalyzed the formation of a politics that was at its core antiracist and antisexist and that underscored the inherent value of women of color.[47]

This was a critical juncture in Baca's personal and professional life, and it seemed to have no clear resolution. She recalls, "I began a very long period of time of straddling two lives—the feminist information and life that supported my growth as a woman, and my community life which was in the Latino community as I worked intently in the neighborhoods. And they never really met. They were constantly separated."[48] However, this straddling of two worlds was a major impetus for the creation of the Social and Public Art Resource Center (SPARC) in 1976.

SPARC was not the author or originator of mural projects. It was the fiscal receiver where Baca could formalize community programs and her artistic innovations. SPARC became a space where Baca could develop artwork that spoke to her sensibilities and forward a new model of feminist identity that did not have to sever a link with her significant cultural experiences. Baca was now able to apply her methods and techniques to a wider artistic community and encourage broader public participation. *The Great Wall of Los Angeles* was conceived by Baca and brought to SPARC. As she remembers, it was "an opportunity over a half a mile-long span of a piece of a mural to define the relationships between ethnic groups and feminism and feminist issues."[49]

Conceptualized and negotiated with the Army Corps of Engineers by Baca, *The Great Wall of Los Angeles*, 1974–83, is the most prominent mural project that SPARC has facilitated. The expansive mural pays historical tribute to interracial harmony. Baca envisioned "another history of California; one which included the ethnic peoples, women, and minorities who were all so invisible in conventional textbook accounts."[50] *The Great Wall of Los Angeles* was the very first project facilitated by SPARC and is a monument not only to the Los Angeles River, where this brilliant composition of public art is embedded, but also a chronicle of the often erased histories of many of California's underrepresented ethnic groups and a rejection of homophobia as well. It is a half-mile-long work of art developed during the civil rights revolution and activism of the 1970s and was realized during California's Chicana/o mural art renaissance.[51] The groundbreaking and collaborative methods developed by Baca and adopted by SPARC resulted in a significant, and more importantly, more democratic history. More democratic in the sense that the knowledge and art produced was not merely an extraction of experiences to be redistributed to a larger audience; rather, these innovative methods encouraged a broader participation in contemporary historical debates by incorporating a more representative set of experiences and values.[52]

Baca developed a collaborative process of innovation that moved far beyond the artist(s) and those who had commissioned the piece. The process brought together artists, historians, community activists, social workers, and young people from distinct communities to promote an exchange of experiences. Often these experiences revealed the memories embedded in the land beneath a "public site." Through this process and within these murals, generations of people have been able to rethink "official" histories.[53] For instance, in a section depicting the circumstances of the Great Depression, Baca and the mural makers rethink those circumstances and provide nuance to a seemingly static historical narrative. Hundreds of thousands of Mexican and American citizens were rounded up in a deportation scheme by the state and forced to start their lives anew, scapegoats for the Depression's economic conditions. Baca and SPARC succeed in restoring the often-omitted histories of our communities, while at the same time disrupting a powerful exclusionary narrative of U.S. history.

The Great Wall of Los Angeles was developed through a process called the Imaging of Content.[54] Inspired by community members and realized through murals, this process was developed over decades and includes a host of elements geared toward a collaborative transformational outcome. The first portion of this process employed a strategy of "multiple ways of knowing." Baca and her team of mural makers combined methods of conventional academic research, including reading and reporting on relevant historical monographs, with an assemblage of popular culture iconography.

Baca also coordinated visits to the mural site by poets, writers, and other cultural informants, which complemented conventional methods of inquiry. A compilation of all of these sources and materials resulted in the construction of a timeline that included many of the major and "not so major" political, cultural, social, musical, and artistic events of the period.

FIGURE 4.4. Judith F. Baca, "500,000 Mexican Americans Deported." Detail from the 1930s section of the *Great Wall of Los Angeles*, © 1976. (Image courtesy of the SPARC Archives, sparcinla.org.)

The next step of the Imaging of Content process typically includes an in-depth analysis of the knowledge and histories harvested. The team then initiates an assessment of the main issue(s) of a particular community and articulates those problematics. From there, the process involves forming an alternative way of understanding the social issues essential to the subject matter of the mural.

Alternatives to the problems are thought through, and innovative solutions to these questions are envisioned. Then a defining metaphor is generated that embodies the variant perspectives of the community—a counternarrative to *official* history is conceived. The culmination of all of these steps and ideas is a visual articulation in thumbnail sketches. The sketches are critically vetted; Baca and other artists and community members carefully talk through the sketches from the prisms of age, gender, immigration status, and sexuality. This vetting process provides another opportunity for Baca to adjust her visual representation.

Painting on *The Great Wall*, which spanned five separate summers, began in 1976 and resulted in an historical re-vision of ethnic peoples in California. The visual survey developed in this mural spans Los Angeles history from its prehistoric roots up to a 1950s postwar metropolis. The wide-ranging themes depicted on the Great Wall include the settlement of Chumash Indian peoples around 10,000 BC and the 1781 founding of "El Pueblo de la Reina de Los Angeles . . . by 46 *pobladores* from Mexico . . . the majority [of which] were Indian, Mestiso,

Mulatto and Black."[55] The mural also charts the tumultuous and often distorted histories of nineteenth-century California, including an homage to a new wave of immigrants. The mural goes on to provide new insights and unearth perspectives of California history regarding World War I, the Great Depression, the Double V Campaign, the displacement of Chávez Ravine residents, and the founding of the Mattachine Society in 1950.[56] This mural offers imagery of forgotten people in public spaces and encourages new ways of thinking about the past.

THE RIVER

An important aspect of this history is the connection between the Los Angeles River and *The Great Wall of Los Angeles*. Baca notes that the river forms the guiding metaphor for this public monument. As early as the 1920s, city planners began planning for concreting the river; Baca viewed that project as a symbol of the hardening of the arteries of the land because it created both disease as well as dis-ease.[57] Baca saw the concreting as a scar on the city, and the relationship "between the scars on a human body and those on the land took shape in [her] mind."[58] From the earliest days of the project, Baca looked out onto the river's edge and imagined how the mural might take form. She envisioned the public marker as a great "tattoo on the scar where the river once ran."[59] Thus, the work of the *Great Wall* was an attempt to reimagine a history of pain, exclusion, and dislocation; it was a way to tattoo over that scar.

Part of the way that Baca and the mural makers at SPARC went about tattooing the scar, or reconstructing these histories, was by centering the history of the river. Baca enlisted the help of oral historians, ethnologists, and troves of community members to tease out the hidden history of the river and of Los Angeles.[60] In the early part of the century, city planners used Mexican memories to disrupt and reroute the river and ultimately segregated many of the Mexicans in Los Angeles, as highlighted in the innovative work of historian Bill Deverell.

In 1914, city planners conducted a series of "oral histories," or interviews, with several Mexican residents of Los Angeles, mainly regarding the history of the river. These histories influenced municipal decisions about how to manipulate the geography of the river and how to physically move Mexican bodies from the land.[61] So a collection of capitalists and city officials used personal memories to manipulate and dislocate a river and its people. Sixty years later, a wide collaboration of artists, historians, and community members also relied on personal

memories to reconnect to the past. In a remarkable example of symmetry, Baca
and the mural makers at SPARC relied on Mexican memories—in addition to
indigenous memories, African American memories, Chinese memories, Japanese memories, and more—but in this case, to relocate and reconnect these
communities with the region, to the river, and to the history of Los Angeles.

The river's history has often been reduced to incomplete fragments of the
past; Allison Carruth astutely notes that for many Angelenos, the Los Angeles
River invokes very little and often includes only the imaginary of films that draw
on dystopian stories about the river as a space of crime and alienation. More
often than not, the river is unseen and unremembered.[62] Precisely for these
reasons, the intervention that Baca and the mural makers at SPARC introduced
provides a space for public imagery that challenges notions of disaffection and
corruption by providing a historical account of distorted or forgotten peoples
of Los Angeles and the United States.

CONCLUSION

This essay traces the lineage of Chicana/o muralism to the work and activism of David Alfaro Siqueiros. That work was shaped by the circumstances of
the Mexican Revolution and led to a flourishing of Mexican muralists in the
United States in the early twentieth century. Siqueiros's six-month sojourn in
the United States in 1932 unquestionably influenced the work of future Chicana/o muralists, including Judith F. Baca. Baca understood and learned from
the artistic and political ethos of her antecedents, yet she had to break with
artists in order to develop a form of muralism with a more collaborative form
of consciousness. The founding of SPARC and the emergence of *The Great Wall
of Los Angeles* represents this critical divergence.

These mural projects are essential reflections of the political and cultural
experiences of Chicanas and Chicanos during El Movimiento and beyond.
The public art projects initiated by Baca and her team of mural makers transform public spaces by rejecting the coercive components of cultural amnesia
and encouraging a different form of remembering. This different remembering inspires its viewers—as well as its makers—to cross the boundaries of art,
social justice, history, and collective memory, and offers a critical lens on how
particular communities envision themselves, their struggles, and their ability to
transform history.

NOTES

1. Eva Sperling Cockcroft and Holly Barnet-Sanchez, *Signs from the Heart: California Chicano Murals* (Venice, Calif., and Albuquerque: SPARC and University of New Mexico Press, 1990), 9.
2. D. A. Siqueiros, as quoted in Philip Stein, *Siqueiros: His Life and Works* (New York: International Publishers, 1994), 74.
3. Blanca Luz Brum, in *El Universal* (México, D.F.), August 17, 1932, as quoted in Stein, *Siqueiros*, 76.
4. Cockcroft and Barnet-Sanchez, *Signs from the Heart*, 10.
5. Michael J. Gonzales, *The Mexican Revolution, 1920–1940* (Albuquerque: University of New Mexico Press, 2002), 59.
6. Social revolutionary movements (SRM) are processes that use a variety of strategies to inspire social change and cannot simply be pegged as a singular discernible set of tactics or polices or phenomena; see Juan Gómez-Quiñones, *Teorizando sobre la Revolución Mexicana: Interpretaciones de sus historiadores y cronistas* (México, D.F.: Secretaría de Educación Pública, Instituto Nacional de Estudios Históricos de las Revoluciones de México, 2015).
7. Shifra M. Goldman, *Dimensions of the Americas: Art and Social Change in Latin America and the United States* (Chicago: University of Chicago Press), 101–6.
8. Anthony White, *Siqueiros: A Biography* (Encino, Calif.: Floricanto Press, 1994), 41–44; quoted in Jean Charlot, "Orozco and Siqueiros at the Academy of San Carlos," *College Art Journal* 10, no. 4 (1951): 362.
9. White, *Siqueiros*, 44–46.
10. Robert H. Patterson, "An Art in Revolution: Antecedents of Mexican Mural Painting, 1900–1920," *Journal of Inter-American Studies* 6, no. 3 (1964): 387. Many artists and their mentors were still influenced by European styles; yet the encouragement to engage with Mexican subject matter, and an explicit focus on the Indigenismo of Mesoamerica, resulted in a less Eurocentric perspective.
11. Quoted in White, *Siqueiros*, 55.
12. Quoted in Stein, *Siqueiros*, 35.
13. Quoted in White, *Siqueiros*, 55.
14. The United States sought to impose a sort of moral imperialism during this period that included military intervention and fiscal control throughout the hemisphere. In 1915 the United States sent troops into Haiti, rewrote the Haitian constitution, and instituted financial supervision of the nation that remained in effect until 1941. Similarly, in the Dominican Republic the United States took control of the customs house in 1905, militarily occupied the nation in 1916, and instituted financial supervision that lasted until 1941.
15. Stein, *Siqueiros*, 54–65.
16. Yankee imperialism can be thought of as the economic or military influence of and coercive domestic and foreign policies developed by the United States to maintain power over subordinated countries and/or groups of people.

17. White, *Siqueiros*, 102–5.
18. White, *Siqueiros*, 133.
19. See Stein, *Siqueiros*, 72; the painting, *Portrait of a Dead Child*, was based on a request that Siqueiros received from a mourning family in hopes that he could capture the memory of their deceased child, a very common custom in some parts of Mexico.
20. Quoted in White, *Siqueiros*, 136–38.
21. Quoted in White, *Siqueiros*, 138–39.
22. White, *Siqueiros*, 142.
23. Jesús Salvador Treviño and KCET, Los Angeles, *América Tropical* (New York: Cinema Guild, 2006), DVD (Siqueiros quoted in film).
24. For more on the "discovery" and restoration of *Street Meeting*, see the KCET documentary on the Chouinard-Siqueiros mural discovery: https://youtu.be/pEd-IwSXdyCM; White, *Siqueiros*, 142.
25. Siqueiros, quoted in film *América Tropical*.
26. Siqueiros, quoted in film *América Tropical*.
27. Chicano artist Gilbert "Magu" Lujan, quoted in film *América Tropical*.
28. Siqueiros, quoted in film *América Tropical*.
29. Cockcroft and Barnet-Sanchez, *Signs from the Heart*, 23.
30. Judy Baca, interview by Karen Mary Davalos, January 29, March 16 and 26, May 10, June 3, September 29, October 13, 20, and 27, and November 3, 2010, Los Angeles, CSRC Oral Histories Series, no. 14 (Los Angeles: UCLA Chicano Studies Research Center Press, 2014), 3–6.
31. Baca, interview by Davalos, 6.
32. *Judy Baca—Artist*, directed by Pedro Pablo Celedón (Barefoot Productions, 2013), HD color.
33. *Judy Baca—Artist*.
34. Judy Baca, "Arte Intimo, Arte Publico: Spirit, Vision and Form, The Art of Judy Baca," Latin American Canadian Projects: Latin American Speakers Series (LASS), March 14, 2014.
35. Baca, "Arte Intimo, Arte Publico."
36. Baca, interview by Davalos, 40; Cockcroft and Barnet-Sanchez, *Signs from the Heart*, 78.
37. Kaelyn Danielle Rodriguez, "Authorship and Memory in Judy Baca's Murals" (master's thesis, University of California, Riverside, 2014), 16–17.
38. Judith F. Baca, "Birth of a Movement," in *Community, Culture, and Globalization*, ed. Don Adams and Arlene Goldbard (New York: Rockefeller Foundation, Creativity and Culture Division, 2002), 112.
39. For a complete history of the Citywide Mural Program, visit the SPARC webpage, http://sparcinla.org/brief-history/.
40. Marcos Sanchez-Tranquilino, "Space, Power, and Youth Culture: Mexican American Graffiti and Chicano Murals in East Los Angeles, 1972–1978," in *Looking High and Low: Art and Cultural Identity*, ed. Brenda Jo Bright and Liza Bakewell (Tucson: University of Arizona Press, 1995), 71.

41. Oral history interviews with Judith Baca, August 5–6, 1986, Archives of American Art, Smithsonian Institution.

42. Sanchez-Tranquilino, "Space, Power, and Youth Culture," 72.

43. Interview with Judith Baca, in *!Women Art Revolution* (Zeitgeist Films, 2010), interview by Lynn Hershman Leeson, October 2, 1992, Catalina Island, California; videotape interviews by Lynn Hershman Leeson for film, 1990–2008, M1639, Department of Special Collections, Stanford University Libraries, Stanford, Calif.

44. Sanchez-Tranquilino, "Space, Power, and Youth Culture," 71.

45. See chapter 5, "L.A. Happenings and Performance Art," in Cécile Whiting, *Pop L.A.: Art and the City in the 1960s* (Berkeley: University of California Press, 2008).

46. Interview with Judith Baca and Suzanne Lacy, in *!Women Art Revolution* (Zeitgeist Films, 2010), interview by Lynn Hershman, July 7, 2004, Los Angeles; videotape interviews by Lynn Hershman Leeson for film, 1990–2008, M1639, Department of Special Collections, Stanford University Libraries, Stanford, California.

47. See Combahee River Collective Statement (1977); Kimberlé Crenshaw, "Mapping the Margins: Intersectionality, Identity Politics, and Violence Against Women of Color," in *The Public Nature of Private Violence*, ed. Martha Albertson Fineman and Rixanne Mykitiuk (New York: Routledge, 1994), 93–118; Cherrie Moraga and Gloria Anzaldúa, *This Bridge Called My Back: Writings by Radical Women of Color* (New York: Kitchen Table: Women of Color Press, 1983).

48. Interview with Baca, in *!Women Art Revolution*.

49. Interview with Baca, in *!Women Art Revolution*.

50. SPARC, *Great Wall of Los Angeles: Walking Tour Guide* (Venice, Calif.: Social and Public Art Resource Center), 2007, 5; Baca, quoted in SPARC, *Great Wall of Los Angeles: Walking Tour Guide*, 9.

51. SPARC, proposal to the Santa Monica Mountains Conservancy (revised, May 2006), 4.

52. Michael Frisch, *A Shared Authority: Essays on the Craft and Meaning of Oral and Public History* (Albany: State University of New York Press, 1990), xxii.

53. Judith F. Baca, "Whose Monument Where? Public Art in a Many-Cultured Society," in *Mapping the Terrain: New Genre Public Art*, ed. Suzanne Lacy (Seattle: Bay Press, 1995), 131.

54. In November of 2004, Baca delivered the Seventeenth Lawrence Kohlberg Memorial Lecture, "The Human Story at the Intersection of Ethics, Aesthetics, and Social Justice," at the Thirtieth Annual Conference of the Association for Moral Education in Dana Point, California. In her speech, Baca gave a clear and concise description of the Imaging of Content process: a "method developed, honed, and systematized at SPARC to create hundreds of murals over the last thirty years." Full text of the speech published in the *Journal of Moral Education* 34, no. 2 (June 2005): 153–69, https://doi.org/10.1080/03057240500137029.

55. SPARC, *Great Wall of Los Angeles*, 20.

56. This is only a brief sketch of some of the major historical circumstances depicted in *The Great Wall*. For a complete history and description of the mural, see http://sparcinla.org/the-great-wall-part-2/.

57. SPARC, *Great Wall of Los Angeles*, 1.

58. Baca, "Birth of a Movement," 116.

59. Baca, "Human Story."

60. SPARC, *Great Wall of Los Angeles*, 5.

61. Bill Deverell, *Whitewashed Adobe: The Rise of Los Angeles and the Remaking of Its Mexican Past* (Berkeley: University of California Press), 121; chapter 3, "Remembering a River," provides an in-depth look at the history of the Los Angeles River, its many incarnations, and its indelible relationship to regional attitudes about race, ethnicity, and culture.

62. Allison Carruth, "A Brief History of Public Art and the L.A. River," March 20, 2014, KCET, https://www.kcet.org/shows/artbound/a-brief-history-of-public-art-and-the-la-river.

5

CHALE CON LA GUERRA

The Chicano Antiwar Movement in Houston, 1965–1975

JESÚS JESSE ESPARZA

T HE JULY 26, 1970, protest march and ensuing rally put on by a group of activists in Houston, Texas, who called themselves the Chicano Moratorium Committee Against the War in Vietnam, was an expression of the larger antiwar movement of this period.[1] The war in Vietnam for the American people quickly escalated following the Gulf of Tonkin Resolution in 1964, which gave President Lyndon Johnson the authority to use military force to thwart Communist activities there.[2] While the United States was already involved in Vietnam through covert, top-secret operations, the American presence on the peninsula did not increase until after August 1964.[3] Emerging simultaneously was an aggressive, unapologetic Chicano antiwar movement that saw this war as another manifestation of American imperialism. This movement expanded rapidly throughout the nation, demanding an end to American military action in Vietnam and a change to U.S. foreign policy, and calling for Chicanos to fight for equality at home and not far away in some strange place.[4]

So, with over a thousand people taking to the streets of Magnolia Park, a historically Chicano section of town, holding signs, banners, flags, white crosses, and a coffin representing those killed in the war, Houston became the site of one of the largest Chicano collective condemnations of the country's involvement in Vietnam.[5] In fact, it was touted as the largest Chicano protest march the city had ever seen.[6] Across the nation, Chicanos were holding antiwar demonstrations. From Austin to San Francisco to East Los Angeles, which would take center stage in the movement to end that war, Chicanos were holding protest marches.[7] In Houston also, Chicanos espoused antiwar sentiments as potent as anywhere else and would organize one of the largest and most memorable protest marches ever witnessed.

But the march was more than an expression of the broader antiwar movement; it was also part of a longer history of resistance by Chicanos in Houston.[8] Using oral histories, this essay intends to craft a narrative of the Chicano Movement in Houston as it relates to protesting the war in Vietnam, because while several seminal works deal with Chicano activism in Houston, almost nothing exists about the antiwar movement.[9] The goal, therefore, is to reposition the city of Houston within the Chicano Movement as an important site of protest against the Vietnam War, to offer a more balanced account of El Movimiento, as indeed it existed in many places throughout the United States. In doing so, this essay will begin to fill the void in the historiography about antiwar activism along the Gulf Coast.

Moreover, while the history of Latino servicemen of Vietnam has grown significantly, with autobiographies of *veteranos* such Charley Trujillo, who in 1990 wrote *Soldado: Chicanos in Vietnam*, and John Trejo's *Carnales: A History of Chicano Vietnam Veterans*, published in 2013, still lacking are an equal number of studies on the antiwar movement that was also a part of this period.[10] The pivotal work on that topic is Lorena Oropeza's *Raza Si! Guerra No!*, which examines the largest Chicano antiwar demonstration in the nation, which took place in 1970 in Los Angeles.[11] In line with Oropeza's study, this essay includes Houston in the larger antiwar narrative. Finally, this essay will demonstrate how the Chicano antiwar movement in Houston emerged, evolved, created alliances across multiracial lines, and, as a result, eventually subsided.

THE ANTIWAR MOVEMENT IN HOUSTON

Houston had a rich history of protesting the war and had already witnessed several demonstrations. In 1967, for example, several activists from Houston took part in a national march on Washington to protest the war.[12] That same year, antiwar protestors in Houston found themselves battered by U.S.

Marines. During a patriotism parade put on by the Citizens Committee to Support Our Armed Forces, several Marines attacked about thirty antiwar demonstrators who showed up to exercise their right to oppose the war.[13] Using sticks from the parade banners, Marines clubbed several demonstrators over the head. Houston police, who were bringing up the rear of the parade where demonstrators filed in, did not intervene but instead proceeded to move forward with the procession. Some recalled seeing police looking on without acting. After the fighting ended, Marines hurried away to catch up to the parade that was now over two blocks away while onlookers applauded them.[14] Once news of the melee reached authorities, victims of the assault hoped for justice, but the commander of the Marines called the fight a "civil act on civil time" and not something that he intended to investigate.[15] Several of the peaceful demonstrators, however, found themselves arrested while onlookers carrying John Birch Society signs along with Confederate flags continued to harass them.[16]

On November 15, 1969, Chicano, Black, and white activists marched through the streets of downtown Houston as part of a nationwide antiwar Moratorium Day.[17] That same month, students from Rice University and the University of Houston (UH) urged their academic communities to oppose the war by holding rallies, teach-ins, and public readings of the names of those killed in Vietnam.[18] They also formed several student-led antiwar groups such as the UH Committee to End the War.[19] Again in November of 1969, residents from the Third Ward, a predominantly African American neighborhood in Houston, held an antiwar march from their community to Hermann Park.[20] African Americans regularly joined antiwar movements, especially those organized by la Raza, because like Chicanos, the Black community suffered from high casualty rates.[21] These shared experiences allowed for deeper alliances to form between the two communities.[22] While there were still issues that divided Chicanos and Black people, during the sixties and seventies alliances developed with greater ease than in previous decades.[23] Moreover, people from the Chicano and Black communities regularly participated in marches launched by radical whites. This is a notable aspect of the antiwar movement in Houston because, more so than with other struggles, opposition to the war in Vietnam was far more effective in creating alliances, albeit sometimes uneasy ones, between Chicanos, Black people, and white activists.[24] As the seventies rolled around, Houston saw several additional antiwar demonstrations, the largest of which was the one put on by Chicanos during the summer of 1970.

A TRAGIC LIVING EXPERIENCE

During the sixties and seventies, Chicanos in Houston lived in neighborhoods with aging infrastructure, declining property values, and increasing abject poverty.[25] They were victims of segregationist laws, systematic disenfranchisement, police brutality, and mass incarceration. The Johnson administration acknowledged this and that Mexican Americans had not only been neglected but were discriminated against in housing, education, and in the workplace.[26] As the war began, Chicanos also became steady cannon fodder, as they seldom were able to circumvent draft notices. Despite these afflictions, and because of them, Chicanos began agitating for change. They voiced their concerns over the war and questioned the motives of the U.S. government, which seemed to have no problem sending young men "halfway around the world to . . . die in a war that seemed to lack a clear objective."[27] Everywhere, not just in Houston, Mexican Americans were participating in more forceful activism for securing change but also to protest the war in Vietnam.[28] Collectively, they challenged the idea that Chicanos should be silent about inequality and willingly serve in the military.[29] Even older leaders and organizations, typically not known for radical activism, began to speak out more forcibly against both the war and the continued injustice toward the Chicano community.[30]

A WHITE MAN'S WAR

While the military objective in Vietnam was to prevent that nation from becoming Communist, for many Chicanos it was an illegal war that manipulated young men and used them as pawns to fulfill American imperialistic desires.[31] The U.S. involvement in Vietnam can be traced back to the 1950s, when President Truman supported France in its war with the Vietnamese.[32] Before World War II, the territory of Vietnam was under French colonial rule. During the war, it fell to Japanese forces; but once Japan surrendered, France attempted to reestablish its authority over the area. The French battled Vietnamese Communist forces who were resisting France's return. By 1950, as part of its policy of containment, the United States was providing France both military and economic support. This proved ineffective. By 1954, France was defeated following the battle of Dien Bien Phu and pushed out of Vietnam, marking an end to French colonialism in Southeast Asia.[33] However, while the Vietnamese people celebrated and hoped for an independent nation, the United States had other plans and quickly assumed responsibility for removing Communist forces from the area through military action that carried into the 1960s. As the United States took over the war, Chicanos in the movement, already disillusioned with the White House's support of France, grew far more critical of the government.[34] They agreed with the sentiments of the Vietnamese-based National Liberation Front, that U.S. imperialists first assisted French colonialists in massacring thousands of Vietnamese peoples and, second, invaded the nation to enslave them and establish a military base there to wage war throughout all Southeast Asia.[35] This led to increased antiwar demonstrations throughout the country.

Early in the war, the perception was that the United States was winning and that the American people were in full support of the military's efforts in Vietnam.[36] But as the war progressed, neither of those things would be true. In 1968, the world would learn of the Tet Offensive, the largest collection of attacks by the Communist forces, which left at least two thousand American and South Vietnamese troops dead.[37] This event showed the American people that the country was not winning the war and perhaps that the war was unwinnable.[38] This was indeed the sentiment expressed by the nation's best-known journalist, Walter Cronkite of CBS News, who delivered an editorial arguing that victory was impossible.[39] The resignation of Defense Secretary Robert McNamara further convinced the American people.[40] In March of 1968, LBJ, haunted by the lives lost and heavily criticized for his dishonesty about the war, announced that he would not run for reelection.[41] Johnson was once a beloved political leader among Mexican Americans, who directly benefited from several programs coming out of his administration, but because of his escalation of the Vietnam War, he would fall from grace, especially among younger Chicano activists, who came to see him as an imperialist. In the early 1970s, the American people revved up their efforts to end the war, holding several marches and rallies against it. In Chicano communities, the antiwar movement was gaining momentum; activists refused to fight in what they considered a white man's war.[42]

THE DEVIL'S DRAFT

Especially repulsive was the draft, which disproportionately affected Chicanos, particularly those not enrolled in institutions of higher learning.[43] Uncle Sam typically provided deferments for enrolled students, but because a vast majority of Mexican Americans lacked "an 8th-grade education," getting into an institution of higher learning was unlikely.[44] Moreover, many Chicano youth were "discouraged from going to college" and urged instead to enter the labor force or join the military.[45] To satisfy its own needs, Uncle Sam initiated Project 100,000, a recruitment program that lowered the standards of the armed forces qualification test and offered remedial support to those who were unable to pass the test so that they would be labeled "fit" for military duty.[46] This was designed to get those with little education into the military. For those with a high school diploma, going to college still proved unattainable, as many were unable to afford the cost of tuition.[47] So for many Chicanos, the draft was both a racist and classist system, since it would be mostly poor people of color who would be drafted into the military.[48] Young white men, on the other hand, often were granted college deferments.[49]

While Chicanos could apply for deferments, as many often did, those applications were steadily denied. Draft boards were typically staffed by older, conservative white men who were unaware of the issues that plagued Chicanos that made them susceptible to draft orders in the first place.[50] This was another reason why Chicanos were disproportionately selected to fight in Vietnam— their inability to qualify for deferments.[51] Not even those enrolled in college, it seemed, qualified for deferments. On graduating from high school in Edinburg, Texas, Antonio González quickly enrolled in Pan American College located in his small hometown.[52] But because of the escalated conflict in Vietnam, he had to leave school and join the military one year before he was scheduled to finish his studies.[53] Because very few Chicanos served on draft boards, requests for student deferments were denied, and draftees had to resort to other methods, such as refusing induction altogether.

Carlos Calbillo, a local Houston activist, recalls undergoing a battery of examinations at the old U.S. Army Depot Recruitment Center, which was part of the U.S. Customs House in downtown Houston.[54] He was asked to raise his hand and swear allegiance to the country, then asked to take one step forward, which indicated his entry into the armed forces. When he refused, he was taken to a separate room and threatened with fines and a five-year prison sentence.[55] Fortunately for Calbillo, he alerted the draft board of his intentions to apply for conscientious objector status, which bought him some time.[56] Also, it did not hurt that he knew one of the members of the board, who intervened on his behalf.[57] Chicanos serving on draft boards were a rarity, but in Houston at least two Mexican Americans

served at one time or another in that capacity, including John Castillo, a member
of the city council, and John J. Herrera, lawyer and president of the League of
United Latin American Citizens Council #60.[58]

Calbillo's experience was an exception. Chicanos who applied for conscientious objector status and got it were few and far between. As if the draft was not
enough, many Chicanos were aggressively recruited a couple of months before
their high school graduation, with recruiters from all branches of the military
visiting schools to sign them up.[59] In 1969, the federal government switched
from the universal draft to a lottery draft system to determine who would be
called to service.[60] But because these lotteries selected men born between the
years of 1944 and 1950, that meant that many Chicanos could still be called on,
as the average age of the American soldier in Vietnam was nineteen to twenty-
two years, putting them squarely within the lottery years.[61] At times the draftees
in Vietnam were even younger. Rick Gutiérrez, for example, found himself
in Vietnam on his seventeenth birthday serving as a paratrooper.[62] Whatever
their age, Chicanos, whether because they couldn't afford college, or because
they were discouraged from attending college, or because their applications
for student deferments were steadily denied, were far more susceptible to draft
orders than their white counterparts. So they fervently opposed the draft. But
what started as a protest against the draft soon transformed into a movement
against the entire war.[63]

THEY'RE JUST LIKE US

One of the most influential organizations of this period was the Third World
Liberation Front (TWLF), a multiracial group established by Chicanos, Black
people, Asians, and others to demand that more classes on their history and
culture be offered at colleges and universities. In its involvement in the antiwar
movement, the TWLF was among the first to make the case that the Vietnamese, like Chicanos, were people of color subjected to military oppression by an
aggressive and imperialist American government.[64] As a result, many Chicanos came to see the Vietnamese people as like themselves: a colored working-
class people invaded and oppressed by a military superpower hell-bent on their
destruction.[65] So standing against the Vietnam War was based in a shared experience of oppression.[66]

AN ILLEGAL WAR

Chicano war protestors needed no convincing that the fighting in Vietnam was illegal and unjust. So when reports about the mistreatment of indigenous peoples by American troops came in, they weren't too shocked, only more angered.[67] The My Lai Massacre, in which American troops executed hundreds of unarmed Vietnamese civilians, particularly angered Chicanos.[68] In March of 1968, an American platoon known as Charlie Company massacred over five hundred women, children, and elderly unarmed men who were falsely believed to be members of the Vietcong, enemy Communist forces operating in South Vietnam.[69] Making matters worse was the government's attempts to cover it up; an entire year would pass before news of the massacre became public.[70] Once revealed, however, there was outcry throughout the nation. In Chicano communities, there was major outrage also over discovering that one of the persons in charge of Charlie Company was a Mexican American. Captain Ernest Medina of New Mexico was in command of the American troops who murdered hundreds of unarmed civilians. While he would be acquitted in the court-martial that ensued, antiwar protestors would never forgive him.[71]

Chicanos were also disgusted to learn that the United States was conducting scorched-earth warfare under something called the Strategic Hamlet Program, a military operation that called for the destruction of Vietnamese homes and communities to destroy potential resources for the enemy.[72] They were equally angered by Operation Rolling Thunder, a three-year hyper-intense bombing campaign of North Vietnam. Moreover, when American intelligence discovered that Communist forces from North Vietnam were using a path called the Ho Chi Minh Trail, which ran through the neighboring countries of Cambodia and Laos, to provide weapons, resources, and soldiers to Communist forces in South Vietnam, American troops on April 30, 1970, went about disrupting and destroying that pipeline.[73] When news broke that the United States had invaded Cambodia, it sparked more protests. For many Chicanos, the constant bombing of Cambodia and Laos was an expansion and escalation of the war. For Chicanos, the My Lai Massacre, along with the search-and-destroy missions under Strategic Hamlet and Operation Rolling Thunder, amounted to mass murder, senseless killings, and were specific examples of how the U.S. involvement in Vietnam was unequivocally illegal and unjust.[74]

THEY'RE KILLING US ALL

What mostly galvanized Chicanos against the war was their high casualty rate, which was reported to be proportionately higher than that of any other ethnic-racial group in the U.S. Armed Forces.[75] In 1967, a study by the Ford Foundation concluded that while Chicanos living in the American Southwest made up no more than 14 percent of the population, they constituted at least 19 percent of all casualties in Vietnam.[76] Two years later the academic journal *El Grito* published a compilation of Mexican American casualties from all U.S. states between the years 1965 and 1969 and found that the American Southwest had the highest percentage of Chicano casualties overall, with Texas and California having the highest death tolls of 28.7 and 28 percent, respectively.[77] Again in 1969, in a study entitled *Mexican American Casualties in Vietnam*, author Ralph Guzman examined the casualty rates of Chicanos from five southwestern states between the years 1961 and 1969 and arrived at similar conclusions: that the death rates of persons with Spanish surnames in Vietnam were at least 19 percent of all casualties.[78] This figure was alarming because the census data of 1960 showed that Chicanos made up only 11.8 percent of the total population of the region surveyed.[79]

A 1970 article in the *Houston Post* stated that at least eight thousand Chicanos had perished in the war.[80] While this number was both premature and ultimately inaccurate, the announcement added to the rage already prevalent among Chicanos, who knew that they were dying in the greatest proportion.[81] While these figures were the result of high draft rates and poor success in obtaining deferments, also responsible were Chicanos' assignments within the military, which often included serving in the infantry or other "high-risk" units with frequent combat duty.[82] Several scholars have successfully documented the inequality faced by Chicano servicemen, who were disproportionately the "grunts," making them more likely to be killed in action, while white servicemen, on the other hand, were either officers, negotiated for if captured, or given assignments that removed them from combat duty altogether.[83] All of this pointed to one conclusion: Chicanos were dying at disproportionately higher rates than any other ethnic-racial group because of blatant, entrenched racism within the U.S. Armed Forces.[84]

By 1970, Texas had 500,000 men who served in Vietnam, with 1,921 confirmed deaths.[85] Of those, at least 434 were Mexican American.[86] Some 358 men from Houston perished in the war, 39 of whom were persons with Spanish surnames.[87] The earliest reported Chicano casualty of the war dates back to November of 1965; Hilario De la Paz Jr. was twenty-six when he died fighting in the Ia Drang Valley.[88] The next year, another five Chicanos would perish, including Corporal Philip Serna, who died on May 20, 1966, from multiple fragment wounds one week before he was to return home.[89] In 1967, an additional seven Chicanos would be killed in action.[90] The year 1968 would be the deadliest; Houston alone would see ten Chicanos killed in action.[91] The next year, the number of Chicano deaths dropped to five.[92] In 1970, the number of Chicano war casualties sat at seven, which included Lance Corporal Macario Sánchez, who was reported to be killed by accidental homicide.[93] In 1971, only one Mexican American from Houston was killed in action; Sergeant First Class William Fernández died on February 19 in an airplane crash over Laos.[94] It is unclear whether more Chicanos from Houston died in Vietnam after 1971, and whether the U.S. government has been able to account for every person deceased or reported deceased also remains unknown.

The fighting was costly for every community, but the recklessness with which the government was handling the war disproportionately affected Chicanos. In all, about 170,000 Chicanos participated in the Vietnam War, and while Mexican Americans made up less than 10 percent of the U.S. population, they had the highest casualty rates.[95] Present figures reveal that at least six thousand Chicanos perished in Vietnam, but death records are inaccurate or inconclusive, and the surname listing of Mexican and Mexican American soldiers makes them difficult to track. Because Mexican Americans were racially categorized as "white," determining who was ethnic Mexican and who was not makes accurate calculations of deaths impossible.[96] Also, these studies covered only parts of the war.[97] So the number of deaths of Chicanos could be higher than official and unofficial records indicate. Still, the figures show that poor Mexican Americans, from barrios across the nation typically "ignored by the U.S . . . [but which] . . . suddenly appeared on Uncle Sam's map," were being killed at higher rates than their white counterparts.[98] In response, Chicanos in Houston organized arguably the largest antiwar demonstration the city has ever witnessed.

OPPOSING THE DRAFT AND WAR

The Mexican American community in Houston has always had a strong political presence, with organizations such as the League of United Latin American

Citizens (LULAC), the American GI Forum, Viva Kennedy Clubs, the Mexican American Political Association, the Houston Civic Action Committee, and the Political Association of Spanish-Speaking Organizations—all of which were hugely successful in politicizing Mexican Americans throughout the city.[99] While many of these older, more established organizations stayed away from the issue of Vietnam, some took it to center stage. Members of LULAC and the GI Forum, along with several other Mexican American leaders, for example, grew frustrated with the government for using monies typically assigned to fund domestic programs to finance the war in Vietnam instead and so engaged in far more direct actions against the war.[100] According to some reports, the U.S. government spent $500,000 to kill a single enemy soldier in Vietnam but spent only about $53.00 on each American person as part of its antipoverty programs.[101]

But the antiwar march was unquestionably influenced by the efforts of the National Chicano Moratorium Committee, the leading antiwar organization for Chicanos.[102] In Houston also, the committee assumed control of the antiwar movement and served in many instances as an umbrella organization to several other Chicano organizations throughout the city, including the Mexican American Youth Organization (MAYO), the Political Association of Spanish-Speaking Organizations (PASSO), the Brown Berets, and the Northside People's Center.[103] The committee sponsored countless antiwar rallies and even started offering antidraft counseling to Chicanos.[104] In California, Chicano Draft Help was instrumental in helping Mexican Americans appeal the draft.[105] In other places like Houston, Chicanos sought the help of the Southwest Regional Draft Counseling Association, which also offered counseling sessions on how to appeal the draft.[106] Local Houston activist Carlos Calbillo served as one of its counselors and provided tips for how to qualify for a student deferment or perhaps apply for conscientious objector status.[107] Calbillo, in fact, already had experience with protesting the Vietnam War, having participated in an antiwar march and rally in Los Angeles in February 1970.[108] Once he returned to Houston, he proceeded to do the same thing there.[109] The message was clear: the war in Vietnam was illegal and unjust, and Chicanos should not be sent there to fight, especially since "la batalla está aquí"; that is, the battle was here on the home front.[110] This slogan had become the battle cry of the antiwar movement. It was taken from a 1970 antiwar booklet by Lea Ybarra and Nina Genera, which pleaded with Chicanos to not go overseas to kill other people of color but to stay at home to solve the problems that plagued their communities.[111] The militant activism of the sixties and seventies sharply contrasted the more reformist methods of activism of previous decades, but leaders of middle-class organizations were falling more in line with the antiwar movement and redefining their strong and long-standing political presence in Houston.

¡RAZA SI, GUERRA NO!

The Houston march of July 26, 1970, was short-lived, lasting only three hours.[112] It proceeded through the streets of the Magnolia Park neighborhood and concluded at a city park called Hidalgo.[113] There, participants heard from an array of speakers who offered fiery speeches against the war and against the racist policies that sent Chicanos to fight in it. The objective of the march was to create awareness certainly, but ultimately it aimed to end the war altogether. Once an end to the war had been achieved, organizers could develop a platform for Chicanos that included self-determination and an alternative to poverty, police brutality, mass incarceration, and overt discrimination.[114] Along the way, shouts of "¡Raza sí, guerra no!," "Chicano power!," and "¡Viva la raza!" could be heard for several blocks in every direction.[115] From the beginning, city officials did everything they could to prevent the march. For starters, city hall refused to grant Gregory Salazar, one of the march organizers, a permit to parade and assemble.[116] In open defiance of city leaders, the march went forward as planned. Even though walkers were told to stay on the sidewalks to avoid fines and arrests, there were just too many people marching, and they eventually spilled onto the streets. What had started with about thirty or forty people grew to more than a thousand persons.[117] Families from the neighborhood came out onto their porches to watch and cheer the procession.[118] Particularly popular were the white crosses with the names of Chicanos who had been killed in Vietnam carried by antiwar protestors. One participant recalls seeing at least eighteen crosses with the names of men from Denver Harbor, the Northside, Magnolia Park, and Second Ward, all neighborhoods and sections of town heavily populated by Mexican Americans.[119]

A who's who of activists, Chicano and non-Chicano, were present at this march. At the ensuing rally, speakers not only criticized the war but also spoke to the grotesque oppression that Chicanos faced at home.[120] Activist and educator Dr. Luis Cano, for example, was there.[121] Leonel Castillo, an iconic leader of the community, also made an appearance.[122] Castillo, a member of PASSO and the first Latino ever elected to office in Houston as city controller, delivered the rally keynote address.[123] The march was also attended by grassroots activists, including MAYO member Gregory Salazar, Alex Rodríguez of the Northside People's Center, and Leo Tanguma, who later became a famous Chicano muralist.[124] Other Chicanos had come from Corpus Christi, Austin, and San Antonio, like Bexar County commissioner Albert Peña, who spoke at the rally in Hidalgo Park and ignited the people when he called the fighting in Vietnam "a gringo war."[125] Peña struck another chord when he addressed the oppression of Chicanos on the home front, comparing the misery of migrant workers in South Texas to the prison systems of South Vietnam, which were notorious for carrying out extreme forms of torture in infamous "tiger cages."[126] These were politically charged statements given Peña's position, but he rarely shied from such tactics.[127]

Several MAYO members from Corpus also made the trip to Houston, including Rey Rodríguez, a Vietnam War veteran turned protestor, who showed up at the march to film it with his old Super 8 camera.[128] Some even came from Los Angeles. Rosalio Muñoz, one of the leaders of the National Chicano Moratorium Committee, flew in on his own dime and was among the speakers that day.[129] Muñoz took the national stage as a war protestor when he publicly refused induction.[130] Also present were a few Black and white antiwar protestors. Some were members of the Houston chapter of the Students for a Democratic Society (SDS), such as Bob Cash and Leonel Jacob Steele, who also spoke at the rally.[131] Never one to pass up a good protest march, activist Gloria Rubac also greeted Chicanos.[132] She would go on to lead the movement to abolish the death penalty.[133] Rubac arrived in Houston in 1968 after graduating from college and quickly aligned herself with militant groups, including Chicano organizations like MAYO.[134] Seeing radical whites at Chicano protest events was common; what was uncommon, however, was receiving public support from liberal whites. A few days later, however, activists received some telegraphed words of encouragement from Democratic senator Ted Kennedy of Massachusetts.[135]

The march went on with no acts of violence, although a journalist for the *Houston Post* was confronted by several Chicanos, who accused him of gathering intelligence for the Houston Police Department, or worse, for the Federal Bureau of Investigation.[136] They believed he was posing as a journalist and taking photos of march organizers, which could later be used as evidence for prosecuting them.[137] Chicanos approached the man and demanded he leave. Several others joined the shouting match that ensued.[138] Eventually, the reporter did leave, and activities resumed as normal. Law enforcement agencies were notorious for infiltrating civil rights groups and activities deemed too radical or "subversive" in order to either sabotage those efforts or gather evidence on the planners.[139] Illegal police surveillance, sting operations, and the opening of files by the FBI were but a few of the techniques used by authorities to censor dissent. Chicanos were aware of this and responded swiftly to anyone suspected of being a part of the criminalization regime.[140]

CHICANO FRONTLINE DEFENSES

The march in Houston was successful because of the frontline protection provided by Chicano organizations such as the Brown Berets and MAYO.[141] MAYO took shape in the late 1960s and, from its inception, became a power-house of Chicano activism in Houston. They "cut their teeth" protesting blatant racism across the city's institutions and occupying various facilities to establish free breakfast programs.[142] MAYO was also instrumental in organizing the march and maintaining the antiwar movement throughout the city. Houston had two MAYO chapters, one formed on the campus of the University of Houston (UH MAYO), the other formed in the community, or Barrio MAYO, as it came to be known.[143] Barrio MAYO was headquartered on the Northside, which had long been a hotbed of activism in Houston. Its members included several militant activists, such as Gregory Salazar, Yolanda Garza Birdwell, Poncho Ruiz, and Alex Rodríguez.[144] While the two MAYOs sometimes took issue with each other, they came together in their support for the moratorium march. In fact, among the many things they did that day was provide security.[145] Rey Rodríguez, for example, a member of the MAYO chapter from Del Mar College in Corpus Christi, remembers driving up to Houston the day before, meeting MAYO activists from the city to work out the details, and then being asked to help keep the peace.[146]

Also there to help keep the peace were the Brown Berets, who were most known for protesting police brutality, but who also ran a platform against the war in Vietnam.[147] March organizers made sure to have Brown Berets present. They were necessary in case vigilantes or the police attacked protestors.[148] The Berets had a peculiar existence in Houston. While there were indeed Chicanos who identified themselves as official members, others admit that an official chapter of this organization did not exist in Houston, or that if it did, it operated as an independent group.[149] Nevertheless, they too were at the march, and along with *carnales* (brothers) from San Antonio, Austin, and elsewhere, protected marchers.[150] Many of the protestors were trained in pacifist methods or were urged to carry an attorney's card along with quarters for a phone call because their march was an act of civil disobedience.[151] But even if protestors had not received that training, they knew well enough to let the Berets handle the police, and so their presence at the march was welcomed.

OPPOSITION TO THE MORATORIUM

Indeed, several groups and factions opposed the antiwar movement in Houston, and at times the pushback was harsh, even violent. In 1969, for example, the Houston chapter of the Ku Klux Klan firebombed a car outside the home of an antiwar protestor.[152] They also repeatedly called and threatened several peace activists.[153] There was also the criticism from the larger conservative white and, at times, Mexican American communities. Moreover, there were threats from federal authorities, who, in addition to keeping surveillance on activists and even starting files on them, had at their disposal regulations aimed at punishing dissenters under the guise of fishing out known or suspected Communists.[154] While most Chicanos were not Communist, their activities were viewed as such, and as a result their loyalties were questioned. In other places, law enforcement was damaging to the antiwar movement. In Los Angeles, for example, the FBI targeted Chicanos for investigation and aggressively pursued them.[155] In San Antonio and Austin, police shouted insults at protestors, sprayed them with tear gas, or set dogs loose on them.[156] At times, employers fired demonstrators, or college administrators suspended them from school.[157] While Houston's experience differed slightly, the threat was still serious. Much of the opposition to the antiwar movement in Houston came from veterans or the families of veterans, including Mexican Americans who had an inherent distrust of leftist or socialist activists and preferred bringing about change through less radical methods.[158] Some were proud that Mexican Americans had received proportionately more citations for acts of bravery in combat since World War II than any other ethnic-racial group. So antiwar activists needed to improve their educational outreach to get more in the Latino community to question and eventually speak out against U.S. involvement in Vietnam.[159] Mexican American veterans, in particular, felt that there was a greater need for them to prove their patriotism and loyalty to the country, and having participated in either World War II or the Korean War, many believed that they had achieved that end.[160] So when antiwar protestors took to the streets, Greatest Generation veterans openly disapproved. Rosendo López of the Twelfth Infantry of the U.S. Army recalls seeing numerous protest rallies once he returned stateside and admitted that he felt betrayed and wondered why persons from his community were angry with him.[161] "I went to serve my country, and . . . there was protesting . . . it was worse here."[162] Complicating matters further was the fact that many antiwar protestors had relatives who had fought in earlier wars. Carlos Calbillo's father and several uncles, for example, were combat veterans and not happy to learn of his activities.[163] Other antiwar protestors had relatives who were veterans and who criticized them and called them Communists for their stance on the war.[164] Homer García remembers even being criticized for his college aspirations, which were perceived as a way for him to get out of doing his military duty.[165] Other veterans considered the entire thing to be unpatriotic and accused protestors of treasonous behaviors.[166] But for those Chicanos who rejected the patriotism felt by many veteranos, the war in Vietnam was another example of U.S. oppression of poor Mexican American communities; for them, to protest was indeed a patriotic act.[167] This, of course, speaks to the division within the Mexican American community. But while war protestors and veteranos seemed to be at opposite ends of the spectrum, they were technically working toward the same thing: to prove their patriotism and secure their rightful place in an equal and just society.[168]

SUPPORT FOR THE MORATORIUM

Many supporters of the antiwar movement were veterans who served in Vietnam. In a statement drafted in 1969, veterans of the Vietnam War made it clear that they believed this war was "wrong, unjustifiable, and contrary to the principles on which [the] country was founded."[169] But veterans who participated in protest marches were often threatened with reprisals of some sort.[170] Active soldiers risked a multitude of penalties from the military if they supported the antiwar movement.[171] Despite that, however, veterans often attended antiwar events and even gave speeches in opposition to the country's involvement in Vietnam. Private First Class Walther Cos, for example, urged the people to resist both the war and the militarism taking place throughout the nation's schools and workplaces.[172] Even while deployed overseas, troops were aware of the sociopolitical turmoil taking place back at home and frequently had those kinds of conversations among themselves.[173] As they began to witness the horrors of war, they grew critical of it and had a "change in consciousness" that aligned with the anger and cynicism of activists stateside.[174] Rey Rodríguez, for example, was fighting in the jungles in Vietnam as early as 1967; once he returned home, he quickly joined MAYO and made ending the war his new mission.[175] Another veteran, Frank Villarreal of the U.S. Army, recalls his time in Vietnam as traumatic and admits that while deployed, he did not quite understand why he was there.[176] John Saenz, with the U.S. Marines, echoed the feeling of not truly knowing the reason for his deployment to Vietnam. But more than feeling left in the dark, he was also immensely angered that many of his friends perished.[177] The same can be said for air force veteran Antonio González, who also witnessed many of his friends killed in action.[178] Rosendo López knew that the United States was not going to win in Vietnam and saw much of his time there as unnecessary.[179] It was these frustrations, then, that motivated many veterans to rethink U.S. involvement in Vietnam.

For other veterans, their "change in consciousness" came not during their deployment in Vietnam, but from their struggles once back home.[180] Cástulo Camarillo's "change in consciousness," for example, came after his return to civilian life and the difficulties he had communicating with folks whom he felt did not like him or who even saw him as a "baby killer."[181] Veteran Frank Villarreal also was called a baby killer, but his awakening resulted more from an inability to cope with the trauma; "when we got back," he says, "we just wanted to forget . . . everything."[182] John Saenz also suffered from trauma following his deployment. He was unable to eat for days, so affected was he by having had to take another life.[183] Manuel Pérez was not part of a combat unit but served as a medic. He saw many dead bodies and recalled the hell it was to have to collect body parts of young men; "I picked [up] body parts like heads . . . [and saw] burning [bodies] . . . [and recall] the smell of people dying."[184] Rick Gutiérrez suffered from a similar trauma and wished that he could forget what he had seen.[185] On returning home, a young Raúl de la Paz, suffering from massive anxiety and unable to be around loud noises, would lock himself in his room for days.[186] Because he was receiving zero help, living with him became extremely difficult for his family.[187] This neglect partly explains why many veterans underwent a "change in consciousness" once they returned home from the war. Even nonmilitary personnel in Vietnam underwent this change. Macario Ramírez, a civilian working for the military, acknowledges that "we should not have been there" and is convinced that U.S. involvement in Vietnam was due in most part to what he called "phony diplomacy."[188] "It was an unnecessary war, and we lost more than 50,000 of our young, and many of them were Latino," he says.[189]

So, while there was indeed opposition to those who protested the war, there was also support for it, much of it from *veteranos*. While many veterans did not participate in the antiwar marches themselves, some, perhaps disenchanted, understood why other Chicanos protested the war in Vietnam and either avoided them or lent their support in different ways.[190] Strangely enough, some of the support for the moratorium march also came through the federal government. VISTA, or the Volunteers in Service to America, a program that came out of the Johnson Administration, was designed to improve the lives of working-class communities via multiple ways, including community outreach.[191] Since 1966, the VISTA program had volunteers assigned to the Houston area, and over time local Houstonians began joining it, including Chicanos who organized the march and who were leaders in the antiwar movement. Carlos Calbillo, for example, worked as a VISTA volunteer.[192] Leo Tanguma was a VISTA supervisor for the Houston area.[193] It would be through VISTA, then, that march planners got access to resources that were generally out of their reach, such as copy machines for making flyers, leaflets, and posters.[194] VISTA was a federal program, and so, technically, activists in Houston were working for the very government they were protesting. But it was a necessary method for achieving their goal: an end to the war in Vietnam.

THE CHICANO MORATORIUM COMMITTEE NO MORE

The antiwar march of July 26, 1970, would be the last one organized by Chicanos in Houston. There would be other antiwar marches and rallies, and Chicanos would participate in them, like in October of 1971 when they joined other protestors in front of city hall as part of a nationwide "moratorium to end the war in Vietnam." However, a march and rally organized specifically by the Chicano Moratorium Committee would not occur again.[195] In other places, activities of Moratorium committees waned because of police infiltration, repression, and violence.[196] In Los Angeles, California, for example, the National Chicano Moratorium Committee was targeted for investigation by the FBI.[197] On August 29, 1970, it would hold the largest Chicano antiwar march in U.S. history, with at least thirty thousand protestors.[198] That march, unfortunately, would be marred by a huge riot started by the Los Angeles County Sheriff's Department, which caused an estimated $1 million in damages.[199] Following the melee, some 152 anti-war protestors were arrested, and three persons were killed, including Lynn Ward, Angel Gilberto Diaz, and Ruben Salazar, a beloved journalist for the *Los Angeles Times* who advocated for Chicanos and covered issues important to them, such as police brutality and the war in Vietnam.[200] Salazar's death horrified Chicanos; he was "a respected member of the establishment," and the police killed him like he was a criminal.[201] Horrifying Chicanos further was their inability to get any justice for his murder.[202] The violence and police repression would ultimately erode the strength of the National Chicano Moratorium Committee.[203]

In Houston, activities declined because the Moratorium Committee joined with and morphed into other organizations. Specifically, it joined forces with the Houston chapter of the Students for a Democratic Society, one of the leading antiwar groups in the United States, with lots of chapters across the nation that were adamant about a full withdrawal from Vietnam.[204] This resonated with many Chicanos. But for a few, groups like SDS were problematic because its members were mainly white, and Chicanos felt that they did not address the concerns of "Brown" people.[205] Or they saw SDS as just another white, liberal, and middle-class organization that lacked a certain perspective on matters related to race and racism.[206]

It would be a difficult balancing act for Chicanos, who understood the importance of ethnic solidarity as well as what might be achieved across multiracial lines. Gregory Salazar of MAYO recalls the difficulty of allying with SDS without upsetting other Chicanos. "We associated with [them] . . . but . . . always maintained a certain distance from [them as well] . . . since . . . we felt that . . . we . . . had no place there."[207] MAYO had a history of forging alliances, albeit uneasy ones, across the color line, specifically with the Black Panther Party, which often worked closely with MAYO on similar issues. Because of that, many believed the same could be achieved with SDS, especially since they too were considered a radical group.[208] Moreover, it did not hurt that several high-profile Chicano activists were official members of SDS. Alex Rodríguez of the Northside People's Center, for example, was a member.[209] Ultimately, then, the Chicano Moratorium Committee in Houston would merge with SDS, and for the most part everyone seemed to get along. They worked on things both groups agreed on and just stayed away from those they did not.[210] What helped also was that a few white people understood that their role was that of allies and not as saviors.[211] So seemingly, the Chicano Moratorium Committee and Students for a Democratic Society successfully came together to end the war in Vietnam. But therein lay the problem. The antiwar movement was far more effective in creating alliances across multiracial lines; however, since SDS was the largest of all groups, the antiwar movement in Houston took on the characteristic of being run by whites, and those kinds of movements rarely ever addressed the concerns of Chicanos.[212]

Uniting with SDS was an example of the multiracial coalition-building that had been taking place throughout Texas since the end of World War II. Indeed, there were several successful instances of cooperation between different ethnic-racial communities, including in Houston. But lost within this coalition-building, especially after 1970, was the nationalism that came to define the Chicano Movement and Chicanos as a separate and oppressed ethnic-racial group. Once the Chicano Moratorium Committee in Houston merged with SDS, their protest was no longer seen as a Chicano issue but had become part of the broader white antiwar agenda, which typically had little concern for the problems that affected Chicanos.[213] Those who opposed the merger, wanting nothing to do with a white-led antiwar movement, redirected their attention and efforts elsewhere.[214] This ensured that the ethnic nationalism espoused by Mexican Americans during this period continued to flourish elsewhere throughout the Chicano Movement.

CONCLUSION

In January of 1973, President Nixon ordered the U.S. military to stop its bombing of North Vietnam, and quickly after that all warring parties on the peninsula agreed to a ceasefire as they awaited coming peace talks.[215] This, of course, was after the military forces of North Vietnam and insurgents in the South prevailed. In 1975, the United States withdrew all its people from the territory; seemingly, the war in Vietnam was over. Not over, however, were the hardships Chicano soldiers and their families suffered in the years following, including post-traumatic stress disorder among the troops; the distress for families from the deaths of their sons, brothers, and husbands; the continued surveillance by law enforcement of antiwar protestors; and a broken Chicano community trying to mend shattered alliances after the fighting in Vietnam had divided an already fractured and splintered community.

Even as the fighting for the United States concluded, members of the Chicano community continued to stand on opposite sides of the conflict. And while there were instances of triumph for some involved in the war, those were few and far between. For most, the war brought nothing but misery and grief. Chicanos already suffered from entrenched poverty, community neglect, segregationist laws, disenfranchisement, police brutality, and mass incarceration, and with the war, they also assumed the role of cannon fodder. This was why antiwar activists protested. Seeing the war as immoral and illegal, Chicanos in Houston took to the streets to condemn American imperialism and held arguably the largest antiwar protest in the history of the Bayou City.[216] In doing so, they repositioned Houston within the Chicano Movement as an essential site of protest against the war. The Chicano Movement existed everywhere throughout the United States, but Houston's part in it rarely gets the attention it merits, especially regarding the antiwar movement. Using the oral histories of protestors as well as veteranos, this essay offers a more balanced account of El Movimiento to include Houston in the larger antiwar narrative and start to fill the void in the historiography regarding antiwar activism along the Gulf Coast.

NOTES

1. Carlos Calbillo, interview, Houston Metropolitan Research Center, February 5, 2018, Houston, Texas. See also Thomas H. Kreneck, *Del Pueblo: A History of Houston's Hispanic Community* (College Station: Texas A&M University Press, 2012), 90.

2. After North Vietnam ships fired on two American destroyers, Johnson responded by asking Congress to give him the authority to use force to defend American forces. When Congress agreed, it essentially handed over war powers to the president. See Steven Rosales, *Soldados Razos at War: Chicano Politics, Identity, and Masculinity in the U.S. Military from World War II to Vietnam* (Tucson: University of Arizona Press, 2017), 92.

3. Rosales, *Soldados Razos at War*, 92.

4. Lorena Oropeza, *Raza Sí! Guerra No! Chicano Protest and Patriotism During the Vietnam War Era* (Berkeley: University of California Press, 2005), 5, 92–93.

5. Calbillo, interview.

6. "News," *Anti-War Viewpoints*, September 1970, p. 6. Houston Committee to End the War in Vietnam, Houston Anti-Viet Nam War Collection, box 1, folder 2, Houston Metropolitan Research Center, Houston Public Library, Houston, Texas.

7. Oropeza, *Raza Sí! Guerra No!*, 74.

8. Kreneck, *Del Pueblo*, 90.

9. Works that focus specifically on Chicanos in Houston include Guadalupe San Miguel's *Brown, Not White: School Integration and the Chicano Movement in Houston* (College Station: Texas A&M University Press, 2005); Arnoldo De León's *Ethnicity in the Sunbelt: A History of Mexican-Americans in Houston* (Houston: Mexican American Studies Program, University of Houston, 1989); Roberto Treviño's *The Church in the Barrio: Mexican American Ethno-Catholicism in Houston* (Chapel Hill: University of North Carolina Press, 2006); Kreneck's *Del Pueblo*; and Tyina Steptoe's *Houston Bound: Culture and Color in a Jim Crow City* (Berkeley: University of California Press, 2015).

10. See also Teresa Moreno Jiménez, "The Mexican American Vietnam War Servicemen: The Missing American" (master's thesis, California Polytechnic State University, 2015), 69.

11. Lorena Oropeza, "Fighting on Two Fronts: Latinos in the Military," in *American Latinos and the Making of the United States: A Theme Study* (Washington, D.C.: National Park System Advisory Board, 2013), 262.

12. "Attention Texans: National Mobilization Logistics for Those Who Plan to Go to Washington," *HCEWV News* 2, no. 8 (October 1967): 18, *Houston Committee to End the War in Vietnam,* Houston Anti-Viet Nam War Collection, box 1, folder 1, Houston Metropolitan Research Center, Houston Public Library, Houston, Texas.

13. "From the Halls of Montezuma to the Edge of Hermann Park," *Texas Observer,* August 4, 1967, p. 7, Houston Anti-Viet Nam War Collection, box 1, file 21, Houston Metropolitan Research Center, Houston Public Library, Houston, Texas.

14. "From the Halls of Montezuma."

15. "From the Halls of Montezuma."

16. "Police Vanish as Marines Attack Peace Demonstrators," *HCEWV News* 2, no. 6 (August 1967): 5, *Houston Committee to End the War in Vietnam,* Houston Anti-Viet Nam War Collection, box 1, folder 1, Houston Metropolitan Research Center, Houston Public Library, Houston, Texas. See also "From the Halls of Montezuma."

17. Brian D. Behnken, *Fighting Their Own Battles: Mexican Americans, African Americans, and the Struggle for Civil Rights in Texas* (Chapel Hill: University of North Carolina Press, 2011), 186.

18. "Announcement," *HCEWV News* 3, no. 1 (January–February 1968): 14, *Houston Committee to End the War in Vietnam,* Houston Anti-Viet Nam War Collection, box 1, folder 1, Houston Metropolitan Research Center, Houston Public Library, Houston, Texas.

19. "Announcement."

20. "Nov. 9 Houston Mass March," *Anti-War Viewpoints,* October 1969, p. 7, Houston Committee to End the War in Vietnam, Houston Anti-Viet Nam War Collection, box 1, folder 2, Houston Metropolitan Research Center, Houston Public Library, Houston, Texas.

21. Behnken, *Fighting Their Own Battles*, 187.

22. Behnken, *Fighting Their Own Battles*, 187.

23. Behnken, *Fighting Their Own Battles*, 187.

24. Behnken, *Fighting Their Own Battles*, 187.

25. Grisel Gómez-Cano and James Ross-Nazzal, *The Spirit of Magnolia Park: Ethnic Pride in a Mexican Barrio, 1909–2009* (Boston: Pearson, 2013), 111.

26. Jiménez, "Mexican American Vietnam War Servicemen," 24.

27. Debbie Harwell, "Letter from the Editor," *Houston History Magazine*, July 28, 2015, https://houstonhistorymagazine.org/2015/07/coming-soon-houstonians-in -action/.

28. Jesús Jesse Esparza, "La Colonia Mexicana: A History of Mexican Americans in Houston," *Houston History Magazine* 9, no. 1 (December 2011): 5.

29. Oropeza, "Fighting on Two Fronts," 262.

30. San Miguel, *Brown, Not White*, 65.

31. John Trejo, *Carnales: A History of Chicano Vietnam Veterans* (Leeds and York, LLC, 2013), 55.

32. Trejo, *Carnales*, 54.

33. Refugio Rochín and Lionel Fernández, "U.S. Latino Patriots: From the American Revolution to Afghanistan, An Overview" (Washington, D.C.: Smithsonian Latino Center, 2002), 17.

34. Calbillo, interview.

35. "The Program of the National Liberation Front," *Viet Report: An Emergency News Bulletin on Southeast Asian Affairs*, February 1966, Houston Anti-Viet Nam War Collection, box 1, file 18, Houston Metropolitan Research Center, Houston Public Library, Houston, Texas.

36. Jerry Zuber, "Returned GI Finds War Attitude Is OK," *Houston Chronicle*, March 30, 1965, Subject File: War Casualties, Houston Chronicle Morgue Collection, Houston Metropolitan Research Center, Houston Public Library, Houston, Texas.

37. Jorge Mariscal, "Cesar and Martin, March '68," in *The Struggle in Black and Brown: African American and Mexican American Relations During the Civil Rights Era*, ed. Brian D. Behnken (Lincoln: University of Nebraska Press, 2011), 148.

38. Mariscal, "Cesar and Martin" 148.

39. Mariscal, "Cesar and Martin," 151.

40. Mariscal, "Cesar and Martin," 151–52.

41. Mariscal, "Cesar and Martin," 165.

42. The earliest known Chicano antiwar march took place on Thanksgiving Day in 1967 in San Francisco, California, and from there it spread throughout the country. See Oropeza, *Raza Sí! Guerra No!*, 74.

43. Gómez-Cano and Ross-Nazzal, *Spirit of Magnolia Park*, 103.

44. Oropeza, "Fighting on Two Fronts," 262.

45. Jiménez, "Mexican American Vietnam War Servicemen," 22.

46. Trejo, *Carnales*, 86–87.

47. Jiménez, "Mexican American Vietnam War Servicemen," 21.

48. "Why Organize Against the Draft?" *New Left Notes* 3, no. 12 (April 8, 1968): 4, Houston Anti-Viet Nam War Collection, box 1, file 2, Houston Metropolitan Research Center, Houston Public Library, Houston, Texas.

49. Jiménez, "Mexican American Vietnam War Servicemen," 23.

50. Rosales, *Soldados Razos at War*, 98–99.

51. Oropeza, *Raza Sí! Guerra No!*, 3.

52. Antonio González, interview, Houston Metropolitan Research Center, April 14, 2016, Houston, Texas.

53. González, interview.

54. Calbillo, interview.

55. Calbillo, interview.

56. Calbillo, interview.

57. Calbillo, interview.

58. Carole E. Christian, "Herrera, John J.," Handbook of Texas Online, http://www.tshaonline.org/handbook/online/articles/fhe63.

59. Homer García, interview, Houston Metropolitan Research Center, April 7, 2016, Houston, Texas.

60. Wesley Abney, "Live from Washington, It's Lottery Night 1969!" HistoryNet, November 25, 2009, https://www.historynet.com/live-from-dc-its-lottery-night-1969.htm.

61. See "Vietnam War Facts, Stats, and Myths," US Wings, https://www.uswings.com/about-us-wings/vietnam-war-facts/.

62. Rick Gutiérrez, interview, Houston Metropolitan Research Center, April 12, 2016, Houston, Texas.

63. Rosalio Muñoz lecture, Sal Castro Memorial Conference on the Chicano Movement, University of California at Santa Barbara, February 27, 2016.

64. Oropeza, *Raza Sí! Guerra No!*, 95.

65. Behnken, *Fighting Their Own Battles*, 186.

66. The record is unclear, however, and more work must be done to find alliances between Chicanos and Vietnamese Americans or refugees that began populating Houston around 1970. Did Chicanos make overtures to ethnic Vietnamese from throughout the city? Certainly, the Vietnamese population in Houston in 1970 would have been small, but that number consistently grew, especially as American troops helped thousands of refugees relocate to the United States; after 1975, at least four hundred Vietnamese families called Houston home. See Tyina L. Steptoe, *Houston Bound: Culture and Color in a Jim Crow City* (Oakland: University of California Press, 2016), 274–75.

67. A Gallup poll measuring American support for the Vietnam War showed that support for the war was at its highest in 1965 but had waned by 1969. See Craig Chamberlain, "Did News Coverage Turn Americans Against the Vietnam War?," *Illinois News Bureau*, September 5, 2017, https://news.illinois.edu/view/6367/551796.

68. Mariscal, "Cesar and Martin," 161. See also Oropeza, *Raza Sí! Guerra No!*, 188.

69. Ivan Moreno, "Ernest Medina, Key Figure in My Lai Massacre Dies at 81," Associated Press, May 14, 2018, https://www.msn.com/en-us/news/us/ernest-medina-key-figure-in-my-lai-massacre-dies-at-81/ar-AAxgD3V?ocid=spartandhp.

70. Moreno, "Ernest Medina."

71. Medina would be charged in the deaths of at least 182 civilians, but during the trial he testified that his platoon was stationed just outside the village and that he was not present when the massacre occurred. This testimony would secure for him an acquittal. See Moreno, "Ernest Medina."

72. Trejo, *Carnales*, 22.

73. "The Invasion of Cambodia," The Vietnam War, https://vietnamawbb.weebly.com/invasion-of-cambodia.html. See also "Who Were the Viet Cong and How Did They Affect the War?," ThoughtCo., https://www.thoughtco.com/the-viet-cong -the-vietnam-war-195432.

74. Among other things that angered Chicanos was the military's use of Agent Orange, a defoliate designed to clear jungle and brush that enemy combatants might use as cover. It turned out that dioxin, the primary chemical used in Agent Orange, was dangerous to troops, causing all sorts of medical problems such as cancer and heart disease. Other problems included illicit drug use by troops, resulting in addiction to dangerous narcotics; a high incidence of mental health issues among the returnees; and growing homelessness among Vietnam veterans. A study of this period reveals that 23 percent of all homeless people in the United States were veterans and that 47 percent of them were veterans from the Vietnam War. See Trejo, *Carnales*, 90, 99–100, 123.

75. Kreneck, *Del Pueblo*, 90.

76. Oropeza, "Fighting on Two Fronts," 262.

77. Nick C. Vaca, Octavio I. Romano-V., Andrés Ybarra, and Gustavo Segade, eds., "Spanish Surname War Dead Vietnam," *El Grito* 3, no.1 (Fall 1969): 6–31. See also figures 1–3 for an illustration of the percentages of Chicano casualties of the Vietnam War for every state within the United States in Jiménez, "Mexican American Vietnam War Servicemen," 54–56.

78. Guzman calculated the number of Mexican Americans killed in Vietnam who were from southwestern states and found that 19 percent of the 7,966 total deaths were persons with Spanish surnames. See Ralph Guzman, *Mexican American Casualties in Vietnam* (Santa Cruz: University of California at Santa Cruz, 1969). See also Jiménez, "Mexican American Vietnam War Servicemen," 56, and Rosales, *Soldados Razos at War*, 99.

79. Jiménez, "Mexican American Vietnam War Servicemen," 56.

80. "Chicanos Told to Organize, Resist," *Houston Post*, July 27, 1970, sec. A, 3.

81. García, interview.

82. Jiménez, "Mexican American Vietnam War Servicemen," 58–59. See also Juan Ramírez, *A Patriot After All: The Story of a Chicano Vietnam Vet* (Albuquerque: University of New Mexico Press, 1999), 174.

83. Jiménez, "Mexican American Vietnam War Servicemen," 23. See also Juan Coronado's *I'm Not Gonna Die in this Damn Place: Manliness, Identity, and Survival of the Mexican American Vietnam Prisoners of War* (East Lansing: Michigan State University Press, 2018) for an examination of the inequality that existed regarding prisoners of war and prisoner exchanges.

84. Behnken, *Fighting Their Own Battles*, 186. See also Rosales, *Soldados Razos at War*, 99–100.

85. Robert Wooster, "Military History," *Handbook of Texas Online*, http://www.tsha-online.org/handbook/online/articles/qzmtg.

86. Jiménez, "Mexican American Vietnam War Servicemen," 57.

87. See the Virtual Wall Vietnam Veterans Memorial, http://www.virtualwall.org/istate/istattx.htm. Officially there were forty Chicano soldiers from Houston that were killed during the U.S. involvement in Vietnam if we include Lieutenant Colonel Donald Alfred Luna, who in 1978, years after the war technically concluded, was shot down and presumed killed in action by what the government classified as "enemy fire" over the Savannakhet Province in Laos. See also the Virtual Wall Vietnam Veterans Memorial, www.virtualwall.org/dl/LunaDA01a.htm.

88. "H. De La Paz Killed by Foe in Vietnam," *Houston Chronicle*, November 1965, Subject File: War Casualties, Houston Chronicle Morgue Collection, Houston Metropolitan Research Center, Houston Public Library, Houston, Texas; see also the Virtual Wall Vietnam Veterans Memorial, www.virtualwall.org/dd/DelapazHx01a .htm. Perishing also in November of 1965 were twenty-three-year-old Private First Class Jesse N. Rodríguez, killed November 17 in the Pleiku Province, and Private First Class Ruben G. Chavez, one of three Texas men to die within the same week. See "Three Harris Soldiers Die in Major Battle," *Houston Chronicle*, November 23, 1965, Subject File: War Casualties, Houston Chronicle Morgue Collection, Houston Metropolitan Research Center, Houston Public Library, Houston, Texas; see also the Virtual Wall Vietnam Veterans Memorial, www.VirtualWall.org/dr/RodriguezJN01a.htm, and "Houstonian, 3 Texas Men Die in Viet Nam in Week," *Houston Chronicle*, November 24, 1965, Subject File: War Casualties, Houston Chronicle Morgue Collection, Houston Metropolitan Research Center, Houston Public Library, Houston, Texas. See also "3 Houston Area Men Die in Viet Nam, Sorrow Marks Tot's First Birthday," *Houston Chronicle*, December 14, 1965, Subject File: War Casualties, Houston Chronicle Morgue Collection, Houston Metropolitan Research Center, Houston Public Library, Houston, Texas. Finally, thirty-three-year-old Marine Corps Staff Sergeant John B. Cordova was killed in action in December 1965; see "Staff Sergeant John B. Cordova Killed in Action in Vietnam," *Houston Chronicle*, December 14, 1965, sec. 17, pp. 20–24.

89. See "Cpl. Philip Serna, 20, Killed in Action One Week Before He Was Set to Return Home," *Houston Chronicle*, 1966, Houston Chronicle Morgue War Casualties Collection; see also the Virtual Wall Vietnam Veterans Memorial, www .VirtualWall.org/ds/SernaPJ01a.htm. Also perishing that year were Private First Class Joel Tamayo, who died in combat on May 21; Private First Class Miguel Fernando Najar, who was killed in action on September 28; Army Private First Class Cesario Calderon, who perished on November 4 from suffocation; and twenty-one-year-old Private Robert R. Martinez, who was killed on December 23. See also "Houstonian Joel Tamayo Dies in Combat," *Houston Chronicle*, May 25, 1966, Houston Chronicle Morgue War Casualties Collection, and the Virtual

Wall Vietnam Veterans Memorial, www.VirtualWall.org/dt/TamayoJxo1a.htm; "Houston Marine Dies in Viet Nam Action," *Houston Chronicle*, October 5, 1966, Houston Chronicle Morgue War Casualties Collection, and www.VirtualWall .org/dn/NajarMFo1a.htm; "Pfc. Calderon Dies in Viet Nam," *Houston Chronicle*, November 9, 1966, Houston Chronicle Morgue War Casualties Collection, and www.VirtualWall.org/dc/CalderonCxo1a.htm; and the Virtual Wall Vietnam Veterans Memorial, www.VirtualWall.org/dm/MartinezRRo2a.htm.

90. Twenty-year-old Private First Class Louis Ferndez Torres died on March 7 in Dinh Tuong Province. Also killed was twenty-one-year-old Private First Class Cipriano J. Pantoja Jr., who died from friendly fire on April 7. In May, three Houston Chicanos were killed in action: Private First Class Frank De Leon Montemayor of the Ninth Infantry Division on May 2; twenty-year-old Lance Corporal Juan Jose Ramírez on May 3; and twenty-one-year-old Private First Class Joseph Arthur Jiménez on May 14. The last two casualties for 1967 were Sergeant Jose López of the First Infantry Division, U.S. Army, killed in action on October 16 in the Binh Duong Province from fragmentation wounds, and twenty-one-year-old Lance Corporal Mike Gomez Ibarra, who perished on November 2. See the Virtual Wall Vietnam Veterans Memorial, www.VirtualWall.org/dt/TorresLFo1a .htm, www.VirtualWall.org/dp/PantojaCJo1a.htm, www.VirtualWall.org/dm/ MontemayorFDo1a.htm, www.VirtualWall.org/dr/RamirezJJo1a.htm, www.VirtualWall.org/dj/JimenezJAo1a.htm, www.VirtualWall.org/dl/LopezJxo2a.htm, www.VirtualWall.org/di/IbarraMGo1a.htm.

91. Sergeant Vicente Garza perished in a helicopter crash on January 8; twenty-two-year-old Specialist Four Raymond González Rocha of the 101st Airborne Division was killed in action on March 11; and Albert Burciaga was only nineteen years old when he was killed in April in the Thua Thien Province. Specialist Four David Adame García of the 101st Airborne Division was killed on May 13; Private First Class Pedro Chavarria Gonzales was listed killed on July 17 by way of drowning or suffocation; Sergeant Ramiro López Salinas died from an explosive device on August 4; and Private First Class Gilbert Trevino Delgado died from multiple fragment wounds also on August 18. There were two confirmed kills in September, Private First Class Lionel Alvarez Ryan and Private First Class Paul Martinez Vara, both of whom died from explosive devices, on September 5 and September 9, respectively. Finally, twenty-year-old Corporal Lawrence Ortiz Jr. was killed in action on December 19. See the Virtual Wall Vietnam Veterans Memorial, www .virtualwall.org/dg/GarzaVxo1a.htm, www.VirtualWall.org/dr/RochaRGo1a.htm, www.VirtualWall.org/db/BurciagaAxo1a.htm, www.VirtualWall.org/dg/GarciaDAo1a.htm, www.VirtualWall.org/dg/GonzalesPCo1a.htm, www.VirtualWall .org/ds/SalinasRLo1a.htm, www.VirtualWall.org/dd/DelgadoGTo1a.htm, www .VirtualWall.org/dr/RyanLAo1a.htm, www.VirtualWall.org/dv/VaraPMo1a.htm, www.VirtualWall.org/do/OrtizLxo2a.htm.

92. Private First Class William Anthony Hernandez died on January 6 from an explosive device; Private First Class Antonio Elizondo Ruiz died on March 14 in a plane

crash; and Specialist Five Roberto Salazar was killed in action on September 23. The last two casualties of the war for 1969 were Houstonians Valentine Berrones Suarez, gunnery sergeant, of the First Marine Division, who died from an explosive device on October 18, and Private First Class Jose Espiridion Ortiz, who died from multiple fragment wounds on October 20 in the Phuoc Long Province. See the Virtual Wall Vietnam Veterans Memorial, www.VirtualWall.org/dh/Hernandez-WAo1a.htm, www.VirtualWall.org/dr/RuizAEo1a.htm, www.virtualwall.org/ds/SalazarRxo1a.htm, www.VirtualWall.org/ds/SuarezVBo1a.htm, www.VirtualWall.org/do/OrtizJEo1a.htm.

93. Twenty-year-old Corporal Xavier Gomez was killed in action on January 8; twenty-one-year-old Private First Class Nick Aguilar of the Twenty-Fifth Infantry Division died from multiple wounds on April 9; and eighteen-year-old Private First Class Jose Jaime Castillo was killed in action on August 8. In November, several Chicano Houstonians perished in Vietnam. Benigno Zamudio Jr. was killed in the Phu Yen Province from an explosive device. Also perishing that year were nineteen-year-old Army Private First Class Jose G. Barrera and Corporal Felipe Morales. See the Virtual Wall Vietnam Veterans Memorial, www.VirtualWall.org/dg/GomezXxo1a .htm, "PFC Nick Aguilar, 21, Killed in Action in Vietnam," *Houston Chronicle*, April 14, 1970, sec. 1, pp. 1–2; Virtual Wall Vietnam Veterans Memorial, www.VirtualWall .org/da/AguilarNAo1a.htm and www.VirtualWall.org/dc/CastilloJJo2a.htm. See also "Bronze Star Recipient Zamudio Dies in Viet," *Houston Chronicle*, November 19–20, 1970, Houston Chronicle Morgue War Casualties Collection, and www.Vir-tualWall.org/dz/ZamudioBxo1a.htm; "PFC. Barrera of Pasadena Killed in Viet," *Houston Chronicle*, November 19, 1970, Houston Chronicle Morgue War Casualties Collection, Virtual Wall Vietnam Veterans Memorial, www.VirtualWall.org/dm/MoralesFxo1a.htm; "Cpl. Macario Sánchez Killed in Da Nang," *Houston Chronicle*, December 2, 1970, sec. 3, p. 5., www.VirtualWall.org/ds/SanchezMxo1a.htm.

94. Virtual Wall Vietnam Veterans Memorial, www.VirtualWall.org/df/Fernan-dezWMo1a.htm.

95. Trejo, *Carnales*, 108.

96. Jiménez, "Mexican American Vietnam War Servicemen," 56.

97. Jiménez, "Mexican American Vietnam War Servicemen," 57.

98. Stella Pope Duarte, *Let Their Spirits Dance: A Novel* (New York: HarperCollins, 2002), 56. See also Jiménez, "Mexican American Vietnam War Servicemen," 53.

99. In 1968, PASSO opened a voter registration headquarters in Houston and was central in the elections of Leonel Castillo as city comptroller, Ben T. Reyes as a state representative, and Armando Rodríguez as a municipal judge. See Esparza, "La Colonia Mexicana," 6. See also Max Krochmal, *Blue Texas: The Making of a Multiracial Democratic Coalition in the Civil Rights Era* (Chapel Hill: University of North Carolina Press, 2016), 241.

100. Julie Leininger Pycior, "Mexican-American Organizations," *Handbook of Texas Online*, http://www.tshaonline.org/handbook/online/articles/vzmvj. See also San Miguel, *Brown, Not White*, 57.

101. See "Calendar," *Anti-War Viewpoints* 4, no. 4 (April 1969): 2, Houston Committee to End the War in Vietnam, Houston Anti-Viet Nam War Collection, box 1, folder 2, Houston Metropolitan Research Center, Houston Public Library, Houston, Texas.

102. Behnken, *Fighting Their Own Battles*, 186.

103. Calbillo, interview.

104. Rosales, *Soldados Razos at War*, 99.

105. Oropeza, *Raza Sí! Guerra No!*, 104.

106. Draft counseling centers operated five days a week and were open to the people for very long hours, typically from 7:00 a.m. until very late in the evening. See "Draft Counseling Service of Houston," *Anti-War Viewpoints* 4, no. 4 (April 1969), Houston Committee to End the War in Vietnam, Houston Anti-Viet Nam War Collection, box 1, folder 2, Houston Metropolitan Research Center, Houston Public Library, Houston, Texas.

107. Calbillo, interview.

108. Carlos Calbillo, "The Chicano Movement in Houston and Texas: A Personal Memory," *Houston History Magazine* 9, no 1 (December 2011): 28.

109. Calbillo, "Chicano Movement," 28.

110. Rosales, *Soldados Razos at War*, 99.

111. Oropeza, *Raza Sí! Guerra No!*, 112.

112. Calbillo, interview.

113. De León, *Ethnicity in the Sunbelt*, 180.

114. De León, *Ethnicity in the Sunbelt*, 180

115. Kreneck, *Del Pueblo*, 90.

116. Gómez-Cano and Ross-Nazzal, *Spirit of Magnolia Park*, 104.

117. Calbillo, interview.

118. Calbillo, interview.

119. Calbillo, interview.

120. "News," *Anti-War Viewpoints*, September 1970, p. 6. *Houston Committee to End the War in Vietnam*, Houston Anti-Viet Nam War Collection, box 1, folder 2, Houston Metropolitan Research Center, Houston Public Library, Houston, Texas.

121. Gómez-Cano and Ross-Nazzal, *Spirit of Magnolia Park*, 104.

122. Denise Gómez, "A Life of Activism: Maria Jiménez," *Houston History Magazine* 12, no. 3 (July 2015): 14. See also interview with Calbillo, and the interview with Calbillo included in the Civil Rights in Black and Brown Oral History Project, Texas Christian University, June 24, 2016, Houston, Texas, https://crbb.tcu.edu/clips/search?filters%5Binterviewees%5D%5B%5D=Calbillo%2C+Carlos&q=calbillo.

123. Calbillo, "Chicano Movement," 28.

124. In 1973, Tanguma would complete what was touted as the largest mural in Houston history, *The Rebirth of Our Nationality*, which was just over four thousand square feet. See interview with Calbillo, and the interview with Calbillo included in the Civil Rights in Black and Brown Oral History Project.

125. Gómez-Cano and Ross-Nazzal, *Spirit of Magnolia Park*, 104.

126. "News," *Anti-War Viewpoints.*, September 1970, p. 6, *Houston Committee to End the War in Vietnam,* Houston Anti-Viet Nam War Collection, box 1, folder 2, Houston Metropolitan Research Center, Houston Public Library, Houston, Texas.

127. Krochmal, *Blue Texas,* 414.

128. Calbillo, interview.

129. Calbillo, interview.

130. Calbillo, interview included in the Civil Rights in Black and Brown Oral History Project. See also Rosalio Muñoz testimony in Mario T. García, *The Chicano Generation: Testimonios of the Movement* (Oakland: University of California Press, 2015), 237–50.

131. Calbillo, interview.

132. Calbillo, interview.

133. Calbillo, interview.

134. Gloria Rubac, interview, Houston Metropolitan Research Center, February 24, 2016, Houston, Texas.

135. Gómez-Cano and Ross-Nazzal, *Spirit of Magnolia Park,* 104.

136. Gómez-Cano and Ross-Nazzal, *Spirit of Magnolia Park,* 104.

137. Gómez-Cano and Ross-Nazzal, *Spirit of Magnolia Park,* 104.

138. Calbillo, interview.

139. García, interview.

140. García, interview.

141. Calbillo, interview.

142. Rubac, interview.

143. De León, *Ethnicity in the Sunbelt,* 181.

144. Rubac, interview. See also the interview with Rubac included in the Civil Rights in Black and Brown Oral History Project, Texas Christian University, June 6, 2016, Houston, Texas, https://crbb.tcu.edu/clips/search?q=rubac.

145. Gómez-Cano and Ross-Nazzal, *Spirit of Magnolia Park,* 104.

146. Rey Rodríguez, interview, Houston Metropolitan Research Center, February 7, 2018, Houston, Texas.

147. Oropeza, *Raza Sí! Guerra No!,* 137.

148. García, interview.

149. Calbillo, interview.

150. Calbillo, interview.

151. García, interview.

152. "Houston, Texas," *SDS New Left Notes* 4, no. 20 (May 30, 1969), Houston Anti-Viet Nam War Collection, box 1, file 8, Houston Metropolitan Research Center, Houston Public Library, Houston, Texas.

153. "Houston, Texas."

154. Ignacio García, *White but Not Equal: Mexican Americans, Jury Discrimination, and the Supreme Court* (Tucson: University of Arizona Press, 2007), 159.

155. Oropeza, *Raza Sí! Guerra No!,* 166.

156. García, interview.

157. García, interview.
158. García, *White but Not Equal,* 13.
159. Calbillo, "Chicano Movement," 28.
160. García, interview.
161. Rosendo López, interview, Houston Metropolitan Research Center, April 12, 2016, Houston, Texas.
162. López, interview.
163. Calbillo, interview.
164. García, interview.
165. García, interview.
166. Calbillo, interview.
167. Jiménez, "Mexican American Vietnam War Servicemen," 40.
168. Jiménez, "Mexican American Vietnam War Servicemen," 39–41.
169. Jan Crumb, "Viet Veterans Organize," Houston Anti-Viet Nam War Collection, box 1, file 21, Houston Metropolitan Research Center, Houston Public Library, Houston, Texas.
170. "Anti-War March Largest Ever Held in Austin," *Anti-War Viewpoints,* May 1969, p. 5, *Houston Committee to End the War in Vietnam,* Houston Anti-Viet Nam War Collection, box 1, folder 2, Houston Metropolitan Research Center, Houston Public Library, Houston, Texas.
171. Jiménez, "Mexican American Vietnam War Servicemen," 43.
172. "Anti-War March Largest Ever Held in Austin."
173. Rosales, *Soldados Razos at War,* 197.
174. Rosales, *Soldados Razos at War,* 197.
175. Rodríguez, interview.
176. Frank Villarreal, interview, Houston Metropolitan Research Center, April 14, 2016, Houston, Texas.
177. John F. Saenz, interview, Houston Metropolitan Research Center, April 12, 2016, Houston, Texas.
178. Antonio González, interview, Houston Metropolitan Research Center, April 14, 2016, Houston, Texas.
179. López, interview.
180. Rosales, *Soldados Razos at War,* 200.
181. Cástulo Camarillo, interview, Houston Metropolitan Research Center, April 14, 2016, Houston, Texas.
182. Villarreal, interview.
183. Interview with John F. Saenz, Houston Metropolitan Research Center, April 12, 2016, Houston, Texas.
184. Manuel Pérez, interview, Houston Metropolitan Research Center, April 14, 2016, Houston, Texas.
185. Rick Gutiérrez, interview, Houston Metropolitan Research Center, April 12, 2016, Houston, Texas.

186. Raúl De la Paz, interview, Houston Metropolitan Research Center, April 14, 2016, Houston, Texas.

187. De la Paz, interview.

188. Macario Ramírez, interview included in the Civil Rights in Black and Brown Oral History Project, Texas Christian University, June 15, 2016, Houston, Texas, https://crbb.tcu.edu/clips/search?q=macario.

189. Ramírez, interview.

190. García, interview.

191. Behnken, *Fighting Their Own Battles*, 133.

192. Calbillo, interview.

193. Calbillo, interview.

194. Calbillo, interview.

195. Calbillo, interview. See also Lindsay Scovil Dove, "A Scream or a Whisper: Images of Activism in Houston," *Houston History Magazine* 12, no. 3. (July 2015): 6.

196. Oropeza, *Raza Sí! Guerra No!*, 182.

197. Oropeza, *Raza Sí! Guerra No!*, 166.

198. Oropeza, *Raza Sí! Guerra No!*, 135, 184.

199. Oropeza, *Raza Sí! Guerra No!*, 147, 170.

200. Oropeza, *Raza Sí! Guerra No!*, 170–72.

201. Oropeza, *Raza Sí! Guerra No!*, 172.

202. Oropeza, *Raza Sí! Guerra No!*, 172, 180.

203. Oropeza, *Raza Sí! Guerra No!*, 182.

204. Krochmal, *Blue Texas*, 390.

205. Oropeza, *Raza Sí! Guerra No!*, 126–27.

206. Gregorio Salazar, interview, Houston Metropolitan Research Center, May 9, 1989, Houston, Texas.

207. Salazar, interview.

208. Calbillo, "Chicano Movement," 27.

209. Rubac, interview in Civil Rights in Black and Brown Oral History Project.

210. Calbillo, interview.

211. Rubac, interview in Civil Rights in Black and Brown Oral History Project.

212. Behnken, *Fighting Their Own Battles*, 187.

213. García, interview.

214. García, interview.

215. "Cease-Fire Goes into Effect," History.com, November 16, 2009, https://www.history.com/this-day-in-history/cease-fire-goes-into-effect.

216. Calbillo, interview.

6

AN INSIDER'S STORY OF THE CHICANO MOVEMENT

Roque García of Santa Fe

ELLEN MCCRACKEN

WHOSE STORIES are written into history? Scholars of the Chicano experience have reconfigured the master narrative of U.S. history by painstakingly constructing the narratives of communities in specific cities and regions, and also writing close-ups of individual leaders and extraordinary figures who had been left out of the master narrative. But scholars have also chosen to focus on lesser-known people, writing individual and collective oral histories that re-center the life stories of ordinary men and women whose daily struggles are at the heart of Chicano history. These oral histories blend the rhetorical strategies of literature with the witnessing voice and first-hand knowledge of history from the bottom-up. Scholars and other creative writers organize and stylize the raw testimony amassed in long hours of interviews—compressing, rearranging, and adding rhetorical elements to create dynamic narratives that will attract readers. Even the most compelling life stories often cannot do this on their own: they need an innovative style of retelling that the joint authorship of the oral history works to achieve. And most importantly, these stories need to be *written* into history and published in a venue that will preserve them.

I am not singling out academics as the saviors of ordinary people and implicitly superior to them. Oral historians have written about the unequal relationships between scholars and their subjects, noting the vast differences in economic privilege and the benefits academics accrue from doing this work.[1] Despite these disparities, I would frame the process of oral history as the joining of two or more people's talents for a greater good, a collective labor in which each person adds value to the project of amplifying knowledge of Chicanos in the United States. As a unique blending of two or more voices, these oral histories enhance the master narrative both by the knowledge they produce and the compelling style they construct, a style sometimes absent in history books.

But despite these new historical accounts written into the revised master narrative, some minority voices have been overlooked. Little attention, for example, has been paid to the role of Hispanos in New Mexico who were involved in the Chicano Movement. Some activists in the better-known movements in California, Texas, and Colorado erroneously believed that there was not much Movement activity in New Mexico, where many defined themselves as Hispanos with long-standing ties to Spain rather than Mexico. The understandable attention paid to the larger segments of the Movement has perhaps unintentionally marginalized a minority within the minority.

After many interviews over several years, Mario García and I wrote the compelling life story of a man born into poverty in rural New Mexico, who, now in his early eighties, still ekes out a living selling his delicious carnitas on the plaza in downtown Santa Fe.[2] Roque García almost didn't make it—having several brushes with the law and moving from place to place—until he became involved with the Chicano Movement in New Mexico in the late 1960s and 1970s. His experiences of eight decades of history in northern New Mexico amplify the master narrative by focusing not only on this neglected state but on an ordinary person's witness to history and participation in it. Roque García is not only the well-known food cart vendor on the plaza, affectionately known as "Roque" by all, but a mover and shaker in history from the bottom-up.

THE EARLY YEARS AND COMING OF AGE IN THE PRE-CHICANO MOVEMENT PERIOD

Born in 1937, Roque spent the first four years of his life in the farming village of Pajarito in northern New Mexico. The town had started as a stagecoach stop (*pararito*) and, because it was easier to pronounce, became Pajarito, as it is known today. His father constructed their house with logs and adobes, and there was a little schoolhouse and about twenty-five other families living there. With no electricity or plumbing, a two-hole outhouse served the family's needs. The children would chase away goats who would jump on top of the roof because it was constructed of boards and dirt, and grass grew on it. His father supported the family by working in mines, doing some farming, and chopping wood to sell in Las Vegas (New Mexico) and Santa Fe. Roque's father was also a Penitente, the lay confraternity of *hermanos* who practiced secret rituals in their *moradas*, including the reenactment of the crucifixion of Christ on Good Friday. Roque learned some of the *alabados*, or songs, from his father, although the secret brotherhood was outlawed by the Catholic Church at that time.[3]

Although they lived in poverty, Roque and the family did not see themselves as poor. "There were no rich people in our village, so we had no one to compare ourselves with," Roque notes. He does remember, however, that once, some passing tourists took his picture as he sat on a pony, wearing overalls and a straw hat, seeing him only as a quaint example of local culture.

During World War II, his father worked for one year in the shipyards of Oakland, California, sending money home to Pajarito to support the family. In 1944 the family moved to Santa Fe where there were better job opportunities and because Roque's mother wanted the children to attend Catholic school. Tuition was $1 a month and a sacrifice for the growing family. Starting first grade there, Roque, along with most of the other children, spoke only Spanish. But the Sisters of Loretto allowed only English, and if they caught children speaking Spanish at recess they would hit them on the back of the head with a stick. "I soon picked up English," Roque jokes. He remembers an awful hole in the basement that the boys had to use for a bathroom. Because it smelled so bad down there, Roque once peed outside. When the nun caught him, he refused to sit in a corner as she insisted and was taken to the principal's office. "I was already quite defiant of authority," he notes. Roque remembers fighting with other kids who teased him about his clothes and his accent in English. Another cruel memory is that the nuns showed movies from time to time and charged five cents. He and his brother were taken out of class to set up chairs for the movie, but then not allowed to attend because they didn't have the money.

Roque was a *travieso* and once in sixth grade brought a gun to school to confront a bully. He shot it at the waste can in the bathroom and the bully never bothered him again. A mini-businessman, he would also capture tadpoles in the Santa Fe River, put them in jars, and sell them to fellow students for two cents. When he was a little older, he travelled with his father and uncle to pick sugar beets in the summer to earn money for the family. They were paid a dollar per mile of crops picked. Surprisingly, although he frequently got into trouble in school, he was also an altar boy and in the summer before eighth grade was sent to Cincinnati with another boy to possibly be recruited to become a Franciscan friar. Roque remembers the long four-day bus ride and being afraid to get off the bus to buy food with the ten dollars the friars gave the boys for the trip. Nonetheless, despite being well behaved at the seminary that summer, and serving as an altar boy at Mass when the archbishop came, he did not enter the Franciscan seminary to become a priest.

Roque did not do well in school and was given a blank diploma at graduation from St. Francis School. With few social programs in New Mexico schools in the 1950s to help poor children succeed, he often played hooky in high school and sought fulfillment elsewhere. He joined Los Corchos, a gang of about twenty kids from his West Side neighborhood. They saw themselves as members of a club, trying to create a supportive environment for themselves. They would sneak out at night, raise money to buy jackets by playing guitars in the street, sometimes carried knives, and walked the streets for a feeling of empowerment. "We were cool," Roque notes. Los Corchos started playing pranks at school, sneaking into dances they couldn't pay for by crawling through a long underground tunnel, even once stealing Fats Domino's piano after he played there and later abandoning it. Their pranks escalated. They distracted an acquaintance who worked at a liquor store and stole bottles of whiskey—not to get drunk themselves but to sell to other students. They engaged in other petty thefts around town—for example, stealing car batteries from a gas station to sell. They were crafty, and when it had snowed, they backtracked on their footsteps to get out of the gas station to make it look like an employee was the thief. Their transgressions progressed to stealing guns and reselling them, and eventually his brother Joe was caught and sentenced to leave the state. Although only in his sophomore year, Roque decided to go with him and dropped out of high school.

After about a year, Roque returned to Santa Fe and, with few other choices, enlisted in the army. Roque credits this period in the army as the beginning of his food career. After training as a quartermaster, he worked in the mess halls and became a "taster" to evaluate various dishes. He was amazed by the quantity of food available compared with that of his poverty-stricken childhood. He also experienced racism for the first time, witnessing segregation in Virginia. A bus driver reprimanded him for sitting with his black friends in the back of the bus. From his $85 monthly paycheck, he sent $30 home to his mother.

After the service, Roque got married and worked in Oakland, California, in charge of the lights for shows at the Holiday Inn nightclub. He met many stars who performed there and remembers comedian Don Rickles openly making fun of Mexicans in his performance: "Ladies and gentlemen, I want to tell you that our great spotlight is by a Mexican. Do you know how to tell where a Mexican is? It's where all the flies are!"

But while he worked at the club, Roque also engaged in burglaries in Oakland and Hayward, stealing liquor and cash, although he and his accomplice were never caught. Once, when he was working for a summer in Lake Tahoe, he was asked to make late-night tacos for Frank Sinatra. The entertainer liked them so much that he and a friend offered to set Roque up in business with a chain of taco restaurants. His lack of self-confidence made him decline the offer, but he wishes he would have accepted and perhaps become a multimillionaire.

After four years, Roque returned to Santa Fe. It was 1964, and at this time Roque's life began to turn around because of new government social programs. He enrolled in a cooking school program run by the state, funded by President Lyndon Johnson's antipoverty program. There he met Senator Joseph Montoya, who said Roque was the best cook in the school and invited him to return to Washington, D.C., with him because he missed Mexican food in the capital. With the senator's help, Roque opened a Mexican taquería called Don Pedro's at Seventh and Pennsylvania. After a dispute with Montoya about the profits, Roque left and opened another restaurant, El Matador, hiring two cousins and a friend from New Mexico to come and help him. He decorated it with serapes and sombreros and allowed a group of Texas orphans sponsored by Congressman Henry B. González to sing at the restaurant. Long lines of customers formed to hear the music and eat. One day Senators Robert Kennedy and Hubert Humphrey came for lunch. But the winters in Washington were harsh, and after a neighbor chastised Roque's son for playing with a black child, the family decided to return home.

REIES LÓPEZ TIJERINA AND THE POOR PEOPLE'S CAMPAIGN IN WASHINGTON, D.C.

Once back, Roque's life took a new direction. He became active in the Chicano Movement, joining Reies López Tijerina and the land-grant movement. Roque's family had lost communal grazing lands to Anglo ranchers and the establishment of national forests. Roque, his brother Joe, and their cousins had been involved in land-grant efforts even before Tijerina came to New Mexico from Texas. In one protest that involved actress Greer Garson, they cut some of the fences that Garson had put up on her land but managed to escape arrest by running away when the police came. Roque was impressed with Tijerina's powerful speeches in Spanish and joined La Alianza, becoming good friends with Tijerina. Roque saw it as a movement not only to regain the lost lands, but one for justice and dignity for Hispanos. He participated in the first major action, the partial takeover of Carson National Forest in October 1966 to bring media attention to the illegal expropriation of Hispano land grants and communal grazing lands. At a press conference, they symbolically arrested two forest rangers for trespassing on Hispano land. In an unplanned action, Tijerina's wife Patty burned the government sign, and Roque's cousins were among the protestors arrested.

A year later in June 1967, Roque and other followers were on their way to the courthouse raid at Tierra Amarilla but were stopped by the National Guard. The objective of Tijerina and his followers was to do a citizen's arrest of District Attorney Alfonso Sánchez, who was harassing the Alianza. In Roque and his friends' trunk were rifles, pistols, and ammunition, but they convinced the guards that they were going hunting. Still, they were turned back and missed the raid itself. After Roque returned to Santa Fe, Tijerina came to his house on Luján Street, and spent several hours there discussing what to do, as the police were looking for the Chicano leader. Roque remembers the tanks on the highway as New Mexico tensed over the raid. Some believed that an armed revolution had begun in northern New Mexico, but Roque points out that Tijerina never believed in violence. Although Tijerina's arrest resulted in the demise of La Alianza, the land-grant movement among Hispanos continues to this day. In the 1970s, for example, Roque, his brother Joe, and others occupied one of the Tierra Amarilla land grants until a court awarded the land back to its original Hispano owners.

Roque continued his political involvement, now seeing himself as a Chicano and part of the militant Chicano Movement. He participated in the Poor People's Campaign in the summer of 1968, working with Tijerina to organize about two dozen people from Santa Fe to go to Washington, D.C. The campaign had been organized by Dr. Martin Luther King Jr. before his assassination as a way for poor people—Black, Brown, and white—to go to Washington, make their voices heard, and bring attention to continuing poverty in America. Roque helped in bringing together a group of Chicanos in Santa Fe. The buses to take the people to Washington from New Mexico assembled first in Albuquerque, where they were joined by participants who had arrived from Los Angeles, and from there they picked up Roque and his contingent at Carlos Gilbert School in Santa Fe and about sixty people from Rowe and Pecos. The buses first stopped in Denver, where participants spent the night at the Crusade for Justice headquarters, hosted by emerging leader Corky Gonzales. During a rally where Gonzales and Tijerina spoke, Roque, feeling that the crowd was not engaged enough, yelled "Viva Corky! Viva Tijerina!" from the back. Others took up the chant. Roque remembers about twenty buses travelling across the country, including Brown Berets from California and Black Berets from Albuquerque. He got to know Corky better on the trip and was impressed with his outspokenness and leadership. In Kentucky, right-wing groups threw rocks and even shot at the buses.

FIGURE 6.1. Roque García and Rodolfo "Corky" Gonzales, 1968. (Courtesy of Roque García.)

FIGURE 6.2. Roque García (lower right) seated with (right to left) Corky Gonzales, the Reverend Ralph Abernathy, Reies López Tijerina, and Andrew Young. Poor People's Campaign, Washington, D.C., 1968. (Courtesy of Roque García.)

Roque's narrative adds firsthand detail to the activities, meetings, and protests that summer in D.C. There, Roque met Chicanos from other parts of the country, such as California and other southwestern states and the Midwest. He also met Latinos such as Puerto Ricans from the East. He notes that some troublemakers tried to get in, but they were quickly thrown out by the Brown and Black Berets, who served as the security for the Chicano contingents. Among the new people that Roque met was Hank Adams, a Native American, who really impressed Roque with his commitment to preserving Native lands and fishing rights in the West, which was similar to what La Alianza was trying to do for Hispano lands in New Mexico. Roque also attended various meetings with black leaders such as Andrew Young and the Reverend Ralph Abernathy. He notes that while there were some tensions between Chicanos and Black people, no serious divisions occurred.

On one very special occasion, Martin Luther King's wife, Coretta Scott King, came to visit the Harwood School, where the Chicano delegation stayed, to thank the Chicanos for participating in the campaign that was part of her husband's dream. Roque was selected to introduce her, which was one of the highlights of his participation in the campaign in Washington. "She was a nice lady," he observes. "She was one of the nicest ladies I have ever met in my life. I remember that she held my hand and said to me, 'you be careful' and she gave me a big hug." This was one of the meetings where Chicanos and Blacks came together to hear Mrs. King. She gave Roque her prepared remarks, but unfortunately he can no longer find the text.

He remembers lengthy discussions among the delegates in the evenings at the Harwood School. They talked about their actions in Washington, about conditions in their own communities, and lots about the Vietnam War and opposition to it. Roque also began a budding leadership role there. He spoke about the land-grant struggle in New Mexico, but also about education and urban renewal and how these affected Chicanos. Now in his thirties, he was looked up to by the younger participants. He was often selected to be one of the speakers at the rallies outside federal departments. He was one of the Chicanos chosen to attend the Arlington National Cemetery burial of Bobby Kennedy after his June assassination.

During their stay in Washington, Roque and the other Chicanos engaged in marches and went to several federal departments and sites to protest the lack of support for Chicanos.

FIGURE 6.3. Roque García (right) with Reies López Tijerina, Poor People's Campaign, Washington, D.C., 1968. (Courtesy of Roque García.)

One major confrontation occurred at the Department of Justice, where Corky Gonzales engaged in a tense debate with Attorney General Ramsey Clark. However, the biggest demonstration, and one that Roque will never forget, was at the U.S. Supreme Court. Hundreds of Chicanos and Native Americans staged a rally on the steps of the court; there were several speakers, including Tijerina. The group tried to enter but was stopped. So the protestors camped outside for a couple of days and nights using blankets and sleeping bags. On the last day, things became tense when one of the protesters threw a rock and broke one of the court windows. When this occurred, Tijerina went to the microphone and said: "Some will criticize us for breaking this window, but what about the government that has shattered more of our people than windows?" At that point, the demonstrators dispersed and began to walk back toward the mall. The Berets kept control and helped people cross the streets. Soon, however, squads of police, some on motorcycles, attacked the group. They hit people, including Roque, with their batons. People were yelling, and Roque fell and hurt his leg. Next to him he saw a young mother with her baby also fall after being hit by the police. She let go of the baby, who might have been seriously hurt but for Roque, who picked up the baby and gave it back to its mother. Roque says that he never had witnessed such an example of police brutality. "We were pissed at the cops; we wanted to kill them for what they did to us but we knew we couldn't." Finally, after about an hour the police left, and Roque and the others found their way back to the Harwood School.

After almost three months—most of the summer of 1968—Roque and the others prepared to go home. They were by now tired and ready to return but proud that they had represented Chicanos and felt that they had made their presence felt in Washington. There were some tensions with the Black leadership, but Roque mostly recalls amiable relations with Black people. The campaign provided some funds for participants to return home on their own. Roque took advantage of this to fly back to Albuquerque with David Tijerina, Reies's son from a first marriage. They stopped in Chicago and met with both Chicano and Native American activists there.

MODEL CITIES, EL VICIO, AND YOUNG CITIZENS FOR ACTION

Back in Santa Fe, Roque helped try to revive La Alianza, but this was unsuccessful because Tijerina's legal problems took all of La Alianza's attention. Although

Roque remained a nominal member of the organization, his interests increasingly turned to working in the Santa Fe community, helping to protect and advance Hispano interests. In 1969 he got a job as a community organizer in the Model Cities Program. Model Cities was part of the War on Poverty program and was aimed at helping local communities upgrade their facilities and integrate citizens into urban planning. Beginning in 1968, and until its funding was cut by President Nixon in 1974, Model Cities coordinated with the Department of Housing and Urban Development to rehabilitate cities through citizen participation and social services, working to rebuild cities through decision-making at the municipal level.[4]

However, not everyone felt adequately represented. Roque and others in Model Cities pushed back against efforts by the city of Santa Fe to bypass Hispanos and their concerns. For one, the city was not hiring Santa Feans for various clerical and administrative jobs but people outside of the community such as from Albuquerque. This was not fair, and Roque and others protested it. More concerning, the city was forcing people, mostly Hispanos, out of their properties in order to redevelop certain areas. As people lost their homes, they were put into public housing. Roque notes, for example, that along St. Francis Drive many Hispanos owned or rented homes, but these were confiscated or subjected to eminent domain so that the city could replace them with stores and restaurants for tourists. On April 8, 1970, Roque and the group Young Citizens for Action (YCFA) presented a petition to the city council calling for a federal investigation of rental policies at a rent-supplement housing development in a poor barrio off Camino Alire. He asked the council to stop the eviction of twenty-three families from the Santa Fe Apartments, which he called "a Chicano concentration camp."[5]

To better combat these city policies, Roque and other Hispanos in Model Cities worked in six neighborhood associations that were formed across Santa Fe: Torreón, Lower Alto, Alvord, Los Amigos, Guadalupe, and Barrio Unido. Roque belonged to the Los Amigos Association. Besides resisting the type of urban renewal that harmed Hispanos, these Model Cities associations also lobbied for pro-Hispano issues. One effort included successfully getting the state legislature to pass a special tax to construct a new hospital in Santa Fe to especially help the poor. The neighborhood committees also assisted in getting the legislature to pass a bill to establish an indigent fund to help those who didn't have money or insurance for the hospital. The bill called for a sales tax on groceries for the fund. The measure, however, had to be approved by voters in the state. Roque and the other neighborhood workers campaigned for the tax, which was passed, although later repealed in 2004.[6] Model Cities also worked on everyday issues such as hunger in the Hispano community. In December 1970, the *Santa Fe New Mexican* showed Roque receiving fifteen hundred cans of food collected by Santa Fe High School students to distribute to needy families in Model Cities.[7]

Roque and others in the Model Cities program also used it to develop the Chicano Movement in Santa Fe. They organized a chapter of the Raza Unida Party. Each neighborhood association linked to Model Cities had organizers paid by the program who used these positions to help organize the Chicano Movement. They ran candidates for the Raza Unida Party and worked to get other Hispanos to vote for these candidates. They encountered opposition from the established Hispano leaders who shunned the term "Chicano" as meaning lower class and too militant. Still, some fifteen hundred in New Mexico joined the party according to Roque. Although they didn't win offices, they used the electoral campaigns to push for community reforms and the issues of the Chicano Movement.

Roque began helping out in El Vicio, an emergency program aimed at education and rehabilitation for drug addicts, whose name was taken from the slogan "Quebrar el Vicio," or "Break the Habit." According to Dan Devereaux, who was the volunteer coordinator of the program for three years, in late 1970 a group of addicts and former addicts approached him to help start a methadone clinic, patterned on one called Quebrar in Albuquerque. The Santa Fe patients, who had been travelling to the Albuquerque clinic for treatment, were about to be excluded from Quebrar because they were from out of town. Heroin use in the early 1970s had become a crisis. Many users were *pintos*, or ex-convicts, both men and women. The Santa Fe clinic received six months' support from HUD, with monies transferred from La Organización de Barrios and Model Cities along with private donations.[8]

To continue funding the center, Roque co-organized a "High Noon" march and fundraising drive on May 2, 1971, calling it "El Vicio Day." It was to raise awareness and financial support for the program, which they wanted to expand to nearby counties. El Vicio hoped to raise $10,000 as matching funds for the program. Some fifteen hundred people walked that day according to Roque, and the march raised $7,000. The Elks Lodge and other civic organizations also pledged their support. With this assistance, El Vicio operated a downtown clinic on Guadalupe Street, right next door to Roque's grandmother's house, that assisted 170 hardcore addicts. In April, before the march, he reported to the city council that El Vicio had treated 35 addicts aged fifteen to forty-one with methadone and placed 17 in jobs. He spoke at the Elks Club, soliciting donations, arguing that they could not make inroads into the heroin addiction problem without "a commitment from people to help their addicted brothers."[9]

As part of raising awareness of the growing heavy drug problem in northern New Mexico, a documentary film about the clinic, *Run Up and Down These Streets*, was produced by Leonard Wood and Gary Young. It was filmed in 1971 in Santa Fe, using patients and former drug users as the actors and in some technical roles. According to Devereaux, the intention was also to teach the methadone patients filmmaking skills that might help them find employment.[10] It opens with a scene of Roque and other program administrators walking into the clinic, talking about their work in Spanish. One former user and dealer, Manuel Montaño, is shown walking through the snowy barrio streets, saying, "As kids, we used to run up and down these streets," which gave the film its title. Devereaux notes that Montaño was a key figure in the clinic because he brought in a number of his former customers for methadone treatment. Roque remembers that one day when they were filming a scene of a simulated overdose with a borrowed ambulance, it turned out that the "actor" had in fact overdosed and they had to use the ambulance to take him to the hospital. The film was shown twice on PBS and won first prize at a film festival in Florida. It was also premiered in Washington, D.C., when Representative Manuel Luján arranged for its showing to federal health officials. Roque attended along with others who had produced the film.

Also in the 1970s as part of his activism in the Chicano Movement, Roque became involved in Young Citizens for Action, a group that worked with youth in the barrios, many of whom took drugs. YCFA had been founded in the 1960s by Brother Godfrey Reggio, a Christian brother who taught at St. Michael's High School, and Richard Moore, a Puerto Rican VISTA volunteer from Philadelphia who worked in the Job Corps program. Obtaining a grant from the Office of Economic Opportunity, Reggio got the youth who belonged to several Santa Fe gangs to work together instead of fighting each other. For example, he got the Lucianito gang to go to the Palace Street gang's headquarters and fix their clubhouse. He also cofounded with Dr. Matthew Kelly La Clínica de la Gente (the People's Clinic), a small neighborhood clinic on West San Francisco Street in the former Monterrey Café owned by community activist "Tisnado" Valdez. Reggio obtained funding for La Clínica by having Santa Fe declared an indigent community, much to the dismay of the local medical community and others. Many Hispanos lacked health insurance, and at La Clínica they could obtain free medical care. Brother Godfrey lived in a small room at the clinic that he called his "cell." He remembers dedicated staff such as Gina Valdez and Silvia Leyva, who worked there many years. Today it is called La Familia Medical Center.[11]

Reggio remembers seeing Roque at La Clínica and El Vicio during that period. In fact, Dr. Matthew Kelly has been Roque's physician for several decades. Reggio notes, "I liked Roque right away. He was part of the huge *familia* of Santa Fe and knew everyone in town. He had a golden tongue!"[12]

Young Citizens for Action also fought against the harassment of young Chicanos by the Santa Fe Police. Reggio bought a police band scanner at Radio Shack and obtained the police "ten" codes (for example, 10–40 for robbery). With five or six cars participating, they would go to crime scenes with a reporter, an attorney, and community members, sometimes arriving before the police. Roque participated in some of these citizens' patrols.[13]

Tensions between the youth and police came to a boil during the Santa Fe Fiesta of 1971 when Chicanos rioted in the plaza. The police responded with force, and eighteen-year-old Gloria Montoya was shot and later died. Roque, trying to calm things down, was arrested, charged with being drunk and disturbing the peace. The riot revealed that behind Santa Fe's Spanish fiesta there were racial problems and tensions. Roque was convicted of a reduced charge of "interfering with the duties of a police officer" and received a suspended sentence. The *Santa Fe New Mexican* included a picture of Roque holding his City of Santa Fe Young Citizens for Action card, which he showed to the arresting officers during the turmoil at the plaza. He claimed that because he was a member of the YCFA peace force, he was not interfering with the duties of an officer: "An incident occurred downtown (Thursday night) and while an arrest was being made, I attempted to discuss what was happening with the officer. I am a YCFA out-reach worker whose role is to aid in relations between law enforcement officers and citizens." Director of Model Cities Salvador Vigil suspended Roque as senior community organizer for thirty days.[14]

Roque's response to the suspension and his later firing was to commit even more to community involvement. He got a job as a counselor in a community center that Godfrey Reggio and YCFA had opened in a two-storey building at 1031 Alto Street in 1966. By 1969 the center had ten employees, who were all from low-income families below the poverty level. Besides recreation facilities, the center had a library, and 102 children registered to take books home. The center also focused on the parents. In February 1969, 18 adults attended twice-weekly night classes. YCFA also reported that they had found jobs for 417 people.[15]

Young Citizens mostly focused on the Agua Fria area on the west side, one of the poorest in Santa Fe and where drug use was a crisis. Roque worked with the group for two years. Youth were into a variety of drugs, including whites and reds. As a counselor, he got paid under a federal grant. There was not enough money to hire him, but his friends in YCFA agreed to cut their pay in order to hire Roque. "A real brotherhood," Roque calls these friends— the director, George Barela, Bernardino (Mino) Martínez, Ruben Lovato, and Jimmy Gallegos.

Roque began to cook for teens in the kitchen of the Alto Street headquarters. He cooked hamburgers and hot dogs, especially for those who were not getting three full meals a day. He also cooked breakfast. In all, each day he fed as many as seventy young men. The teenagers loved his cooking, although sometimes they stole food from the kitchen. They would ask, "Roque, when are you going to cook again for us?"

"When you behave yourselves," Roque replied.

In fact, before he fed them, Roque insisted that they work for their meal, doing jobs such as cleaning out the weeds and debris from the adjoining empty lot. The program didn't have enough money to feed the youngsters; however, Roque had a friend who worked at one of the Safeway supermarkets and who agreed to "contribute" the hamburger meat and hot dogs along with the buns and all the fixings for free.

Roque also helped to start a boxing program for the kids with the assistance of his younger brother Tommy, who had been an excellent boxer in his youth. They built a boxing ring for the boys to hold matches.

However, not everything went well in Young Citizens. On the Wednesday before Thanksgiving in 1973, six boys boycotted Roque and the other counselors. The group staged a sit-in at the building and refused to let the staff in because they had punished a couple of the teens. They also claimed that the staff charged for the boxing matches held in the gym and pocketed the money, instead of giving any of it to the boxers. The protestors demanded the resignation of YCFA director George Barela and other staff members, including Roque.[16] Roque says that the staff only took some of these funds for expenses and to buy more boxing equipment. On Thanksgiving Day, Roque helped defuse the takeover by

FIGURE 6.4. Roque García (left) with the Reverend Jesse Jackson, Santa Fe Plaza, 1988. (Courtesy of Roque García.)

delivering a Thanksgiving dinner cooked by his mother. The meal had a New Mexico touch; instead of gravy, his mother provided chile. After seven days with little food, the boys finally gave up and opened the doors.

In the mid-1970s, Roque got a job doing social work for County Social Services. He had earlier enrolled in a sociology class for future social workers at the College of Santa Fe, but didn't get credit because he couldn't afford to pay the tuition when the bill came due. Now he accompanied social workers on various cases, checking to see if children were going to school and working with delinquent Hispano youths to get them out of gangs and to stop doing drugs. Once, he found one of his clients burying his mother in the backyard because the family could not afford a funeral home or cemetery burial. When the funding for his job from CETA (Comprehensive Employment and Training Act) ran out, Roque got a position as a homemaker, caring for the elderly and disabled who could not care for themselves. He had been told that only women could work as homemakers, but citing his long experience in cooking, he threatened a lawsuit for gender discrimination. He became the only male homemaker in New Mexico. He worked among poor Hispanos in both urban and rural areas, making fresh tortillas, beans, and chile while cleaning and taking care of them.

Roque participated in local marches and demonstrations during this period, including hosting César Chávez when he came to town to support the grape boycott and a nurse's strike in one of the Santa Fe hospitals. Roque and others picketed Safeway and participated in anti-Vietnam War protests. Even though he was a veteran, he opposed the war. He was especially concerned that many young Chicanos in northern New Mexico were being drafted, including those from Santa Fe neighborhoods. In 1988 he was chosen to introduce presidential candidate Jesse Jackson, who was speaking in the Santa Fe plaza.

He presented the Rainbow Coalition candidate a small plastic statue of San Martín de Porres, the first black saint of the Americas and the patron of the poor, the homeless, the old, and the sick. Roque told the *Santa Fe New Mexican*, "I wish [Jackson] could be nominated to the second-in-command so he could go on with the issues."[17]

PEOPLE'S CANDIDATE

In the 1980s Roque became involved in local politics and ran for office. He was a member of Save Our Cities, working to control growth in Santa Fe. At a meeting on October 18, 1983, at St. John's Methodist Church attended by about seventy-five people, Save Our Santa Fe handed out antigrowth petitions. Roque spoke about key concerns, such as the construction of the First Interstate Bank building, the Sangre de Cristo Water Company rate increase request, the demolition of the Big Joe Lumber lot to make way for the Hilton hotel, and the use of the historic Santuario de Guadalupe church for classical music concerts. The group also protested the proposed construction of Metro Inns on 520 acres of city-owned land in northwest Santa Fe.[18]

A few months later, in early 1984, Roque ran for city council, believing he had the credentials to be a voice for barrio residents. Although Santa Fe County had district elections, candidates for the city council and school board elections had to run citywide. The Southwest Voter Registration Education Project, which advocated for Hispano voters, was targeting cities in New Mexico that had at-large elections, and the issue was widely debated in the 1984 election in Santa Fe. Roque took a strong public position supporting district elections, noting that he could much more effectively represent the issues of his own area rather than those of everyone in the city of Santa Fe.[19]

Because the 1984 city council election was citywide, Roque needed to campaign in the entire city with meager funds of only $1,300.[20] He ran on a platform of getting more parks in the barrio, more youth facilities and programs, and more senior centers. He called for a more effective police presence to protect against robberies, including car thefts and gang violence. He fought against the Metro Inns, a 520-acre development on city-owned land by a Dallas corporation that, in Roque's words, "would benefit only the wealthy" and was "a Fantasy Island type complex." At a candidates forum he spoke out against the proposed residential resort that would have three hundred condominiums and nine hundred housing units.[21]

Despite many votes from the barrios, he went down to defeat, with 2,702 votes out of the 10,679 citywide, a smaller turnout since it was not a mayoral election year.[22] Roque ran again in 1986 after district elections were established, for a seat from District 3 that covered the poor west side but also did not win. This time, he raised $1,486, while his opponent, Hispano David Schutz, a former land-use administrator and pro-growth candidate, raised $5,306.[23] Roque ran in an informal coalition with candidates John Coventry and Peter Gómez. Roque saw himself as a "people's candidate" and spoke out against the eroding support for established social services. At an arts forum for the candidates, he called for the preservation of Santa Fe's heritage. He also proposed a 2 percent tax on all large developments to expand human services such as recreation and transportation. He called for more police protection, especially in the poor Hispano neighborhoods, more funding for youth programs and senior transportation, and maintaining the downtown area for locals rather than tourists. "I grew up on the West Side and I have seen few programs over the years that benefit the people of the West Side . . . [and address] our social problems. . . . I will be a voice for social services and I will particularly be a voice for the West Side."[24]

After Roque lost the city council election in 1984, he decided to open a food cart, an idea suggested by a friend who had tasted a delicious beef roast with chiles and onions that Roque prepared one day. When he hit roadblocks getting a permit from the city, he used the political skills learned in the movement and called an acquaintance, Lieutenant Governor Casey Luna, who interceded with "people who owed him" in city government. On the cart Roque cooked beef carnitas with peppers, onions, and salsa, wrapped in a warm flour tortilla. Hardworking Roque sold food from the cart from 10:00 to 2:00 every day of the year, even in freezing winter. He rose early to shop and cut the ingredients and then haul the colorful cart to the plaza. Now a mainstay for locals, tourists, and even celebrities, Roque and his delicious food cart have been written up in dozens of national venues such as *Bon Appetit*, *Gourmet*, the *Washington Post*, and the Food Channel. Everyone knows Roque, and one commentator called him "Santa Fe's Senior Senator for welcoming visitors to the plaza."[25] He continues to speak out on local and national political issues and advocate for social justice at every opportunity.

CONCLUSION

What does Roque's story tell us about one of the have-nots from the second poorest state in the United States (by household income), whose life was significantly changed by his participation in the Chicano Movement? First, it alters the mistaken view that New Mexico was peripheral to the movement because its people saw themselves only as Hispanos, with deep-rooted connections to Spain, not Mexico. We see that Tijerina's land-grant movement was especially resonant with a variety of Spanish-speaking people in New Mexico because they saw this struggle as their own, dating back many years. For Roque and others in New Mexico, the Poor People's Campaign of 1968 was a natural outgrowth of their involvement with Tijerina in the continuing land-grant struggle. It was precisely their Spanish heritage and the legacy of the U.S. conquest that drew them into the burgeoning political activism of the Chicano Movement.

Second, we see a changing sense of ethnicity throughout Roque's life and the variety of social and political issues to which Chicanos like him were committed throughout their lives. Born in a village with a strong Hispano community whose traditions, beliefs, and cultural practices dated back centuries, Roque nonetheless experienced the reification of exoticism by Anglo tourists, racial bullying in grammar school, discrimination based on poverty from the nuns, low self-esteem, and the new subcultural identity he found as part of the Los Corchos gang. He was publicly ridiculed as a Mexican by Don Rickles in Oakland, and in 1995 by white youth gangs on the plaza who called him a "little wetback."[26] The Chicano Movement and War on Poverty social programs in the 1960s helped to turn his life around. He worked in antidrug and other social service programs and ran for office as a "people's candidate," campaigning for social justice issues. Having dropped out of high school, he struggled to earn a living his entire life. Nonetheless, he blossomed as a leader in the everyday struggles of the community, forged ties to other minorities, and continues to work for social justice issues on many fronts. Roque's story demonstrates the variety of social and political community issues that veterans of the Chicano Movement became involved in. Their activism branched out on many fronts and continues to this day.

Roque recently discovered through genetic testing that he is 29 percent Native American. Since President Trump began making nativist pronouncements, more tourists ask him on the plaza, "Where are you from? You speak pretty good English!" While he is extremely proud of his Hispano origins, he agrees that the annual Entrada parade and performance during the Santa Fe Fiesta, which celebrates the reconquest of Santa Fe in 1692–93 from Native Americans and which Native Americans and others successfully fought against in 2017 and 2018, should be discontinued or removed from the plaza. He is thinking of making a T-shirt that says, "Speak Indian. You're in America." Without doubt, Roque's political analysis, the positions on issues he takes, his continued political work, and his own identity were all shaped by the historical and life-changing Chicano Movement.

NOTES

1.   See, for example, Daphne Patai, "Ethical Problems of Personal Narratives, or Who Should Eat the Last Piece of Cake?" *International Journal of Oral History*, February 1987: 5–27.

2.   See Mario T. García and Ellen McCracken, *Roque's Corner: The Life and Times of Roque García and His Santa Fe* (Santa Barbara, Calif.: Adelante Press, 2019).

3.   Except where otherwise noted in notes, the story of Roque García's life recounted here is drawn from twenty-eight interviews conducted with him between 2013 and

2018 in Santa Fe by Mario García and Ellen McCracken. Additionally, because of memory gaps and imprecise information in the interviews, nearly two hundred newspaper and magazine articles about Roque and the events he participated in were researched for our book *Roque's Corner*. We also conducted interviews with several of Roque's friends and relatives.

4.   Santa Fe's program received HUD approval in September 1968 with a $91,000 planning grant for its Model Cities neighborhood. "The Past 100 Years," *Santa Fe New Mexican*, September 6, 2018.

5.   Ron Longto, "City Council Calls for Probe of Housing Supplement," *Santa Fe New Mexican*, April 9, 1970.

6.   Gail Cole, "New Mexico Clarifies Gross Receipts Tax on Food," *Avalara*, October 11, 2012, https://www.avalara.com/taxrates/en/blog/2012/10/new-mexico-clarifies-gross-receipts-tax-on-food.html.

7.   "School Students Help," *Santa Fe New Mexican*, December 28, 1970.

8.   Don Devereaux, interview by Ellen McCracken, September 23, 2018; "SF Elks Pledge El Vicio Fund Support," *Santa Fe New Mexican*, April 23, 1971.

9.   "Drug Abuse Groups Mobilize Campaigns," *Santa Fe New Mexican*, December 20, 1970; "Community Spirit," *Santa Fe New Mexican*, January 5, 1971; "'El Vicio Day' Set in Santa Fe," *Santa Fe New Mexican*, April 19, 1971; "Addict Talks on Drug Life," *Santa Fe New Mexican*, April 1, 1971; and "SF Elks Pledge El Vicio Fund Support."

10. Devereaux, interview.

11. Godfrey Reggio, interview by Ellen McCracken, September 22, 2018.

12. Reggio, interview.

13. Reggio, interview.

14. "Garcia Intends to Appeal," *Santa Fe New Mexican*, September 23, 1971. Roque's version of the events is that he and three others, Antonio Mendoza, Roberto Mondragón, and Roque's brother Joe were visiting schools, doing cultural awareness work as part of Model Cities outreach during fiesta week. Afterward, they were eating in the Plaza Café downtown, when Ernest Trujillo made a derogatory remark to the group. Antonio took Ernest outside to settle things, and in the scuffle lost the fancy belt buckle he was wearing for fiesta. With a borrowed flashlight, Roque was helping Antonio look for his buckle under a car when the cops were called to stop a fight at El Sombrero bar next door. They tried to arrest Roque, and even when he showed them his YCFA card, charged him with drunkenness in public, resisting arrest, and disorderly conduct by striking an officer (Roque García, interview by García and McCracken, September 14, 2018, Santa Fe). A few months later in January 1972, Jim Maldonado, a newspaper columnist, noted that Roque had been fired from Model Cities amid budget turmoil, political wrangling, and a possible HUD investigation. Maldonado wrote that Roque "tends to speak out against the [Mayor] González administration, and as a result, he is terminated. This time it looks like it's for good." Maldonado, "Pepe and Pepito," *Santa Fe New Mexican*, January 26, 1972.

15. Bill Dunning, "Young Citizens for Action Involved in Many Programs," *Santa Fe New Mexican*, February 6, 1969.
16. "YCFA Dissidents Stay in Building for Protest," *Santa Fe New Mexican*, November 23, 1973.
17. "Jesse Jackson's Trailing Campaign," *Santa Fe New Mexican*, June 4, 1988.
18. Helen Gaussoin, "Residents Protest Local Growth," *Santa Fe New Mexican*, October 19, 1983.
19. See Jocelyn Lieu, "Candidates Split on Districting"; William Heimbach, "Group Promises to Sue If At-Large Voting Continues"; and Jack Hartsfield, "Mayor Carrying Banner for Voting Districts"—all in *Santa Fe New Mexican*, February 26, 1984.
20. The newspaper noted that Roque raised $1,300 for his campaign and had expenses of $1,904; "Contributions," *Santa Fe New Mexican*, February 7, 1984.
21. "Know Your Candidates," *Santa Fe New Mexican*, March 5, 1984; Kathy Haq, "Metro Inns an Issue at Candidate Forum," *Santa Fe New Mexican*, February 29, 1984; "City Council Hopeful Lists Issues," *Santa Fe New Mexican*, March 1, 1984. Roque managed to get an entire article publicizing his campaign issues in the newspaper on March 1, 1984, claiming that he did not receive the letter mailed from the newspaper asking all the candidates to outline their issues for an article previously published. He argued for "a ceiling on Santa Fe's development to keep the entrepreneurs and opportunistic developers from defacing or destroying the second oldest city's true tourist attractions, its ancient landmarks." The large developers fill their higher paying jobs before coming to Santa Fe, he noted, and leave the locals only minimum wage jobs. Among other issues, he campaigned for drug prevention programs that would attract youth to the arts, hobbies, and sports; better salaries and training for police; and the revocation of the current water franchise in favor of a city-owned water company. "City Council Hopeful Lists Issues."
22. "City Council Hopeful Lists Issues." Robert Storey, "Great Turnout, Support from South, Help Seal Victory for Big Winners" and "Unofficial Results" (table), *Santa Fe New Mexican*, March 7, 1984.
23. J. W. Schomisch, "Districting Fosters New Campaign Style in the City," *Santa Fe New Mexican*, February 2, 1986; Robert Storey, "Pick Outspends All Opponents," *Santa Fe New Mexican*, March 4, 1986.
24. "Candidate Responses," *Santa Fe New Mexican*, March 2, 1986; Ron Franiscell, "Candidate Coventry Doesn't Yet Know His Opponent," *Santa Fe New Mexican*, January 5, 1986; Inez Russell, "Candidates Agree on City Growth, Arts," *Santa Fe New Mexican*, February 21, 1986; "Endorsed by the *New Mexican*," March 2, 1986. The newspaper endorsed Roque's opponent, Schutz, a former county land-use administrator and "professional planner" in its words.
25. Pancho Epstein, "Bites," *Santa Fe New Mexican*, May 7, 1997.
26. Ben Neary, "'Punks' Draw Wrath of Plaza Merchants," *Santa Fe New Mexican*, October 13, 1995.

7

TAKING CHICANOA AND SOLIDARITY MURALS SERIOUSLY

HOLLY BARNET-SANCHEZ AND TIM DRESCHER

WHILE STUDYING the murals at the Estrada Courts Housing Project in eastern Los Angeles, known as East Los, we realized that murals are often treated primarily as visual sources for discussions of topics or theories, with little or no attention paid to the implications of the mural medium itself.[1] Murals have taught us a great deal because we look at them again and again over time; we look at where and how they are situated. One could say we "listen" to what they have to say; we take them seriously. The murals at the Estrada Courts Housing Project are particularly loquacious, and part of their lesson, of course, is bound up with the normal meanings derived from content (in many cases during the early years of El Movimiento, both representing and helping to construct *chicanismo*), the very characteristic that is so attractive for use as illustrations for other topics. We discovered, however, that meanings also derive from the medium itself, from intrinsic characteristics that add to image-based content, yielding a more complex, but potentially more satisfying expression of chicanismo—for example, as seen in the murals at Estrada Courts and Ramona Gardens.

Intrinsic characteristics include the several simultaneous locations the mural inhabits and, by way of emphasis, its relation to architectural characteristics. We want to open up a discussion about murals' intrinsic elements by looking specifically at the importance of location and architecture in a selection of

Chicanoa and Latinoa and solidarity murals painted over the last four decades in Los Angeles and San Francisco. These murals are a subset of the much larger international community murals phenomenon. Community murals were outgrowths of and contributors to civil rights movements, liberation movements, and to the creation of new communities that the murals themselves helped to conceptualize and represent.

We now take for granted exterior murals in locations such as housing projects. At the time they went up in the late 1960s and early 1970s, painting them at all and painting them on building exteriors in primarily working-class neighborhoods was a revolutionary act. These murals were phenomenologically different from any prior iteration of frescoes and murals, including those from the Mexican mural renaissance and from the New Deal era in the United States during earlier decades of the twentieth century. They aspired to be a people's art. They were created by, for, and with the communities of which they were a part—very urban, public, accessible mediums of expression that helped create and portray community and individual identities and aspirations. As such, their locations on housing project walls is of utmost significance for the creation of meaning in these murals. That being said, many of the observations explored here are applicable to murals anywhere, within any cultural context.

A mural's meanings emerge dialectically from relations between its content, its location, and its architectural setting. Content is always the primary source of a mural's meaning that resides in the subject matter, the symbols and image details and their interrelationships as they are given nuance by size, scale, color, style, and other formal aspects—that is, standard art historical analysis. But murals can be different from other kinds of artworks because of the ways in which community muralists utilize location and architecture, primarily having to do with a mural's relation to space. Spatial relations are always in play with murals, but are not always examined as a potential source of meaning.[2]

By "location" we mean where the mural is placed physically, where in a housing project, where in geographical or topographical relation to contiguous and otherwise relevant parts of the city, perhaps of the state and, indeed, the planet insofar as that raises the question of cardinal (compass) direction. In other words, location, an intrinsic characteristic, exists in several relational spatial modes simultaneously. The mural's meaning relates to all these things at once, but it helps to discuss physical location separately from the metaphorical, by which is meant such categories as art-historical location, socio-historical location, and so on, the typical categories used to unpack a mural's meaning.

By "architecture," we mean the ways in which a given mural relates to the structural characteristics of the building on which it is painted. Is an air duct an obtrusive visual blight or has it been incorporated into the design so as to invoke the building's mass in the thrust of the design? In East Los and in San Francisco, several murals exhibit these potential relationships and in doing so wrest more complex meanings for a viewer to consider than are available in the painted surface alone.

A particularly apt example of both location and architectural utilization is Michael Rios's *BART Mural* above the BART plaza at 24th and Mission Streets in San Francisco.

Rios turns the mural wall's horizontality into a forceful design component by showing a BART train coming from downtown (the left side of the mural) into the Mission District where the mural is located. The elegant line of the long mural curves up from downtown (also the actual direction where downtown is located) and swings around to the right as it terminates and dips toward the escalators at the station entrance, taking passengers down to and up from the trains. Aesthetically elegant, and also functional, the depicted BART train points the way, a kind of "this way" arrow placed over the plaza.

FIGURE 7.1. Michael Rios, *BART Mural*, 1975, Mission District, San Francisco. (Photograph by Tim Drescher.)

While the *BART Mural* is an excellent example of the use of location and architecture to enhance meaning within a single work of art, as well as within the broader place it occupies, mural clusters present a different set of possibilities for the creation of meaning within and between the murals, as well as between the murals and their location, environment, and their community. Mural clusters present multiple and complex avenues for their study across disciplines. Within our context, they are particularly fruitful sources of meaning because in clusters there is an immediate opportunity to consider how the murals interact with each other. A viewer does not have to walk or drive several blocks to compare examples. A cluster automatically emphasizes, because several voices speak louder than one. Clusters also uniquely contain the possibility of murals not only "speaking" to each other (interrelating), but also establishing new meanings not available to single examples of the medium. The Estrada Courts murals teach that.

Location and architecture, especially in clusters, serve to create and amplify meaning over time, and help viewers to conceptualize newer meanings as times change and the murals are still there to be considered. Location and architecture always work on a subliminal level, but once one starts to consider them actively, they become powerful tools for understanding a fuller, more nuanced meaning.

The more than ninety murals painted between 1972 and 1978 at the Estrada Courts Housing Project exemplify the coming together of three communities within the Courts (figure 7.2). This can be observed through the interactions of location and imagery, and by studying the uses of architectural features, such as dihedral (double angled) and lower walkway walls within the projects. These murals exemplify the predominantly Mexican American families who resided there, the members of the VNE (Varrio Nuevo Estrada) youth gang who were located within the projects, and the young people—residents and invited artists alike—who called themselves Chicanas and Chicanos, participants in the Chicano civil rights and arts movements of the 1960s and beyond. The process of painting those murals between 1972 and 1978 made those communities' interactions visible.

Those murals that are most publicly visible, what we call the Entrance Guardians and the Olympic Façade, constitute the public, Chicanoa face of the projects.[3] They are located on Olympic Boulevard and Lorena Street, two thoroughfares that come together at a busy intersection, the site of the keystone dihedral wall mural *Give Me Life*. These murals' locations vis-à-vis the Courts,

FIGURE 7.2. Long shot of the Olympic Façade, ca. 1986, Estrada Courts Housing Project, Boyle Heights. Photograph by Marcos Sanchez-Tranquilino. (Courtesy of the Housing Authority of the City of Los Angeles [hereafter HACLA]. Courtesy of Marcos Sanchez-Tranquilino.)

the wider Boyle Heights community, and each other create a dynamic set of meanings addressed to the "outside world" and Estrada Courts residents alike.

Two of the Entrance Guardians, *The Virgin of Guadalupe* and *Aztec Deity*, are located at opposite intersections entering the Courts. *The Virgin* faces out toward southbound drivers on Lorena at the corner of Hunter Street, the northeast corner of the projects. *Aztec Deity* faces outward toward eastbound drivers on Olympic Boulevard at the corner of Grande Vista Avenue, the southwest corner of the New Estrada Courts addition where the murals are located. Both are located at access points: *Aztec Deity*, a depiction of ancient civilizations, guards the official roadway into Estrada Courts leading to the administrative and recreational buildings. *The Virgin*, a timeless figure of religious faith and political resistance whose origins lie in the early Spanish colonial era, protects not only Courts residents but also passersby and those who live outside of the Courts on Hunter Street. Both Grande Vista Avenue and Hunter Street are used by residents and the public to enter and leave the more private areas of the projects. In Los Angeles driving culture, these access points are significant. They are both welcoming and gatekeeping/protective; they point the way to the interior of the Courts and, in reverse, to the outer world beyond Estrada. They acknowledge and even "bless" those who are leaving.

The next three Entrance Guardian murals are close to each other on Lorena, separated by a large lawn next to the driveway leading to a parking lot for the Courts (figure 7.3). *United Farmworkers* brings ancient and revolutionary eras in Mexico together with the Mexican American/Chicano UFW, all equally protected by another image of the Virgen de Guadalupe facing south toward *Orale Raza!* and *Farmworker Family*. *Orale Raza!*, the middle and most prominent mural combining a contemporary pop-art style and overt messaging, faces outward toward Lorena and the public, beckoning everyone to pay attention and to join together in El Movimiento. The third mural in this triumvirate, *Farmworker Family*, provides the familial center that supports all community, especially those who work in the fields, serendipitously represented by the swath of lawn in front of all three murals. It faces north towards *Orale Raza!* and *United Farmworkers*.

This grouping of three murals presents a pointed Chicanoa activist section of Estrada Courts—a declarative statement. These three balance the equally

FIGURE 7.3. Frank Fierro, *Orale Raza!*, 1974–79, Lorena Street, Estrada Courts Housing Project, Boyle Heights. *United Farmworkers* mural by Alex Maya is in the background. Photograph by Tim Drescher. (Courtesy of HACLA.)

powerful *movimiento*-embedded declarations of *We Are Not A Minority!!*, the proof-sheet documentary-style *The Black and White/Moratorium Mural*, and the erstwhile critique of the Vietnam War, *Wonderful World of Corruption* on the Olympic Façade (see figure 7.2). These six calls to activism bring together on the two most public faces of Estrada Courts the local, regional, national, and international scope of Chicanoa political engagement.

Give Me Life, located at the intersection of Olympic Boulevard and Lorena Street, is situated physically, geographically, and conceptually at the center point between these most public declarations of chicanismo, of identity, activism, and international solidarity (figure 7.4). Painted on a large dihedral wall, its theme is grounded in the immediate community and is very ambitious: life and death, the demand for a chance for the children of the Courts, the wider community, and for the planet itself.

Give Me Life is also the centerpiece of a smaller grouping of contiguous murals that work together: a mini-cluster. The building on which it is painted contains another large mural, *The Sacrifice Wall*, a depiction of human sacrifice on an ancient ball court in El Tajín. This key mural is located on the reverse side of

FIGURE 7.4. Charles "Cat" Felix and The Kids of the World, *Give Me Life*, first version with original walkway wall, ca. 1973, corner of Lorena Street and Olympic Boulevard, Estrada Courts Housing Project. Photograph by Kazuo Higa. (Courtesy of HACLA. Courtesy of Estate of Kazuo Higa.)

the same double apartment block as *Give Me Life*, facing a pedestrian entrance to the Courts, and visible from both inside the Courts and from Olympic Boulevard when driving or walking east. The walkway walls surrounding this end of the building complete the group, while serving to reinforce the meanings of *Give Me Life*.

The Sacrifice Wall is a cautionary tale using the ancient Mesoamerican ball game and human sacrifice as a metaphor for war/gang violence, life in the projects, even life itself as perceived by young men in the projects. It is the necessary counterbalancing companion to *Give Me Life*.

A rendering of the pachuco cross is painted on the small walkway wall perpendicular to *The Sacrifice Wall*. Based on the well-known tattoo found on many men's hands since the 1940s, it symbolized resistance among Chicanos, especially in California. In this particular location, the cross becomes a temporal link between the ancient Mesoamericans and the contemporary world as lived in the Courts and depicted in *Give Me Life*. The walkway walls that surround that mural visually expand and reinforce its message.

Give Me Life, along with all the public murals on Olympic and Lorena, separates the smaller community of Estrada Courts from the surrounding Boyle Heights neighborhood while also attracting neighbors and outsiders as viewers. *Give Me Life* can therefore be seen as a welcoming gesture, a declaration, and a manifesto. Its location on the corner and the large dihedral wall accentuate its significance vis-à-vis the Courts and the rest of the murals. It is also important to note that *Give Me Life* is *not* located at the official entrance to the Courts, or anywhere near the administrative offices, which are in a different, older section of the projects that has no exterior murals owing to architectural constraints. This physical separation of the murals from the official domain of the Housing Authority of the City of Los Angeles (HACLA) enhances the perception (real or not) that the communities of residents and invited artists have created something of substance that is their own, separate from the various governmental agencies that daily impact their lives.

Given the location of *Give Me Life*, one has to acknowledge that any mural painted here, by virtue of geography and architecture, is a very public statement with the potential for an expansive, powerful, and significant message to both the residents of the Courts and the wider communities of which the Courts are a part. The nature of that statement was determined by the artist Charles "Cat" Felix and his group of young assistants from the Courts, Los Niños del Mundo, by their choices of subject matter, content, composition, style, form, and color for *Give Me Life*. The initial success and subsequent impact of the mural are the result of the interactions between the mural, its location, its architectural framework, and the responses of those who have viewed it over the years. The resulting mural, as seen here in the first version from 1973, including the imagery on the walkway wall, took full advantage of space and place.[4]

Give Me Life's themes and imagery speak to several communities at once: the Kids of the World's families and friends, the VNE gang that resides at the Courts, the administrators of the projects, the residents and politicians of Boyle Heights, of Los Angeles, and a wider, even global community—the universe. Earth's place and potential futures determined in part by games of skill are shown by pool balls as planets connected by the thinnest of threads representing nuclear potential and threats, and by the element of chance. The earth-encircling merry-go-round with its brass ring held aloft by the black-robed figure of death holding an hourglass while standing on the eight ball emphasizes the precariousness of existence. The walkway walls as first painted contained a line of figures carrying planet Earth, bookended by the symbol of nuclear energy and a pulsing hot sun. To the upper left of the composition is a large sunflower filled to overflowing with seeds, people yet to be born into this world, this universe, demanding a chance at life. The entirety of the composition floats in a blue-black sky heated and lit by an enormous yellow and orange sun at the topmost point of the dihedral split. That split wall enables the people in the sunflower to look directly at the floating earth merry-go-round with its accompanying death figure. The composition utilizes the dihedral wall to simultaneously open and close, to present both danger *and* hope as real.

The lower right side of the walkway wall takes the viewer into ancient history with the depiction of an abstracted serpent, Quetzalcoatl, the feathered serpent of the ancient Mesoamerican ancestors of present-day Mexicans, Mexican Americans, and Chicanoas. The lower left side apparently provides another reference to Mesoamerican architectural designs. In essence we see the ancient past encircling and protecting the present and future of the center composition. On closer inspection, those abstract designs camouflage the initials of the local resident gang, the VNE, bringing everything in the mural back to the immediate present.[5]

The murals were seen by housing authorities as a means to eliminate gang graffiti; the hidden VNE logo at the central point of the murals at Estrada Courts indicates the gang's continued presence, and its desire to both protect the Courts and be stealthily visible in doing so. Once discovered by the Courts

administrators, that design was painted out, replaced by pre-Columbian protective tomb figures, an ostensible removal of the gang graffiti that served as
a symbol of the gang's presence throughout the Courts, while simultaneously
representing the ties between the ancient past and the current residents.

The spiritual and mythological foundations of a certain conception of El
Movimiento ground the pre-Columbian heritage of the Courts' messaging, seen
on Entrance Guardian murals and the walkway walls that surround and protect.
Its use as a metaphor for the continued presence and role of the VNE serves
to replace the all-important graffiti. By including pre-Columbian imagery on
the walkway walls, especially at the entrances and exits, the gang's self-assigned
protective role is acknowledged by the Chicano artists and organizers and is
tied directly to the symbolism of the Chicano movement. These locations, the
architectural features of the walkway walls, are where the Chicanoa Movement
artists and the Mexican American gang youths intersect most visibly at Estrada
Courts.

In terms of the importance of architecture for the meaning of the Courts'
murals, we note four separate phenomena: where the walls are located and
toward what direction they are pointing; the size of the painted walls that
are eighteen by twenty-three feet on average; the use of the walkway walls
throughout the Courts; and the use of dihedral walls for the murals.[6] For most
of the walls, architecture does not usually play a role in creating meaning but
serves primarily as an emphasizer. In two instances architecture has a material
impact on meaning. One is *Give Me Life* on the most public exterior face (looking away from the Courts). The other is *Mi Raza Primero* on an external wall
surrounded by Estrada apartment buildings (facing inward toward the center
of the Courts), in an area designated for residents' recreational use (figure 7.5).
Together, these two murals speak to the complexities of the identities of the
residents of the Courts. *Mi Raza Primero*, located on the only patch of rising
and grassy land on Courts property, presents a fiesta where everyone from inside
and outside the courts is welcome. *Mi Raza Primero* can be understood as the
cultural expression of *Orale Raza!* on Lorena, and perhaps as the celebration of
the life so wished for and demanded by *Give Me Life*.

The location of Estrada Courts at the intersection of Olympic Boulevard and
Lorena Street unintentionally creates, by virtue of the already extant urban grid,
what one could call a "reverse dihedral," with the actual dihedral wall of *Give
Me Life* situated at its apex. This is slightly apparent if one stands catty-corner
across the wide intersection, but is really only visible when one looks at a map

FIGURE 7.5. Robert Chavez and students from East Los Angeles College, *Mi Raza Primero*, 1974, interior area of Estrada Courts. Photograph by David Botello, 1970s. (Courtesy of HACLA. Courtesy of David Botello.)

of the Courts' layout with the Olympic Boulevard side about twice the length of the Lorena section. This particular, primarily subliminal factor of location and architecture may resonate in the subconscious. It may be one of the ways by which we understand *Give Me Life*'s role and significance as the keystone mural.

The imagery and meaning of *Give Me Life* are expansive, realistic, surreal, and hopeful. This was Cat Felix's vision for the mural. It was by (under the direction of Cat Felix), for, and about the kids and the rest of the world. That being said, its ultimate resonance, complexity, and power are also the result of the dynamic relationships among all the elements we have discussed. In fact, the overwhelming nature of the entirety of this mural cluster, this sense of an urban sublime as we drive by or walk through the Courts, results from the sheer scale of this project, and the multiple simultaneous and often serendipitous interactions among the murals, location, architecture, and communities within and beyond Boyle Heights.

There are two muralized housing projects in East Los, both in Boyle Heights: Estrada Courts at the southern edge of the neighborhood, and Ramona Gardens at the far north just south of Lincoln Heights. There are profound differences in their respective locations and relative size. Estrada Courts apartment blocks are densely compacted in the middle of a typically mixed use (residential and commercial) working-class urban environment situated at a very busy intersection of streets that connect East Los to greater Los Angeles and beyond. Ramona Gardens, on the other hand, is built on a significantly larger, more spread out section of land that is isolated from busy streets. Muralized during the same years, the location, setting, and architectural features of Ramona Gardens presented different opportunities than those presented the artists at Estrada Courts.

Although there are more apartment blocks and administration buildings at Ramona Gardens, they are not densely packed and sit at more angles to each other in less of a classic grid pattern. The roads through the Gardens are curved for aesthetics and to slow traffic. Hills and open spaces within Ramona Gardens are more open. There are far fewer murals at Ramona Gardens, approximately twenty-seven in contrast to the over ninety at Estrada Courts. In addition, because there are no walkway walls as an integral architectural feature, there were no opportunities to create a connecting thread of smaller murals that wend their way through the projects to reinforce the meanings of the larger ones. Architectural and spatial relationships between several apartment block end walls created the opportunity for mini-clusters within the larger overall Ramona Gardens cluster. Perhaps because of the greater isolation of this housing project, none of the murals are overtly directed to an outside audience, and almost none are visible from beyond the Gardens. They were painted for the residents and those administrators and other housing authority employees who worked there. There is no serendipitous opportunity to drive by these murals; one must make a special trip to see them. The dynamic between the public and private at Estrada Courts is functionally absent at Ramona Gardens. The mural clusters within each housing project reflect that essential difference.

Perhaps that is why there is more dramatic imagery at Ramona Gardens, more overtly gang-related imagery, and, interestingly enough, far more of a focus on the significance and contributions of women than is seen anywhere at Estrada Courts. There are not really any murals one could label entrance guardians at Ramona Gardens. However, there are two "sort of" entrance guardians. *Homenaje a las Mujeres de Aztlàn* on Lancaster Avenue faces into the projects, and *Adelita* at the north end of Alcazar Street faces outward, protective rifle in hand. This emphasis on powerful women is balanced by the young men and their ancestral shades in *Ghosts of the Barrio* on the other end of Lancaster, conceptually triangulating historical and contemporary imagery directly connected to the Gardens' residents and the broader communities of East Los.

Even though the murals are more spread out, and fewer "conversations" are possible between them as one walks through the Gardens, the longer one looks, the more resonances and shared themes appear. However, the openness of the Gardens, the larger spaces between the buildings, the broader expanses of lawn and concrete mitigate against an automatic sense of being overwhelmed by the enormity of the mural project. Although a cluster, or perhaps better said, a series of smaller clusters, it does not present in the same way as Estrada Courts. Individual murals here are impressive and have become historically important, even iconic. Just as Ramona Gardens does not feel like an urban space, this location does not evoke a sense of the urban sublime.

At the time the murals at Estrada Courts and Ramona Gardens were being painted in the 1970s, there was only one effort in either housing project to paint an indoor mural: *My Life in the Projects* at Ramona Gardens. This mural provides a worthy counterpoint to *Give Me Life*, its surrounding walkway wall murals, and its companion murals of the *Sacrifice Wall* and *The Pachuco Cross*.

My Life in the Projects was even more isolated from general viewing than the rest of the murals at Ramona Gardens. In an already isolated geographical location, its presence in a room designated for gatherings of youths, as opposed to the more general population of the projects, brought an entirely different set of challenges than those found on a dihedral wall at a busy intersection.

Willie Herrón III painted *My Life in the Projects* in 1973. It was located in a fairly large low-ceilinged room designated as a recreation center. Notably, it was directly adjacent to the Ramona Gardens administrative offices. Only a few years after it was opened the center closed, and the room was turned into a storage space, making the mural inaccessible. During a remodel of the offices in the early 1990s, the mural was partially destroyed, partially covered by wallboard. During its short time of operation, it was officially called the drop-in center; the kids who used it claimed the space as their own and renamed it the dropout center, with all possible references to school and life embedded in this not-so-subtle reflection of their perceptions of the world and their places in it. The mural covered almost the entire wall, floor to ceiling, and was composed of vignettes and imagery provided to Herrón (at his request) by the young people who used the facility. While the ceiling was not actually unusually low, that feeling came from two interrelated factors: the larger dimensions of the room relative to its height, compounded by the oversized scale of many of the key images within the composition as it wrapped itself around the room, enveloping those within.

Since it was the youths' space, Herrón wanted it to represent what they wanted to see and be surrounded by on a daily basis. As such, this mural has much in common with *Give Me Life*, even as it is a profoundly different work of art and statement. Geography, location, and architecture are determining factors in the differences, as is the intended audience, deriving in large measure by the differences in place. Other differences result from the contrasting artistic sensibilities of the two artists, Cat Felix and Willie Herrón.

As far as is known, Herrón painted without assistance, but created the imagery entirely based on what Ramona youths suggested: violence within and outside the projects, a tropical sunset from Puerto Rico for a young boy who missed his home there, motherhood as requested by several girls, the presence of religious practice and belief, hope and danger (which could translate into the promise of life balanced by the threat of death). The final series of vignettes was created from Herrón's imagination and artistic sensibilities. These include local East L.A. Chicano cultural references (including Day of the Dead celebrations, with their community and art events originating at Self-Help Graphics) and personal touches from Herrón's collaboration with the other members of Asco, the performance art collective that included Patssi Valdez, Gronk, and Harry Gamboa Jr.

The mural features the potent image of the Sacred Heart of Jesus—rather than the less fraught and more nurturing Virgen de Guadalupe—floating at the corner top of the room, connected to the other images via blood vessels originating from a suspended fetus in a womb at the center of the wall to its left, and from blood vessels coming directly from the heart. Multiple large, small, and hugely oversized faces populate much of that same wall. Phantasmagorically distorted, they stare out at the viewer, reminiscent of those seen in *Caras*, a mural Herrón painted with Gronk at the handball court in Hazard Park at about the same time. A young girl protectively holding her doll is placed at the edge of a cemetery surrounded by threatening faces. Figures of Gronk and Herrón from one of Asco's performance pieces also turn up in the cemetery (in one of the room's corners).[7]

The enormous, voluminous, cloud-shaped mother holding three small children shares the first wall with the floating fetus (figure 7.6.). They are loosely attached to each other by the many vessels and arteries connecting all life in this mural, conceptually comparable to the threads of nuclear energy gently binding together the floating pool-ball planets in *Give Me Life*. This mother is both monstrous and comforting, and fills up the entire space, floor to ceiling, seemingly causing the wall to burst at its joints. Horrific in size and shape, yet gentle in her pillowing volume, she presents a safe haven juxtaposed to oversized torsos and faces of men fighting and knives stabbing on the next wall, all of which are forced to the very front of the picture plane, also covering the wall from floor to ceiling (figure 7.7).

This graphic violence is followed by the tropical sunset as if viewed through a break in the wall, or on a black velvet painting hung there. Below the palm trees swaying in the red sunset is a supine *calavera*, "bouncing" in the air buoyed by flames. Life and death, hope and danger: not only is this an actual interior space, this mural becomes what the Chilean surrealist artist Matta called an inscape, an interior psychological state or experience.[8] The combination of the specific images with their jumbled, disjointed connectedness, the ways in which they are depicted, and their location in the dropout center create this psychological interiorization of external experience modeled on the hopes and fears of the youth living at Ramona Gardens. The proximity of the administrative offices may also contribute to the contradictory sense of being safe while also being

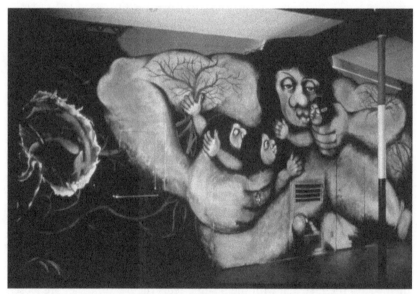

FIGURE 7.6 Detail of mother and fetus, from Willie F. Herrón III, *My Life in the Projects*, 1973, entire room interior, Ramona Gardens Recreation Center ("dropout center"), Lancaster Avenue, Ramona Gardens Housing Project. Photograph by Eva Cockcroft. (Courtesy of HACLA. Courtesy of Willie F. Herrón III, © 1973. Courtesy Estate of Eva Cockcroft.)

FIGURE 7.7. Detail of stabbing, from Willie F. Herrón III, *My Life in the Projects*, 1973, entire room interior, Ramona Gardens Recreation Center ("dropout center"), Lancaster Avenue, Ramona Gardens Housing Project. Photograph by Eva Cockcroft. (Courtesy of HACLA. Courtesy of Willie F. Herrón III, © 1973. Courtesy Estate of Eva Cockcroft.)

threatened; there is little separation from authority even though the youths are technically in their "own space." Ultimately, it was made clear by the center's closing that this room with its all-encompassing mural did not really belong to the youths (or to the artist who could have saved the mural panels), but rather to the administrators of Ramona Gardens.

Both murals address the lives of youth in housing projects; both murals combine hope with danger. *Give Me Life*, with its small mural cluster, directly addresses a much larger world with the solar system as its setting. Whereas *My Life in the Projects* addresses the more immediate and mundane environment as expressed through an interiorization of external experience. The geographical and architectural openness of the location for *Give Me Life* contrasts with that of *My Life in the Projects*, demonstrating the significance of these factors for the compositions of these two murals.

A major difference between Los Angeles and its northern neighbor San Francisco is the dominance of Chicanoa muralists in L.A. and their presence among residents of multiple homelands in San Francisco. While these origins matter for the variety of each city's restaurants and mural references, artists in both places have utilized awareness of locations and architectural characteristics in their mural work.

Cities facilitate many things, one being the possibility of mural clusters because of the relatively dense urban layout. This is true of extensive Los Angeles, and also of San Francisco, which is smaller in scale and population. The primary living area of people of Latin American descent/origin is the Mission District. "The Mission" has gone through several demographic periods, but in the second half of the twentieth century its ethnic composition and dominant culture were Latino. "Reflecting on the mid-1970s, writer Alejandro Murguía described how San Francisco's Mission District 'teemed with painters, muralists, poets, and musicians, even the occasional politico or community organizer who acted beyond the rhetoric and actually accomplished something. . . . We had no problem being understood because La Mission was a microcosm of Latin America, and the whole barrio seemed in perfect sync.'"[9] It has some of the best weather in the city, and several hundred murals. Buried in the heart of the Mission is Balmy Alley.

Before it is anything more, Balmy Street (its official designation) is a typical one-block-long alley in San Francisco's Mission District. Its most important intersection is at the north end, where it meets 24th Street, the main thoroughfare for the Mission's Latino population. Located where 24th Street crosses Mission Street, the main commercial link to downtown and the financial district, is Michael Rios's *BART Mural*. In the 1980s, Precita Eyes Mural Center, the Galería de la Raza, and Studio 24 (an exhibition space and a store selling Latin American artifacts) were located between this major intersection and its other end. The Galería has a billboard attached to its Bryant Street side, which it controls and which offers rotating images promoting its shows and also neighborhood issues such as good nutrition and anti-gentrification. The cross street of Folsom was the site of Paco's Tacos and its mural—a declaration of ethnicity in the face of a McDonald's scheduled to be built two blocks away. 24th Street itself is a major mural cluster. The walk from Mission Street to Potrero Street houses one of the densest collections of community murals in the world. About halfway along 24th Street is the entrance to Balmy Alley. Balmy is at the geographic and cultural heart of Mission muralism. It has a central presence as well as a central location, thus magnifying its murals' significance.

Balmy Alley is an extension of the dense urban environment of 24th Street but too small to be awe-inspiring, consisting of fences and garage doors that open directly onto the alley (figure 7.8). Nevertheless, the close proximity of

FIGURE 7.8. Long shot of Balmy Alley, Mission District, San Francisco. Photograph by Tim Drescher, ca. mid-1980s.

murals within the cluster defined by the alley, and/or by 24th Street and the Mission District writ large, enables the murals to be viewed simultaneously, not only showing that Central American culture is composed of different aspects, but making the point that, in some ways, Balmy Alley *is* in Central America and vice versa. That's what murals can do. Especially in clusters, murals can bring other places into ours and show how ours is also a part of a larger world.

In 1984, walking through the space delineated by Balmy's murals was akin to walking through Central American political struggles. The murals' Central American background is also a background of the Mission District neighborhood, yielding a double location: where Balmy is located in the city of San Francisco, and where its varied murals are located within the alley itself. Although the alley includes murals painted earlier, it was not fully muralized with coordinated imagery until Ray Patlán brought mural activists together as PLACA in 1983 and explained his conception of an entirely muralized alley, to be dedicated in 1984.[10]

According to Cary Cordova, "In the late 1970s and 1980s, world events transformed the content and iconography of Mission District murals. Political upheavals and dramatic influx of refugees and immigrants from Central

America forced new community signifiers. . . . And while the mural movement may have seemed spontaneously local, the art reflected an extensive international network of communications and an expansive political consciousness."[11] The Balmy Alley Mural Project was based on a dual theme: opposition to U.S. involvement in Central America, and celebration of its indigenous cultures. Some of the murals demonstrated awareness of their architectural sites, but the key to Balmy's local importance was its expression of anti-U.S. politics in Central America. Nicaragua in particular was engaged in open warfare, fighting a losing battle against the U.S.-financed Contras. Balmy's varied murals also represented the various cultures coexisting in the Mission District. All the muralists working in Balmy painted in solidarity with Central America's struggles, each focusing on an aspect of their choice. As such, Balmy Alley's conceptual structure more closely resembles the organizational principles of the mural cluster at Chicano Park, in the Barrio Logan district of San Diego, than it does those at Estrada Courts and Ramona Gardens. The main difference is that Balmy had an overriding dual theme.

The project reflected a period of intense political activity in San Francisco as well as in Central America, especially Nicaragua, where the U.S.-financed Contras battled with the Sandinistas for control of the country. Contra supporters were rumored to have trashed apartments of Sandinista supporters in San Francisco; so the struggle was playing out in San Francisco as well.

The alley is narrow, so the figures in the murals often appear to be too close to the viewer. The mural that most clearly takes advantage of this was painted in 1984 by Ray Patlán and Francisco Camplís, called *On the Way to the Market / Camino al Mercado* (figure 7.9.). Their mural manipulates the viewer, as does Jane Norling's *Give Them Arms, but Also Teach Them How to Read / Darles Armas y Tambien Ensenarles a Leer*, by moving the vanishing point and giving the mural depth. *Camino al Mercado* identifies Balmy Alley with Central America by being painted as if someone in the alley were looking down on it, thus erasing the alley's narrowness and making viewers a bit more participatory because they have a privileged place from which to view it. The scene shows two women going to market, something that happens millions of times a day throughout Central America. In the background, standing in a shadowed doorway, is a soldier, clearly identified by his helmet, and made more threatening by being only a silhouette—the scariest moment in Balmy. A close inspection of the two women reveals the mural's special punch: under their shawls and visible to a viewer in the alley, but not to the soldier, each woman carries an automatic rifle. Everyday

FIGURE 7.9. Ray Patlán and Francisco Camplís, *On the Way to the Market*, 1984, Balmy Alley. Photograph by Tim Drescher.

life in Balmy Alley is depicted as the location of armed struggle, as it actually happens in several places in Central America. This portrayal of citizens fighting back is unique in Balmy Alley's murals, although a few murals contain weapons.

The mural uses the alley's narrowness to create a scene of danger and, because of its location and who its residents are in the Mission District, Patlán and Camplís assumed tacit approval of the implied armed response, manipulating the physical viewpoint to make witnesses of viewers by effectively bringing them into the action of the mural.

Another example of architectural exploitation in Balmy is the work of muralist Osha Neumann, an Anglo painting in solidarity with the struggles of Central American countries against the inimical presence of the United States (figure 7.10). Neumann's *Regeneración* is across from Jane Norling's *Give Them Arms*, a mural whose title captures PLACA's dual theme most clearly. Norling's mural is near Terry Brackenbury's untitled one (see below). Neumann extends the cactus growing in the backyard behind the fence, down onto the fence, connecting the alley and its murals' themes to the horticultural landscape. Plants regenerate as does the country via revolutionary struggle. But along with the cactus (in both its horticultural and acrylic modes), another form of regeneration is portrayed on the fence via automatic rifles. The mural makes the point that there are two kinds of regeneration: as in plant life so in socio-historical life, here demanding armed conflict. That much is evident from the mural itself, with its left side filled with weapons but connecting the acrylic to the horticultural brings the alley itself into the scene: one that is now and simultaneously Balmy and Central America.

Neumann's focus on a cactus is no accident. It brings the U.S. Southwest into the alley, cacti being more typical of that area than of Central America, but it is nevertheless well chosen for its role in Balmy, having both flowers (and the tasty nopalitos) and prickly spines. The mural is an example of Balmy's overarching theme, recognition of culture and military struggle in Latin America, of which the Mission District is a part.

Across the alley from *Regeneración*, Terry Brackenbury, Gary Crittendon, and Marsha Poole also make use of the narrowness of the alley in their untitled mural, filling the foreground of the picture plane with a bamboo forest and showing behind its myriad stalks a small village in the middle distance (figure 7.11). At first, the mural seems to depict a typical, not to say stereotypical, scene of Central American jungle and domestic tranquility, until a viewer notices among the trees along the bottom of the scene, at its interface with the asphalt

FIGURE 7.10. Osha Neumann, *Regeneración*, ca. 1984, Balmy Alley. Photograph by Tim Drescher.

FIGURE 7.11. Terry Brackenbury, Gary Crittendon, Marsha Poole, untitled mural, ca. 1984, Balmy Alley. Photograph by Tim Drescher.

of the alley, a large snake, partly camouflaged by the forest through which it slides. When a viewer notices that the snake is red, white, and blue, the political threat to the village is clear. The snake is also, significantly, situated between an observer standing in the alley and the scene; in other words, the United States stands (slithers) between Balmy Alley and Central America. The literal background of the mural coincides with the figurative political background of the Mission District at the time the mural was painted: a threatening presence to Central America, *and* also to the site and different people in the Mission District, *and*, most immediately, to someone standing in Balmy Alley appreciating its murals.

One of the most effective uses of the alley's architecture is in Mary Nash's later addition in which women artists bear witness to the alley, looking out from the garage door on which they are painted: Frida Kahlo, Elizabeth Catlett, Georgia O'Keefe. To the right, on a portion of the building jutting at ninety degrees to the alley, is *La Virgen de Guadalupe*, watching, as it were, the other female figures on the garage door.

This space, because it is recessed from the alleyway, provides a modicum of privacy, or at least nonvisibility from the alley, and thus was used as a toilet by homeless residents and drug users. But with the addition of *La Virgen*, those who used the space as a toilet were confronted with doing their business in front of a representation of a venerated religious figure, and many could not do it. When *La Virgen* was placed to watch over the short three-foot driveway entrance to the garage, what had become a toilet for the homeless suddenly remained clean. People said they could not defecate beneath the female figure, "not with the Virgin of Guadalupe watching."

A major change in Balmy occurred between the painting of PLACA's murals in 1984 and the end of the century. Balmy's murals have changed over time as old fences and garage doors have been replaced; unused walls became sites of new murals. During that time, murals at each end of the alley were converted from a political orientation to a spiritual/religious theme, which turned the alley from being a politically oriented gallery to a religious one. By the turn of the century, religious icons signaling this transformation overlooked each entrance/exit—as guardian figures: the bodhisattva Manjushri and the Virgen de Guadalupe at the southern end, *Five Sacred Colors of Corn* (1990) at the northern end, at 24th Street.

This spiritualization makes it possible to expand the themes of Balmy's murals to include AIDS, Nepalese women's rights, and Palestinian struggles as well, destroying its original unity and thereby diluting the impact of its content, while also expanding the project's subjects. As new alley locations become available, no doubt other topics of significance to the community will be introduced into Balmy Alley.

The mural clusters at Estrada Courts, Ramona Gardens, and Balmy Alley demonstrate the various simultaneous ways in which location and architecture create, inflect, and enhance meaning in and between murals, as well as between the murals and those who live among them or come specifically to view them. Those at Estrada Courts and Ramona Gardens represent the early years of dynamic artistic and political collaboration of the Chicano civil rights and arts movements of the 1970s. As such, they are present-day survivors, speaking to the specific historical moment of their genesis. Their multiple interactive meanings and their dynamic physical and conceptual interactions with each other and their communities are created and intensified by their locations and artful uses of key architectural features.

The Balmy Alley project represents a different circumstance: it has become, by virtue of the waves of changing murals at this one site, a location for muralistic conversations that demonstrate changing demographics and neighborhood priorities. In the 1980s, the moment addressed in this essay, the intense socio-political focus on solidarity with those in Central America whose lives and countries were assaulted by U.S. economic hegemony and military interven-tion created the desire to make that activist solidarity visible through the dual themes found in the Balmy Alley murals. The resounding impact of those murals during those years was multiplied by their location in this small, narrow roadway, and through the judicious use of architectural and horticultural fea-tures found there. By focusing on location and architecture as intrinsic sources of meanings for community murals, we have expanded our understanding, not only of the meanings of the murals and mural clusters discussed in this chapter, but also of the ways in which the medium itself functions, never separate from its environment, always specific to its community, and often also "speaking" beyond itself, addressing other times and differing territories.

NOTES

1. We want to thank Mario García for his kind invitation to discuss our recent book, *Give Me Life: Iconography and Identity in East LA Murals*, at the Sal Castro Memorial Conference on the Emerging Historiography of the Chicano Move-ment, February 23 and 24, 2018, at the University of California, Santa Barbara. This essay develops ideas presented at that conference, and we express our appreciation to Mario García and Ellen McCracken for their encouragement.

2. Scale has been discussed by Francis V. O'Connor in *The Mural in America: Wall Painting in the United States from Prehistory to the Present*, pt. 1, chap. 1, sec. F, http://www.muralinamerica.com.

3. See Holly Barnet-Sanchez and Tim Drescher, *Give Me Life: Iconography and Iden-tity in East LA Murals* (Albuquerque: University of New Mexico Press: 2016), 45–71, 73–98.

4. There have been multiple changes over the decades to both the larger mural and the walkway wall imagery. Most have diminished its visual impact or meaning. See chapter 3, "Estrada Courts Entrance Guardians," 48–56, in *Give Me Life*, for an itemization of the changes and a complete history and analysis of the mural *Give Me Life*.

5. Marcos Sanchez-Tranquilino, "Mi Casa No Es Su Casa: Chicano Murals and Bar-rio Calligraphy as Systems of Signification at Estrada Courts, 1972–1978" (master's thesis, University of California at Los Angeles), 67–69. Sanchez-Tranquilino was the first scholar to notice and analyze the relationship between gang graffiti and pre-Columbian designs.

6. It is interesting that although there are seven dihedral walls at Estrada Courts, only four were painted, three of those in the public areas. One was painted over

in the mid-1970s (see Barnet-Sanchez and Drescher, *Give Me Life*, 86–89, for details about the painting and destruction of *The Wonderful World of Corruption* on Olympic Blvd.). One of them does not carry the visual or conceptual strength of the best of the murals at Estrada Courts. And two of them—*Mi Raza Primero* and *Give Me Life*—make excellent use of their locations and architecture.

7.   It is most likely a version of the local Evergreen Cemetery in Boyle Heights, with its Jewish, Buddhist, and Catholic gravestones, and its public crematorium, and also the location of several Day of the Dead celebrations and performances.

8.   See Rocío Aranda-Alvarado, "Wifredo Lam's *The Jungle* and Matta's 'Inscapes,'" in *Latin American and Caribbean Art: MoMA at El Museo*, ed. Miriam Basilio (New York: El Museo del Barrio and the Museum of Modern Art, 2004), 103–7.

9.   Alejandro Murguía, *The Medicine of Memory: A Mexica Clan in California* (Austin: University of Texas Press, 2002), 118, qtd. in Cary Cordova, *The Heart of the Mission: Latino Art and Politics in San Francisco* (Philadelphia: University of Pennsylvania Press, 2017), 126.

10.   One of the co-authors of this essay, Tim Drescher, was a founding member of PLACA.

11.   Cordova, Heart of the Mission, 145, 149.

8

BLOWOUT!

The Testimonio of Mita Cuarón and the 1968 East Los Angeles Walkouts

ANDREA MUÑOZ

INTRODUCTION

WAS SITTING in the front row of my Chicano Studies 133 class when I first heard Mita Cuarón speak. Professor Ricardo Stanton-Salazar invited her to talk to the class about her role in the 1968 East Los Angeles walkouts. As she recounted her story, she spoke with conviction and desire, not only causing us to reflect but inspiring us and propelling us into motion.

A few weeks later I ran into Mita again. I was at the 2018 Sal Castro Memorial Conference listening to a panel that featured a presentation about her father, Ralph Cuarón, by Dr. Enrique M. Buelna. Once again, she spoke with conviction. She did not focus on herself and her role in the walkouts this time, but rather about her father's work in the community. I was not previously aware of Mita's life outside of her role in the walkouts. Her father's story intrigued me and brought so many questions to mind. I was thinking, there has to be so much more to Mita's life. I did a quick Google search. I was confident that someone with such an extraordinary story would be easy to find. I was sadly mistaken; I could not find anything.

As a result, I decided I would focus on Mita Cuarón's story for the honors program in the Chicano Studies Department at University of California at Santa Barbara. From dialogue with Professor Mario T. García and through networking connections with Professor Stanton-Salazar, I contacted Cuarón to ask if she would collaborate with me on this project.

WHO IS MITA CUARÓN?

Mita Cuarón has been an invisible player in the Chicano Movement. As a student at Garfield High School, Cuarón helped organize students to challenge the inferior conditions at the school. During the 1968 "blowouts" in the East Los Angeles schools of the Los Angeles Unified School District, thousands of Chicano students walked out to protest a history of discrimination and poor schooling. It was one of the largest mass protests by high school students in the history of the United States.

Cuarón was an important leader in the East Los Angeles walkouts, and her role as a Chicana leader should not be ignored. She deserves as much recognition as the many Chicanos and Chicanas whose names have been recorded in history. This oral history, *testimonio*, attempts to show the importance of Cuarón's role in the walkouts, as well as recount her life story.

THE CHICANO MOVEMENT

Mita Cuarón's story is rooted in the Chicano Movement, which was the largest, most expansive civil rights and empowerment movement among Mexican Americans in the United States up to that time.

The Chicano Movement was a civil rights and social movement that included issues of education, political representation, and overall empowering identity and community. The role of women in the movement was complicated. Chicanas had to walk a fine line between not conforming to stereotypes but also not destroying those stereotypes. Chicanas did not stay within the domestic sphere or in secretarial work. Still, there was gender discrimination and sexism. The women faced a triple oppression; they wanted gender equality but they also had to acknowledge their racial and class oppression.[1]

MITA CUARÓN AND CHICANAS AS LEADERS IN HISTORY

Chicanos, for the most part, look at the walkouts from a traditional paradigm and fail to recognize the important contributions of Chicanas. There is something faulty in leadership paradigms that do not allow us to understand and explain the lived experiences of Chicanas. The Chicano Movement idealized a subaltern masculinity to decolonize Chicano people and through this configured a construction of gender in the movement that was supposed to be "traditional."[2] Chicanas were denied roles as leaders and were often relegated to "female" roles such as cleaning, cooking, and secretarial work, while men executed the orders. Many Chicana leaders emerged during the Chicano Movement; however, due to the male-centered leadership, women were often ignored, and this has translated into history, where women's stories have been recorded much less often. Chicanas were important organizers in the walkouts and must be acknowledged as leaders. By relocating Mita Cuarón to a central position in this historical narrative, we gain a different perspective. Through a paradigm of cooperative leadership, with women included, we open an alternative view of the walkouts.

METHODOLOGY

I conducted several in-person interviews with Mita Cuarón. The questions for the interviews were mostly open-ended to allow for an organic recounting of her story. The questions and topics were introduced in chronological order, though this was sometimes abandoned to allow a natural flow of conversation. To organize my research I utilized the oral history *testimonio*. The testimonio as a narrative emphasizes an oral discourse where the single speaking subject portrays her own experience in the name of a group or class marked by marginalization, oppression, and struggle.[3] Additionally, I utilize an oral history testimonio because Mita's narrative does not claim to be an objective account of events that she witnessed firsthand, but rather stories that she is retelling and reconstructing from memory. Lastly, I chose to use the testimonio because telling Mita's story in the first person as the protagonist of the events is more powerful than using the third person.

I look up the steep stairs, ponder for a few seconds until I get the courage to take that first step. I look down and up as I ascend the stairs toward the shaded porch. I stare at the dark wooden door, then quickly and shyly knock. The door opens and Mita's warm and welcoming smile greets me. She embraces me in a hug and welcomes me into her home. The walls are full of art, and every corner of her home seems to tell a different piece of a story, a different piece of her story.

***

MITA CUARÓN'S *TESTIMONIO*

MY ROOTS

I am bicultural. My father is Mexicano and my mother is Jewish. These are my roots.

My father's family came from Chihuahua, Mexico. They immigrated to the United States in the late 1880s as a family and settled in Arizona. They were forced to continue migrating due to social and financial changes. They eventually immigrated to Los Angeles, working as day laborers in the Southwest along the way.

My mother's family came from Ukraine. They travelled with several other extended family members during the pogroms, which were attacks on Jews in the Russian empire that took place largely during the nineteenth and twentieth centuries. They became store merchants in Brooklyn, New York, and shortly after moved to Los Angeles and opened up a little grocery store on Brooklyn Avenue, now César Chávez Avenue.

In 1948, my parents met at a housing forum on the issues in the community of Boyle Heights. Soon after they married and bought a little house in East Los Angeles. I was born in 1952, as a premature baby by three months, at Queen of Angeles hospital. I weighed one pound and twelve ounces. I remained in the hospital for three months, until I was a little over five pounds and was discharged home with my parents.

My parents are very progressive and were members of the Communist Party. My father joined the Communist Party of the United States in 1942, at age nineteen.[4] During the 1950s there was a second Red Scare in the United States, with horrendous condemnation and hysteria. My father became unemployed and could not find work, even in the unions. As a result, my mother worked outside the home in various job positions within different unions. Throughout my life, my mother was the breadwinner and my father was the organizer and activist. He never had a steady clock-in job during my childhood. My parents did as best they could given their financial situation and for the most part were able to make do with what they had. Sadly, it was not always enough. Due to financial hardships, my parents more or less handed me over to my *tía* Marjorie ("Marjie"). She never married and was a devout Catholic. When she got a hold of me, I became consumed in Catholicism. I think I said enough Hail Marys and Our Fathers to wrap around the world. I became very distant from my Jewish background. I always find it somewhat of a contradiction that people as progressive as my parents placed me in the hands of somebody so steeped in religion. The only justification I find is that they needed childcare.

GROWING UP IN EAST LOS ANGELES

I am the oldest of four siblings: Margarita ("Mita"), Rafael ("Ralph"), Adela ("Adele"), and Fernando. We grew up in East Los Angeles, within walking distance of Rowan Avenue Elementary and Stevenson Junior High School. I flourished in my classes, my grade point average was above average, and as a result I was inducted into the Lamp Lighters for High Achievement. By the time I was in middle school, I had already made my Catholic confirmation and I migrated toward the arts. As I became more involved in my studies and arts, I became more creative in my classes. My father helped me with a project for science class investigating the California condor. I wrote a research paper but went above and beyond by creating a papier-mâché bird. I was so fascinated by the arts and enjoyed making fun pieces out of papier-mâché. I made a papier-mâché mask and entered into a contest and won first place. I loved it so much and became really good at it.

I was the oldest in the family, so I took on a caretaker role. Some of the duties that I had were food shopping and cooking. I learned how to cook with my grandmother, which was wonderful and was a great way to connect. We were able to build a beautiful relationship through our time spent in the kitchen. My own childhood was interrupted by being ladened with the responsibility of being in charge of my siblings. I think the responsibility was in part because of my age, but there was also a gender component. Regardless, I was in charge and had to take on those additional responsibilities. Nobody told me to do certain things such as delegate chores, but I did that and much more. All of the added responsibilities and expectations would sometimes get to be too much for me. There was a lot of anger and a lot of frustration at home. At times I would get to my breaking point and demand that everyone help me or I would break their toys.

From my seventh- into my eighth-grade year, my father became even more involved in the community. During this time, he chose to focus his energy on housing by embarking on an innovative experiment in community housing and community building.[5] He founded the East Los Angeles Improvement Council (ELAIC) and was championing the cause of affordable housing in East Los Angeles. At 3726 Princeton Street, my parents cultivated a home away from home for many people. The house on Princeton came to be used as a hub for my friends and I to come together; it became a beacon for local youth. A core group of my friends, including Kenny Ortiz, John Ortiz, George Rodríguez, Marti Rodríguez, Aurora Carreon, Cassandra Zacarias, Harry Gamboa, Steve Valencia, George Reyes, Moctesuma Esparza, and others, frequented my home.[6] We had a place to congregate and discuss issues that piqued our interest. As a result, my father created a student group; it was a movement to include the youth in the community. As part of the youth group, we frequently travelled to Tijuana to deliver food and clothing. We became involved in the VISTA program and Volunteers for America. At the house on Princeton Street, my father also had a "school" in the upstairs unit of the apartment complex. He would hold classes about philosophy, political struggle, unions, know your rights, as well as other topics. As the student group, we participated in reading circles, sometimes up to four times a week.[7] The house on Princeton Street was a training ground for activism and political consciousness.[8]

MY TRANSITION TO GARFIELD HIGH SCHOOL

The train tracks decided my high school placement. I was on the east side of the train tracks, so I had to attend James A. Garfield High School, as opposed to students on the west side of the tracks who attended Theodore Roosevelt High School. I received no guidance or preparation to go from middle school into high school. There were no transitional meetings, orientation, or parent groups. There was nothing to prepare us, and I did not expect anything. The very essence of preparing children and young teenagers in their formative years did not exist in East L.A. We were being conditioned to accept what was given to us without questioning. I entered high school in the fall of tenth grade. I was fifteen and I felt like I was being sequestered in East Los Angeles.

When I arrived at Garfield, the gates were ominous and unwelcoming. There was a population of around three thousand students. Due to the high number

FIGURE 8.1. Mita Cuarón, tenth grade, 1967. (Courtesy Mita Cuarón.)

of students enrolled, Garfield had a track system in place. Students were put into one of three tracks: A, B, or C. There was no educational equity between the tracks. Students in Track A received the most opportunities, while students in Track C received the least. I was placed in Track C. In many ways my placement determined the opportunities or lack thereof in my high school education. Despite my placement in Track C I tried to be hopeful about my classes. At Garfield, just like at most schools, students were supposed to have the opportunity to meet their counselor during their first semester to plan out their classes. Meeting with the counselor was supposed to set the foundation for a student's high school experience. I was never referred to the counselor and did not have the opportunity to meet with someone at all my first year. This was the reality for most students at Garfield; the counselors were inadequate. This was in part due to overcrowding, but it was also an overwhelming lack of interest on behalf of counselors for their Chicano students.

The same lack of interest was also evident in many teachers at Garfield. It felt like most teachers had no regard for their students. Too often teachers used derogatory terms toward the students. They responded to students as if we were cattle. They did not care to even feign any sort of connection to students. Teachers had very low expectations of their Chicano students. All too often teachers seemed satisfied to not have students fall out of windows. They were content with simply moving us along the broken educational system. Most teachers expected us to become skilled laborers, soldiers, or unwed parents. There were no goals, there were no incentives, there were no aspirations. Teachers did not provide enough encouragement for students.

As a student in Track C, the classes available to me were very limited and rudimentary. We had homeroom, which was the only time that teachers would take roll during the day. Through roll call in only one class, the administration sent the message to students that they did not care about our education; they made it very easy for students to ditch classes. No one cared if we stayed at school; they got their money for our attendance and then almost urged us to leave. It was difficult for students to remain engaged. Even for students who were trying their very best to succeed, it was not easy. Going into high school I really enjoyed science, but as a student at Garfield in Track C science was dull at best. The curriculum lacked substance and the walls in my usual class were empty. There were no diagrams, nothing to instill curiosity. On one occasion I wandered into a Track A science room, and when I opened the door it hit me like a ton of bricks. I was shocked to see all of the props on the walls and on the desks. I was angered and devastated. In the midst of all the frustration and disappointment that plagued my first year at Garfield, art class was my lifesaver. Art was taught by one of the very few teachers who showed appreciation for their students; he connected, engaged, accepted, and appreciated us. This was the one ray of sunshine and my lifeline.

Although the schools failed to prepare and motivate students, we received encouragement from the community, especially through programs such as Camp Hess Kramer. In 1963, the Los Angeles County Commission on Human Relations began sponsoring an annual Mexican American Youth Leadership Conference at Camp Hess Kramer, in Malibu, for students in Los Angeles County.[9] The conference was first called the Spanish-Speaking Youth Leadership Conference but changed names in 1964. In the 1970s the name changed again to Chicano Youth Leadership Conference, which is the name it still has today.[10] Students are selected a few weeks before the conference is to be held. The organizers did not just focus on the Eastside schools or inner-city schools but drew from a variety of public, and some Catholic, schools throughout the county.[11] The students were selected by a school, community person, or an organization based on their ability to contribute to the group but also return and create progress in their own communities.[12] The students chosen had good grades and also displayed leadership through participation in student government, sports, or other activities, on and off school premises.[13] I was fortunate enough to be chosen to attend the camp. The official goal of the camp was to improve self-image and intergroup relations so that Mexican American students "may be free to develop themselves into the mainstream of Anglo-American life."[14] As a result, we were encouraged to be traditional school leaders, run for school offices, and go on to college. We were provided with a framework to understand inequities and with a space to develop a sense of community responsibility. Despite the camp's assimilationist perspective, it fostered civic responsibility and school leadership, and many students left motivated to organize around more radical and progressive issues. For these reasons, the conferences were important to the development of the 1968 walkouts because many of the organizers of the walkouts, like myself, participated in the conference.

THE STRIKE COMMITTEE AT GARFIELD

My group was the political group, the Garfield Strike Committee. We were the same group of young people who had come together on Princeton Street, organizing around the East Los Angeles Improvement Council. When I started at Garfield some of the members were already there, but the group had not been formed. It was really the year that I arrived when the whole apparatus formed, and it all started to ferment and crystalize. The main members of the committee were Harry Gamboa, John Ortiz, Ken Ortiz, Cassandra Zacarias, and myself.

The committee was all I knew; it was all I had. At school, we would have lunch together, and after school we would walk as a group to get the bus on Whittier Boulevard. As a committee we met weekly for the most part, but it could be inconsistent at times. When we were not meeting and discussing strike details we would pick up random topics because we were all good friends. Although we were all friends it did not mean that the group dynamic was perfect. There were times when the guys seemed to have the upper hand. I would pick up on subtleties, but back then I was quiet, so I would often end up letting them take the lead. It was not that I did not know to speak up, but as young women we were not necessarily socialized to speak up; the whole socialization process was off.

As a member of the Garfield Strike Committee, I met Sal Castro the January before the walkouts took place. Up to that point I was not aware that he had been around to different community centers and parent groups to talk to the community at large. Meeting Sal was motivating because it showed me that the community at large had similar concerns about our education. After meeting Sal, the Garfield Strike Committee decided to start the process of a proposal for a leaflet to inform students at Garfield about the poor conditions at our school and the inadequacies of our education system. This was one of the Garfield Strike Committee's main focuses. It provided a forum in which students and community members were able to articulate their discontent with the school.

The leaflet had an emphasis on social, cultural, and political activities relevant to students and was directly informed by our experiences in Eastside schools. Many of the Eastside schools could be thought of as "Mexican schools" because they had many of the negative attributes, including the tracking system. "Mexican schools" were established mostly in the Southwest, within barrios as segregated schools. By the 1960s, school boards no longer legally maintained separate schools for Mexican Americans but due to geographic concentration in barrios, such as East L.A., students continued to attend predominantly Mexican American schools.[15] During the 1960s, East Los Angles high schools had an especially bad education record for Chicano students, with a dropout/pushout rate of over 50 percent, in comparison to 3.1 percent and 2.6 percent dropout rates in Palisades and Monroe, as well as the lowest reading scores in the district.[16] The high dropout/pushout rate was a reflection of the poor conditions at the Eastside schools. Classrooms were overcrowded and teachers had little understanding of the Mexican working-class communities in which they taught. Teachers made derogatory comments about their Mexican students and prohibited the use of Spanish at school; if you broke that rule you faced punishment. They did very little in East Los Angeles, and this translated to insensitivity and lack of understanding of their students. The schools did not attempt to understand the lived experiences of Chicano students.

All of this informed our purpose for the leaflets and the content of the leaflets. Hence, some of the content of the leaflets was pushing for bilingual education, culturally sensitive staff, and history that was centered on our culture. The leaflets also advocated for activities such as school luncheons and after-school activities. Our leaflets were distributed on a small scale at Garfield because we had limited access to print. We relied on a mimeograph machine that my parents owned; my mother would type everything up for us and then we would print it out with donations from the paper company. We would distribute the leaflets by placing them around campus during recess and lunch. Our leaflets served as a catalyst for discussion and organizing of the walkouts at Garfield.

Inside Eastside actually did something similar to what our leaflet was doing but on a larger scale. As part of the Chicano underground press, *Inside Eastside* had an emphasis on social, cultural, and political activities relevant to students and for the most part was written and edited by high school students.[17] Frequent themes were the poor quality of East Los Angeles schools and the cultural insensitivity of teachers. Raul Ruiz, under the pen name Lazaro Q., wrote a piece for *Inside Eastside* titled "Picket, Brothers, Picket," in which he clarified that walkouts, boycotts, and pickets were not against the law and that under the First Amendment they had the right to assemble and petition for the redress of grievances.[18] This piece was very relevant because as students we were in the midst of meeting and planning possible actions and it emphasized our rights. Looking at the title more critically, we see the culturally mediated concepts in Chicanismo of masculinity, such as brotherhood, or *carnalismo*. The newspaper community included many Chicanas. Chicanas, like myself, were integrally connected to the community newspapers, including Paula Crisostomo, Tanya Luna Mount (daughter of Julia and George Mount), Celeste Baca, Cassandra Zacarius, Rosalinda Méndez González, Vicki Castro, and Rachel Ochoa Cervera.[19] Not only did the newspaper include high school reporters from the different schools, but we also helped distribute the paper to other students.[20] Initially, students took stacks of newspapers to distribute at school; however the schools later prohibited the distribution of the newspaper on campus. Students instead placed the newspaper in conspicuous places such as the bathroom and cafeteria without physically distributing it themselves.[21] In these forms, our leaflets and *Inside Eastside* were pivotal in bringing additional attention to the poor educational conditions of East Los Angeles schools.

THE BLOWOUTS AT GARFIELD

The walkouts happened in the spring of my tenth-grade year. The walkout at Wilson was due to the cancellation of the school play *Barefoot in the Park* by the administration. We knew the walkouts were brewing, but that was really the catalyst for the timing of the rest of the walkouts. The following afternoon, on Tuesday, Garfield had its own walkout. I was sitting in class when we all heard the fire alarm go off. Teachers and students proceeded to follow the fire drill procedure. Students calmly walked out of classrooms and into the hallways in an orderly manner. To everyone it appeared to be a routine fire drill. We all followed the evacuation procedure and made our way outside. When we made it outside and to the front of the school the energy shifted. Students seized the opportunity and started chanting, "Walkout! Walkout!" We took full advantage of the fire alarm.

I found myself among a group of students chanting "Walkout!" over and over again. I continued to chant and made my way toward the gates. I momentarily hesitated but continued past the gate. Once I had made it to the other side of the gate I felt invigorated. I proceeded to march forward and crossed the street. I was so engulfed in the action that it felt like my body was moving ten times faster than my mind. On the spur of the moment I took a cone, jumped on a car, and started yelling "Walkout!" I could hear "Walkout!" coming from what seemed to me to be every direction. Students were mobilizing and making their way out of the gates. The bliss of the moment did not last long. Shortly after, the county sheriffs arrived at Garfield. The quick arrival of the sheriffs was not surprising because their offices were so close to campus. The sheriffs surrounded Garfield and were doing line dances to corral us. I felt two hands on each side of my body; they grabbed my arms and pulled me away. I could see everyone starting to become a distant picture. I was being dragged away from the other students. The sheriffs that had a hold of me were accusing me of being an outside agitator as they continued to take me farther away. The sheriffs intervened and declared the walkout an unlawful assembly. Officers continued to use physicality against students, and due to the spontaneity of the walkout we were not prepared for the violence. Students were beat up; some officers were using their batons on students. Chaos ensued due to a false bomb threat. As sheriff officers continued to turn on students, fire trucks began to arrive on the scene. The presence of the fire trucks made us more wary; we were afraid that the firefighters would turn their hoses on us.

Students inevitably retaliated. Some students started to throw bottles and cans. Students were attempting to protect themselves from the unwarranted violence being inflicted. I saw two students being arrested, but I did not understand; we were not doing anything illegal; we were protesting. As everything continued around me, I noticed the arrival of a TV news reporter. By now things had started to die down, but the arrival of the news outlet impelled us to continue striking until about three that afternoon.

At the end of the first day of the walkouts I called my father, who, accompanied by Kenny Ortiz and Steve Valencia, had just arrived in Washington, D.C., for low-income housing advocacy. Everything spilled right out of my mouth. I explained to him how the students at Garfield had just walked out; I described the events, the sheriffs, the helicopters, the pandemonium, kids running everywhere. Immediately he decided they had to return to East L.A. and drove another three thousand miles.

The walkouts at Wilson on Monday and at Garfield on Tuesday forced the organizers, Sal Castro, high school students, college students, and community members to decide that the rest of the school had to walk out the following day.[22] Sal Castro had hoped that a bluff of a mass student civil disobedience would be enough to get the attention for the changes we wished to see in the schools, but unfortunately it was not.[23]

The next day, Wednesday, we walked out again at Garfield. This time it was planned and the rest of the schools were ready to go. There was coordination between the schools, but each school had its own distinct character and each school administration and police reacted differently. The reactions ranged from peaceful and controlled to brutal police violence. At Lincoln the cops were there and kept out of sight on the periphery of the school. The county sheriffs surrounded Garfield. At Wilson they had to climb the school fences and had problems with the cops. Roosevelt had the worst conflict with the police. Belmont did not go out on Wednesday due to communication problems.[24]

At Garfield, the walkout started out with only 500 students, but it grew to approximately 2,700 students out of 3,750 total students.[25] We continued to walk out, with the Brown Berets and college students present for backup and protection. Sal made specific arrangements with them that if there was any violence their heads were going to protect our heads. Throughout the blowouts, many individuals were arrested, including five Brown Beret members, who were later indicted by the Los Angeles County Grand Jury for their participation.[26]

On Wednesday, after the walkout at Garfield, we made our way to Hazard Park. The Board of Education offices located downtown were too far from the Eastside; instead we protested in front of the local area offices that were housed at Hazard Park. Students from all the Eastside schools walked or drove to the park. Most Garfield students had no choice but to drive since we were the farthest of the Eastside schools. When we arrived at the park I noticed that there were news crews waiting for us. There were so many faces that I did not recognize since there were students from all of the Eastside schools. At the park we did some more chanting and heard from various speakers. The energy naturally died down, and it indicated that it was time for everyone to go home.

On Thursday, the walkouts continued at all of the Eastside schools. Again, even though the walkouts were now coordinated between the schools, the reactions continued to be different across the campuses. Thursday was Belmont's first walkout, and students faced immediate assault from the cops. All the schools were dealing with some level of police presence. Despite the harsh police reaction at some campuses, we could not turn back until we got a response from the school board; so we continued to walk out. On Friday, we were met with rain but we did not let that deter us. From Garfield we began to march to Hazard Park, but the rain started to come down harder. We sought refuge from the rain in the Catholic church near Garfield, Saint Alphonsus Parish. The priest opened the door and said, "You get what you deserve," and slammed the door in our faces. We realized that not everyone in the community was supporting us.

Throughout this experience, the organizers would meet to reflect and assess the happenings of the day. These meetings would be held at Sal's home on the Westside, or people would come to East Los Angeles. In East L.A. we met at the plaza, my house, the Episcopal Church with the late Father John Luce, or La Piranya, the Brown Berets' coffeehouse located on East Olympic Boulevard. I could feel that we were a part of something historical, because the meetings were being watched; there were even helicopters at times. One night, we were in the middle of a meeting at home when there was a knock on the door. In comes Congressman Roybal and Judge Sánchez. These people with authority, who were Mexican, were telling us to stop this movement. Did they not know the problems that existed? They were imploring us to stop. There was a dam and the water was flowing with such ferocity, with great force and energy, how can we stop this by putting a peg in the hole? It seemed so absurd, ridiculous, and impossible. The tone, the magnitude of what was happening was unprecedented.

Despite all the pushback we were getting, we continued to strike for two weeks. Every morning we would get ready to go to school with our picket signs. As a result of the continued walkouts, a contingent of concerned parents mobilized during the first week of protests to provide protection for their children, including my mother, Sylvia Cuarón, and Dora Esparza.[27] On March 6, we had an assembly meeting on the Garfield football field, and as I arrived, two security guards and a teacher came up to me, furious, because they thought I was some sort of ringleader in the strikes. Dora Esparza tried to set me free from the guards, but she failed—they were too strong. She continued to struggle against them physically, asking them to release me and reiterating that I was a student. The security guard pushed Esparza with his elbow and knocked her away.[28] As organizers, we were being targeted, and it became quite violent.

The second week of walkouts we would go home after our meetings and turn on the news only to see George Putnam demonize us, chastise us, and make us into criminals. The whole attitude was that we had no power or rights. We were just kids causing trouble and chaos. The news continued to reinforce the stigmatization that we were rampant and wild without reason to our cause. There were parents who were petrified and ashamed that their children took such a position of walking out. In their minds teachers always knew best. They did not understand how their children could question authority; they did not understand the systemic oppression, that there was an actual plan to keep us inferior. As a result, a lot of students could not go back home and stayed at my house; it was a sanctuary. I was fortunate to have parents who were progressive, with a sense of class awareness. We had kids sleeping in different apartment units on the floor, and the Episcopal church brought us food, blankets, and other provisions.

By now my sense of identity was cemented. I grew up in East L.A; so I subscribed, assumed, became familiar with my community as a Chicana, and the walkouts made that even more evident to me. We were surrounded by freeways; it was like a concrete jungle. We were trapped, hoarded, enclosed; it physically and symbolically prevented us from seeing the world. Through the walkouts I witnessed brutality, I witnessed exploitation, I witnessed unfairness, I witnessed a school system that was just a big warehouse. Our education was mediocre at best; it was educational injustice, it was human injustice. The system was rigged to create a working labor class that produced people who had no options and who were expected to be beasts of burden. We were made to believe we had no options. The walkouts changed that for many of us.

ARREST

On March 15 there was a parent committee meeting formulated by my father because he had been designated as the official representative by concerned parents and community leaders to deal directly with Principal Reginald Murphy at Garfield.[29] My father, my tía Dora Carreon, Ken Ortiz, and myself entered the main office to take care of some last-minute details about a meeting that would be held later that day. There were several other students and parents, and we had to force our way in. As soon as we got in, the doors were shut behind us. The principal, Murphy, who was ex-military, came out and addressed my father in a very demeaning manner. He said, "Buster, you are a nobody, you represent nobody, and you should be ashamed of preventing your daughter from getting an education." The audacity for him to tell my father he should be ashamed of preventing me from getting an education when in fact it was institutional and systemic educational barriers. He continued, "Buster, if you do not leave the campus I am going to call the sheriffs." My father answered, "Well, I guess you have to do that." Within fifteen minutes, six to ten sheriffs marched in from the same doors that we had entered. They were dressed to the nines; they had their helmets, batons, and guns. There I am standing, with my tía, my father, Ken, and we are all holding hands with our backs facing each other. Within minutes they threw us to the ground, handcuffed us, dragged us up and out the door, maced us. The only weapon that I had was my voice. I was not going to let them get away with this. I screamed and I hollered and I yelled at the horror. As we climbed down the stairs I could see the students looking out the windows as they put us in the car. They booked us and put us in jail. I could not even be in the same cell as my tía. Our cells were next door, and there was a wall; so she put her hand out and I put my hand out and we held hands and talked and cried until we were bailed out. My father and my tía were charged with resisting arrest, and my father was additionally charged with disturbing the peace on school grounds. They had to go to criminal court, which took place a year later, and was quite lengthy. My father was ultimately found guilty on both counts and sentenced to two weeks in the county jail and fined, and my tía was found guilty as well and sentenced to a short probation.[30] During the hearing my mother was called up to the stand, and she made it a point to include a remark about the poor school conditions. She stated that she had never been in a school where bathrooms were closed. She elaborated on what I had told her about my experience with bathrooms at Garfield. Whenever a student wanted to use a bathroom, they would have to ask permission and be excused. Additionally, certain bathrooms would be closed during certain hours of the day. Sometimes if they were closed others would be open in other areas far removed from students' location. It was not a free thing to go to the bathroom. For a girl to use the bathroom at will, it was not a free thing.

SUSPENSION

I was suspended for two weeks directly following the two weeks of striking. During my suspension I would go to the Board of Education meetings for the Los Angeles Unified School District. We would have small meetings outside; and if nothing was happening outside, then we were inside at the meetings. Students generated a list of grievances and pushed for the board to hold a special meeting in which we could present them. The official list of student grievances to be presented to the board consisted of thirty-six demands, including smaller class size, bilingual education, more emphasis on Chicano history, and community control of schools.[31] Through our actions we were able to force the board to officially meet with us and discuss the Chicano community and our grievances about the schools.

Chicano parents, community members, high school students formally created the Educational Issues Coordinating Committee. The EICC continued the work from where we as the students left off. The committee had its roots in a Saturday evening parents meeting at Julia Mount's home. Community organizations such as the Mexican American Political Association, the East Los Angeles Improvement Council, the East Los Angeles Democratic Club, and the Mexican American Opportunity Foundation became charter members of EICC.[32] My father was part of this group as a parent and organizer. EICC also included college students, who were the driving force although they did not assume public leadership. Reverend Vahac Mardirosian became the nominal leader and spokesperson. The EICC met regularly with the Board of Education, rehashed the demands, including problems at the individual schools, and coordinated the actions the board would be required to take to meet those demands. Parents also discussed their concerns about their children being expelled and suffering retribution, being hurt by the police, and stigmatization by teachers. The EICC was important because it was the continuation of the efforts put forth through the walkouts.

When my suspension was over, I had to go back to school with my father and face the principal again. I experienced a lot of shaming and villainizing on my return, especially from one teacher. My history class was taught by a Chicano, Mr. Tuncole. On my first day back when I walked into class, he looked up and said, "Oh look who decided to come back to school, the troublemaker. She is responsible for causing all this mess, disrupting your education; it is all her fault." I stood there looking at him, and he said, "I do not care what you do in my class. I do not care if you try to make it up. I am going to fail you." And guess what? He failed me, but he demonized me, he villainized me, as I stood there and I took it. He berated and insulted me and continued to blame me for the whole ruckus, for the whole experience, me and the leaders. He believed we were being selfish for imposing our will on the entire student body. He completely ignored the valid reasons for our actions, including our freedom of assembly, speech, and redress. There were other teachers who were actually very supportive and willing to help me catch up on schoolwork. I did miss a lot of work during the walkouts and during my suspension, but I did try to make up as much work as I could. My art teacher was one of the teachers who was very supportive after the walkouts and would often encourage me to continue to pursue art. At school, the experience of the arts got me through the year.

The school year following the walkouts, I continued to face repercussions for my participation. Someone on the campus threw a Molotov cocktail, a bottle filled with gasoline and lit with a cloth wick. It landed nearby and exploded right in front of me. I was with a girlfriend and I asked her if she would support me and speak on my behalf. She was so fearful and said she could not do that for me. I really thought it was important to do

FIGURE 8.2. Mita Cuarón, eleventh grade, 1969. (Courtesy Mita Cuarón.)

something about it and make it known, especially because it took place on school grounds. I went to the principal's office accompanied by my father, but nothing ever came of that.

There were many individuals who were still facing the repercussions of participating in the 1968 East Los Angeles walkouts. Thirteen men, the "East L.A. 13," were arrested for "conspiracy to disturb the peace" as organizers of the walkouts. The L.A. 13 were Sal Castro, Carlos Muñoz, David Sánchez, Carlos Montes, Ralph Ramírez, Gilbert Cruz Olmeda, Eleazar Risco, Joe Razo, Fred López, Richard Vigil, Henry Gómez, Pat Sánchez, and Moctesuma Esparza. Each person was charged with two counts of disturbing the peace and disturbing the peace of the schools, in addition to fifteen counts of conspiracy, turning the charges from misdemeanors to felonies, with a total of thirty counts. If convicted they would have faced forty-five years in jail.[33] The men were arrested on a Friday to prevent quick bail and were kept in jail over the weekend until Monday. On their arrest the East L.A. 13 declared a hunger strike until their release and issued a statement. The community drew on the conceptual connections among community protest and repression. As a community we all rallied in support of the East L.A. 13 and mounted a community defense that organized demonstrations outside of the Parker Center, the main police jail in downtown Los Angeles. At one point there were two thousand people at the protest.[34] ACLU lawyers, including Abraham Lincoln Wirin, Michael Hannon, and Paul Posner, represented the East L.A. 13. The Mexican American Legal Defense and Education Fund footed almost all of the attorney fees. In 1970 the California Second Appellate Court ruled that the indictments based on the conspiracy charges were illegal because they violated the First Amendment rights of free speech and the right of redress of grievances.[35]

From the walkouts I had gained a sense of empowerment and I was not satisfied. I wanted to see more change around me. Myself and a core group of students continued to be involved in the community, especially through work that my father organized for the housing movement. As organizers, the young women noticed discrepancies of treatment. My father seemed to side with the guys a lot, and the girls seemed to be secondary. In retaliation, I organized my girlfriends in the backyard and we made protest signs. We had a protest against my father and the guys for equal rights. We were being silly in part, but we were also serious about wanting to be treated as equals. The walkouts gave me that identity of speaking up, speaking out, and protesting.

MY MOVE TO THE HIGH DESERT

After the walkouts, time passed and we eventually went our separate ways. Once Sal was reinstated, I had lost track; the momentum had died down. I dropped out of high school and became involved in other activities. It was a lot of flux, a lot of change and stressors. My father had spearheaded a proposal to create affordable low-income housing for the working-class poor. His proposals were so dynamic that TELACU (East Los Angeles Community Union) hired him. As soon as he was hired and the first project got off the ground, he was fired. My mother was working for Edison and somehow she got fired too. My parents both lost their jobs, and the house we called home in East L.A. went into bankruptcy or insolvency.

We were in the midst of moving, changing from this environment in East L.A. and going to a whole different environment of the high desert. My parents bought a house in the mountains because San Jacinto residents urged my father to carry out a similar affordable housing plan that he had spearheaded in East Los Angles. He had previously been commuting to the high desert, creating and spearheading meetings and putting forth the proposals. The transition was the clear next step for our family. My father purchased a house in the mountains that had just a small generator for electricity; we also had to pump our own water. I went from being in the midst of a tremendous dynamic that was organically evolving into the Chicano civil rights movement to the quietness of the mountain. This was a whole different experience.

With the change of environment I wanted to pursue the arts, but I focused on nursing. I grew up in poverty and wanted to have a lifestyle where I could take care of myself. I worked as a nurse's aide while I attended a local college, Mt. San Jacinto College, and graduated in 1974. I completed and passed the exam boards for LVN, and I started to pursue classes to become a registered nurse. I ran into a bit of a problem since I had dropped out of high school and did not have my diploma. I had to attend night school to finish the one class to get my diploma. When I received my diplomas, I officially continued with my studies to become an RN. Throughout my studies I was constantly working. My parents would drive down the mountain to take my two younger siblings to school. They would go to work, and I would go to work and school. We would all meet in one central location and drive back up to our house in the evenings. Sometimes we would turn on the generator at home, but other times we would not have enough propane. I graduated in 1983 and became an RN.

RECENTERING ART IN MY LIFE

I relocated to Riverside because there was trouble up on the hill; it was hard to maintain. Riverside was not ideal, and eventually I moved back to Los Angeles. In Los Angeles I was able to volunteer through different programs as a nurse. In the eighties I went to Nicaragua on a rewarding health brigade to take some medical supplies, and I volunteered for the Flying Samaritans, an organization that went down to Baja California on weekend trips to provide free health care. I often went as an interpreter. We travelled in little twin-engine planes that seated four to six people from Burbank to Baja California.

I did not get seriously involved in my art until I was in my thirties and started exhibiting. At this point I also started to learn more about my culture; it allowed me to recognize the beauty of our culture. Art also allowed me to revisit my heavily Catholic-influenced childhood. Through art I was able to reinterpret the Virgen de Guadalupe. Growing up I had come to resent Catholicism since my tía Marjorie was so religious. Art was a way for me to deal with this and reconcile in some ways on my own terms.

With my transition to Los Angeles, I decided to go to California State University, Long Beach, to pursue art. This was my way of trying to figure out my artistic side. I was thirty-one; I took one class at night or a class in the week when I had my day off; I was not a full-time student. During this time I took my first Chicano art class. The class was wonderful; it was about what had happened in the sixties, the revolutionary practices, the civil rights movement. It was about how the arts were parallel to the movement and the inspiration that often came directly from the great artists of Mexico. We focused on the relationship and the connections between art and revolution and how the arts evolved from the revolution.

I continued to work throughout this time, at various clinics, family practices, and hospitals in orthopedics, maternity, and gastrointestinal practices. Work gave me financial stability, and I was able to pursue the arts in my free time. I was able to fuse art with nursing as a mental health counselor RN. Various disciplines acknowledge music, poetry, writing, the visual arts and their benefits for mental health. In my life I have found the arts to be multifaceted; art has been political and healing.

The relationships with those who I knew that were active in the Chicano Movement are very strong. You have academics, activists, and community people. Our family is small and some of us are linked more so than others.

CONCLUSION

Overall, I want to highlight Mita's life story to emphasize the larger picture of Chicanas' participation during the movement and their subsequent continual work in the struggle. I challenge the historical and ideological representation of Chicanas by relocating Mita Cuarón to a central position in the historical narrative. Mita's testimonio helps us reconceptualize and overcome popular stereotypes of Mexican women as docile, passive, and apathetic. In the face of Chicanos' perception of the feminist critique as an assault on their cultural past and their power, Chicana leadership continues to push those bounds. Ultimately, we need to recognize and corroborate Chicanas' activist leadership in the 1968 walkouts.

NOTES

1. Adelaida R. Del Castillo, "La Visión Chicana," in *Chicana Feminist Thought: The Basic Historical Writings*, ed. Alma M. García (New York: Routledge, 1997), 44.
2. Maylei Blackwell, *Chicana Power! Contested Histories of Feminism in the Chicano Movement* (Austin: University of Texas Press, 2011), chap. 2
3. Annette Portillo, "Writing Photomemories: Crossing Borders, Crossing Genres in Norma E. Cantú's *Canícula: Snapshots of a Girlhood en la Frontera*," *Chicana/Latina Studies* 11, no. 1 (2011): 84–123, http://www.jstor.org/stable/23345301.
4. Enrique M. Buelna, *Chicano Communists and the Struggle for Social Justice* (Tucson: University of Arizona Press, 2019), 14.
5. Buelna, *Chicano Communists*, 154
6. Buelna, *Chicano Communists*, 161.
7. Buelna, *Chicano Communists*, 163.
8. Buelna, *Chicano Communists*, 163.
9. Dolores Delgado Bernal, "Grassroots Leadership Reconceptualized: Chicana Oral Histories and the 1968 East Los Angeles School Blowouts," *Frontiers: A Journal of Women Studies* 19, no. 2 (1998): 113–42, doi:10.2307/3347162.
10. Mario T. García, *Blowout! Sal Castro and the Chicano Struggle for Educational Justice* (Chapel Hill: University of North Carolina Press, 2011), 313.
11. García, *Blowout!*, 106.
12. Delgado Bernal, "Grassroots Leadership Reconceptualized," 118.
13. García, *Blowout!*, 106.
14. Delgado Bernal, "Grassroots Leadership Reconceptualized," 118.
15. García, *Blowout!*, 13.
16. Delgado Bernal, "Grassroots Leadership Reconceptualized," 119.
17. Delgado Bernal, "Grassroots Leadership Reconceptualized," 119.

18. Mario T. García, *The Chicano Generation: Testimonios of the Movement* (Oakland: University of California Press, 2015), 41.

19. Buelna, *Chicano Communists*, 174.

20. García, *Blowout!*, 144.

21. García, *Blowout!*, 140–47.

22. García, *Blowout!*, 150.

23. García, *Blowout!*, 148.

24. García, *Blowout!*, 168.

25. García, *Blowout!*, 174.

26. Ernesto Chavez, *Mi Raza Primero! Nationalism, Identity, and Insurgency in the Chicano Movement in Los Angeles, 1966–1978* (Berkeley: University of California Press, 2002), 48.

27. Buelna, *Chicano Communists*, 179.

28. Buelna, *Chicano Communists*, 180.

29. Buelna, *Chicano Communists*, 180.

30. Buelna, *Chicano Communists*, 184.

31. Delgado Bernal, "Grassroots Leadership Reconceptualized," 122.

32. García, *Blowout!*, 195.

33. Ian F. López, "Protest, Repression, and Race: Legal Violence and the Chicano Movement," *University of Pennsylvania Law Review* 150, no. 1: 205–44, 207, doi:10 .2307/3312916.

34. García, *Chicano Generation*, 290.

35. García, *Blowout!*, 230.

9

THE CHICANO MOVING IMAGE ON WALLS AND MEDIA ACTIVISM

MICHAEL ANTHONY TURCIOS

There will be no pictures of pigs shooting down brothers
There will be no pictures of pigs shooting down brothers
—GIL SCOTT-HERON, "THE REVOLUTION
WILL NOT BE TELEVISED"[1]

O N NOVEMBER 5, 1970, Chicanas and Chicanos organized the Mexican American Conference at Beverly Hills High School, where they detailed persistent systemic and institutional inequity. The Chicana/o community voiced concerns and frustrations about exclusion, lack of visibility, and racism in society. Speakers such as Ray Andrade, former Green Beret and chairman of Justice for Chicanos in the Motion Picture and Television Industry (Justicia), delivered statements chiefly criticizing the entertainment industry's denigrating images of Brown people. This fascinating event illustrated that the Chicana/o community would no longer accept racist televisual and cinematic representations; they demanded the entertainment industry do its part in undoing these stereotypes. The community was eager to drive its petitions forward, even going as far as disrupting the escapist pretense of award shows, such as the Forty-Second Academy Awards in 1970 (figure 9.1). The speakers called on Hollywood to redress negative images of Brown people, to cease misrepresentation, and to employ Chicanas and Chicanos across various positions in the industry. Despite the community's efforts, mainstream media continued manufacturing moving images that propagated racist tropes of Chicanas and Chicanos to global audiences. So Chicanas and Chicanos found alternative means of creating, circulating, and displaying images of cultural affirmation through political posters and prints, photographs, local newspapers and magazines such as *La Raza*, and other visual and print mediums. The community's investment in helping foster an accurate and positive image of the cultural group was a decolonizing and political act that echoed the planetary calls for negating centuries of visual oppression. In this sense, the community's goal of deconstructing popular culture and making art with themes of self-respect functioned to raise skepticism of mass entertainment in which cultural imperialism, fact distortion, and coded racism were disguised.

This chapter proposes that we consider the Chicano "moving image" as a theoretical framework for studying the unconventional and yet important historical role played by visual culture with televisual and cinematic components during the Chicano Movement. I specifically study murals in order to place emphasis on the intertextuality and intermediality of the social movements for liberation that took place in the 1960s and 1970s. I call attention to perception and mobility in muralism. Murals were more than decorative large-scale pieces

FIGURE 9.1. Protestors demonstrate against the film industry for the lack of representation and negative representation of Latina/os. (©*La Raza* Staff. From the *La Raza* Photograph Collection [#1000]. Courtesy of the UCLA Chicano Studies Research Center.)

adorning bland walls in urban space; their grandeur delivered didactic messages to the public and mobilized action. I will specifically attend to Willie Herrón III and Gronk's *The Black and White/Moratorium Mural* (1973) and David Botello's *Read Between the Lines (Cuídense Amigos)* (1975) as Chicano moving images used in the service of liberation.

Both murals openly critique mass media, in particular film and television. These large-scale images were created during a political period that catalyzed a radical visual culture inspired by the community's decolonizing and political engagement and the desire to create alternative images that reified self-worth. Although the term "moving image" is associated with film and television, I argue that Chicana and Chicano artists with limited means available to them were ingenious in creating pieces of work that resembled cinematic strips and television screens. These artists were not using cameras to shoot back at mainstream media but using brushes and urban walls to project realities, dreams, and desires that disputed stereotypes. Through this creative endeavor, artists visualized themes and topics that would offer the community the opportunity to contemplate their histories, which were generally ignored and grossly misinterpreted. I reclaim the concept of moving images from the territory of film and television to contest the notion that only people equipped with cameras created moving images. Although this chapter does not focus on the history and evolution of moving images, I would point out that moving images predate cinema. For example, magic lantern shows and the zoetrope made it possible for artists to experiment with mobility and perception in order to create images that came alive and inspired the imagination. Muralists such as Herrón, Gronk, and Botello painted large-scale works that gave the impression that spectators were gazing at television screens. The term "moving image," in my estimation, gains greater currency in this essay when we consider how the perceptual and affective registers in these murals activated the spectator to respond, inspiring political action. The magnificent scale of murals and the themes they undertook lead me to complicate my interpretation of what Chicano "moving images" visualized that film and television disregarded. Considering that the entertainment industry did not promote positive images of the community, these muralists brought the cinematic and televisual media to the walls of East Los Angeles.

I suggest that we position Chicano "moving images" as depicted in murals within the history of Chicana/o media activism and the Chicano Movement. Studies of the entanglements between murals and media activism of the

1960s and 1970s have received only minor attention despite their interconnected trajectories. Focusing on murals does not dismiss the central role of photography and its evidentiary value for the community.[2] In addition, this contribution to Chicano Movement historiography encourages us to analyze murals in opposition to the acculturation and assimilation messages of film and television and within the multitudinous efforts of the community's media activism.

Why have scholars not studied murals as alternative visual productions to those of Hollywood? For example, why have murals such as Judith F. Baca's *The Great Wall of Los Angeles* or Barbara Carrasco's *LA History: A Mexican Perspective* (1981) not been studied as Chicana "moving images"? Does Baca's half-mile-long mural not resemble a cinematic montage of historical narratives unfolding spatiotemporally? Moreover, while Baca references Hollywood histories in selected panels—such as Charlie Chaplin, McCarthyism, Jewish people in entertainment, and the proliferation of antennas and television sets in suburban 1950s Los Angeles—the cinematic nature of the wall alongside the Los Angeles River visualizes histories pertinent to Los Angeles and its surrounding areas, acknowledging communities in the margins of the entertainment industry. We can identify a comparable trait in Carrasco's mural, where "minor" histories and spaces of Los Angeles are woven into the hair of a young Chicana woman, who is actually Carrasco's sister, thus visualizing relational histories. To revisit Chicana/o murals in the history of media activism of the Chicano Movement is to emphasize the importance of protests and how murals created counter moving images as a practice of decolonizing minds, screens, and histories.

The first part of this essay provides context, putting the Chicana/o media protests at the intersection of the Chicano Movement and the community's struggles against the entertainment industry. I draw from articles in *La Raza* magazine to show that the community wrote about these issues in order to inform readers about the ways in which advertisements and motion pictures were detrimental to the community, and especially to youth. In the second part I perform a close reading of Herrón and Gronk and Botello's murals and argue for their inclusion in Chicano Movement history of media activism and their importance as moving images outside the realm of the cinematic and the televisual. The actions of the community prove to us that their organizing was critical for shifting representation and history, even if it meant going against an unrelenting institution.

MOVING AGAINST CINEMATIC CURRENTS

To move against currents is to plunge oneself into the spontaneity of turbulent and directionless movements. A current can go down unknown channels and take everything it picks up along the way with it to uncharted territories. When Chicanas and Chicanos organized to denounce injurious representations of their community, they were going against the institutional and systemic currents of the entertainment industry. The cinematic misrepresentations of the Brown community that emanated from studios to screens and to minds flowed from popular stock imagery of the bandido, the lazy Mexican, the seductive señorita, and the dirty "other." Cinema is a medium that conditions the affective and visual registers of audiences, meaning that conventional plots and characters are replicated time and again to make the stories relatable to the expectations of viewers. The negative portrayal of Chicanas and Chicanos on screen created digestible stereotypical flows of images for non-Brown audiences perceived as accurate. So the Chicana/o community engaged in demonstrations against Hollywood, stressing that defamatory representations affected the community psychologically, causing an inferiority complex.

In "Chicanos and the Motion Picture Industry," a 1970 paper co-authored by Professor Thomas M. Martínez and José Peralez and delivered at the Mexican American Conference, the speakers elaborated on how Hollywood stereotypes enacted violence on the community. The authors cite as a chief example how the Western genre turned Brown bodies into "moving targets," pointing out how these cinematic stereotypes depended on romantic colonial subjection and other violent imaginaries.[3] Early fiction and nonfiction culture derided Indigenous and Mexican people by inflicting violence on their bodies, objectifying them in dehumanizing ways. Martínez and Peralez call attention to the consumption of traditional cultural forms replete with normalized violence when they write, "story writers have been utilizing the appeal of the wild and dangerous life in the west for about a century."[4] The adaptation of Western genre literature for films brought in high revenue for the studios; violence and racism were profitable and well received. In other words, the Hollywood industrial complex's preeminence hinged on an optics of violence that harmed racialized groups.

At the November 1970 conference, Andrade remarked that the films nominated for Academy Awards in 1970 objectified and subjected people of color to violence.[5] The critiques he read at the conference, composed by Professor Martínez, undermined the "credibility of the Hollywood movie industry as a creative force in society," due in part to the "simplistic plots based upon historical inaccuracies . . . to the detriment of oppressed people."[6] The statement charged motion picture studios with dismissing nonwhite histories and called attention to the bigotry entrenched in Hollywood as a system, institution, and spectacle.

In the 1970s, *La Raza* magazine published articles covering racism in the entertainment industry and the boycotts against films, many of which were Westerns. In a bilingual article published in 1971, "El Mexicano Through the Eyes of the Gavacho" [*sic*], the writer explains that "the movie and broadcasting media is one of the institutions most guilty of creating stereotypes," calling it a system of "exploitation."[7] *La Raza* included articles that targeted specific films that distort the image of the community and asserted that such images had global repercussions. This is clearly illustrated in an article from 1972 titled "Rated X: Racist Films," where the writer explains, "In the Philippines and in many other countries a person that is lazy and sleazy is called a Mexican," and outlines why the community needed to mobilize against the entertainment industry.[8] The publication also paid attention to the minor movements within the Chicano Movement that staged actions against Hollywood. Chicanas/os took a critical posture against organizations that failed to address the needs of the community. For instance, a 1972 article, "Justicia o Muerte," argued that the organization NOSOTROS, an advocacy group founded in 1970 to promote visibility of Chicanas/os in the entertainment industry, was not sensitive to the struggles of the Chicana/o community when it invited to their dinner event then Los Angeles City Council member Art Snyder and then Los Angeles mayor Tom Yorty as guests of honor. Council member Snyder and Mayor Yorty advocated for the city to pay the legal fees of Los Angeles Police Department officers involved in the deaths of Guillermo and Gildardo Sanchez. The article condemns NOSOTROS: "If the leadership of NOSOTROS has fallen so out of contact with the Chicano community that it can pull a stunt as dumb as the one it did at the installation dinner, then it should cease to exist an [*sic*] an organization dedicated to LA CAUSA for it will only do more harm than good."[9] This history of media activism, while expansive and heterogenous, shows us that the community was fully committed to seeking rightful representation in the industry provided that the actions were generative.

Since Hollywood and the television industry were not covering stories about Brown people, Chicanas and Chicanos turned to other means to create images that gave more accurate representations. Well documented is the history of the explosion of Chicana/o creative energy channeled in performance, art, and music during El Movimiento. These cultural texts impressed on the Chicana/o community cultural pride and self-determination not visible to mainstream audiences.

We should not overlook, however, the fact that Chicanas and Chicanos have worked in the film industry and that Latin American actors have been under contract, notably during the Golden Age of Hollywood. Nor should we assume that Brown people did not have access to personal film equipment. Many of them filmed documentaries, such as David García with *Requiem 29* (1971), detailing what transpired during the Chicano Moratorium of August 29, 1970, and some developed provocative experimental projects, such as the East Los Angles art collective ASCO with the performance pieces of *No Movies* in the early 1970s. According to Max Benavidez, ASCO's *No Movies* performances subverted and rejected the Hollywood institution by mailing promotional press material and stills of nonexistent films "while constructing the group as media celebrities" in response to Hollywood's discrimination against Chicanas and Chicanos.[10] The absence of a complete film by ASCO might be seen as a metaphor for the limited visibility of Chicanas and Chicanos in motion pictures, heightened by the fact that they were always subsumed in the subplots as antagonists to white characters. And although ASCO's performance initially did not include actual footage of *No Movies*, one of the members of the collective, Harry Gamboa Jr., would go on to produce moving image content by the 1980s.

Aside from studies of ASCO, there is more historiographic work to be done on Chicana/o cinematic works. For example, the University of California at Los Angeles Chicano Studies Research Center restored a Chicano independent film, *Please, Don't Bury Me Alive! / Por Favor, No Me Entierren Vivo!* (1976), directed by Efraín Gutiérrez.[11] We have to support ongoing archiving, digitizing, and scholarly projects of moving images and recognize that many films have yet to surface.[12] We need to remember that this was the era when personal home video cameras emerged and that some recorded material was not meant for public consumption. We must therefore rethink how we write the histories of films made during the Chicano Movement, especially if the content refers to the political and cultural struggles of the period. When studying film and television, we must acknowledge that Spanish-language media institutions were subjected to scrutiny, including surveillance, thus forcing them to self-police.

Local and national television stations were not innocent of problematic representation and limited inclusion of Chicanas and Chicanos. The local

Spanish-language television station in Los Angeles, KMEX-34, covered the walkouts and student protests of 1968, which were key moments of the Chicano Movement. This led authorities to surveil the station. For example, the LAPD monitored KMEX's coverage of police brutality. In a confidential report that included a newscast transcript, the LAPD paid particular attention to the way that the news station framed the coverage of police arresting students at Roosevelt High School and how Captain William Smith of Hollenbeck Division attempted to obstruct KMEX cameramen from shooting footage of the arrests "by either grabbing at the lens or sticking his hands in front of the camera."[13] Officer C. Quiñones monitored the newscasts and summarized: "The presentation of the news broadcast failed to be objective and makes [sic] its presentation impartial. . . . All police actions were condemned and were labeled as 'BRUTALITY.'"[14] Because of police threats, the conditions of Chicanas/os were not suitably addressed, aside from community newspapers and magazines, and their voices were silenced. These instances of surveillance and policing did not deter the community from expressing its contentious relationship with authorities; rather, it inspired them to organize and demand inclusion and visibility, even if it meant taking direct action.

Chicanas and Chicanos who worked inside the entertainment industry were exteriorized. And those who were prevented from accessing those opportunities were conceived as an "other." This neglect led the community to support the media activist movement for an equitable and fair representation. For example, at the Mexican American Conference, Andrade's proposal to the film industry listed proactive steps to remedy negative images of Chicanas and Chicanos: to provide equitable employment onscreen and in production; to allow Chicanas and Chicanos to embrace their identity without feeling forced to Anglicize their names; and to provide fair remuneration.[15] The tone of Andrade's delivery matched the determination for justice seen in manifestos and proposals drafted by racialized and colonized peoples around the planet at that time. He specifies Brown people's encounter with moving images and the inferiority complex it induced: "In a time of social upheaval and the need to change the structures that divide man against himself, we can still stroll into a movie theatre and lose ourselves in the myth of anglo-white [sic] supremacy."[16] Andrade's document demanded liberation and integration, but also called for cultural self-determination, resonating with the calls made in "El Plan de Aztlán" delivered at the 1969 National Youth Liberation Conference in Denver, Colorado. On the point of cultural values, "El Plan" stressed the need for an assured cultural identity among Chicanas and Chicanos:

"We must insure that our writers, poets, musicians, and artists produce literature and art that is appealing to our people and relates to our revolutionary culture."[17] Although written in a nationalist and heteropatriarchal context, "El Plan" nevertheless played a critical role in instilling cultural pride in Chicanas and Chicanos at a time when mainstream media ignored the needs of the community, or when authorities were surveilling the Spanish-language press. Reading Andrade's proposal to the entertainment industry in conjunction with "El Plan" illustrates the ways in which Brown people embodied the ethos of liberation and decolonizing struggles central to the Chicano Movement.

Chon Noriega writes that the community's media activism ran parallel to the Chicano Movement in that both "worked on three levels at once: challenging the state, regime, and government."[18] Chicanas and Chicanos mobilized against the three interconnected systems of violence and erasure.[19] Noriega organizes his analysis of Chicana/o media activism into three prominent periods. The first is between 1968 and 1977, a watershed moment when the community used a "discourse of violence." The activists made demands of the entertainment industry, and especially the news media, since the latter were mostly regulated by the state, to fully represent the Brown community. Between 1974 and 1984, Chicanas and Chicanos made radical demands for inclusion, all the while depending on noncommercial funding for filmmaking and aligning themselves with the emergent Latin American Third Cinema movements that reshaped the landscape of moving images. The third period is in the 1980s, which saw proliferating roles for Latin Americans in film and television.[20] The first two periods are relevant to this study, with global movements impacting the community. Noriega and other scholars have made critical interventions in showing how Chicanas and Chicanos organized against the state and the entertainment industry during the Chicano Movement, and alluding to how the policing and entertainment institution intersected, as evinced by the Ruben Salazar case.

When authorities used batons against and fired tear gas at protestors participating in the Chicano Moratorium of 1970 in Laguna Park, the death of Ruben Salazar foregrounded questions of Spanish-language press censorship in Los Angeles. And while the history of censorship predates the Chicano Moratorium and Salazar's death, this period raised questions about the role of moving images and the ways that Chicanas and Chicanos were given visibility only when they were typecast or framed through limiting representation. As I will elaborate on shortly, authorities had scrutinized Salazar's activities, and his death only raised suspicion in the community. In this moment, artists and journalists turned to other media as sites where they could speak directly to the community and record histories of determination.

Examining murals as an alternative medium for making moving images would greatly benefit Chicana/o scholarship. While the community protested the entertainment industry, artists and community members made moving images on street walls for public consumption. I am unsure if Herrón and Gronk and Botello considered themselves moving image makers, or even if they intended their murals to stand in for what was overwhelmingly absent on television and cinematic screens. Whatever their intents and approaches, it is generative for us to include the murals in the history of media activism of the Chicano Movement. What do the murals *The Black and White/Moratorium Mural* and *Read Between the Lines (Cuídense Amigos)* reveal about the community's suspicion of mainstream media? How does the form and content of each mural inform our reading of them as Chicano moving images? What would we gain by incorporating these works into the history of Chicana/o media activism?

MOVING IMAGES ON WALLS

The exclusion of Chicanas and Chicanos from motion pictures and television meant that nuanced issues from the perspective of the community, such as substandard housing, police brutality, immigration, spatial displacement, and labor exploitation did not reach mass audiences. Those who needed to see and hear the stories of ostracized people did not receive this information, and so stereotypes continued to shape their ideas of cultural otherness. Fortunately, artists used their talents in other media, including murals along the corridors and within the public housing projects of East Los Angeles. During the Chicano Movement, muralists experimented with form and content to visualize and uncover histories ignored by mainstream institutions. The production, circulation, and exhibition of images representing struggle were imperative for decolonizing and political action. Images of self-determination mostly traveled from space to space via political posters and prints. Murals themselves did not travel, but their themes reflected the concerns of the Chicana/o community. Whatever the medium in which community struggles were visualized, we can argue that Chicana/o visual culture functioned as evidence; whether photographed or drawn, the images acknowledged the people's oppression and empowered resistance against cultural hegemony from institutions like film and television.

In interpreting historical events and visualizing them on a large scale, muralists recuperated narratives and experiences, offering counter-histories to sanitized and misleading stories by rendering visible what had been dismissed and displaced to the periphery. In other words, muralists reimagined archives and worked against official histories in visualizing historical discrepancies and omissions. On the function of photography as an activist-oriented praxis in what he calls the "Chicano photographic," Colin Gunckel writes that muralists drew inspiration from historical photographs, corroborating my point that murals embody a kind of photographic and cinematic-like quality.[21] Furthermore, murals have also been photographed for preservation efforts. If still photography functioned as primary source material for murals, film and television provided artists with purpose for unsettling and raising suspicion of spectacle, such as Herrón and Gronk and Botello set out to do in their respective works.

Noriega writes that Chicano cinema emerged alongside television industries. He argues that in addition to studying Chicano cinema against Hollywood, we should also consider the role of television in relation to the Chicana/o community. Television, a product of the nation-state, emerged amid post–World War II boom consumerism, spatial demographic shifts as a result of white flight from urban setting to suburb, the rise of automobile culture, and the valorization of the nuclear family arrangement. Television was indisputably the tool of assimilation and a nationalist project; the ideal American family was expected to own a television set and consume both images and commodities. Noriega explains that television was part of the public sphere, whereas film was situated in the social imaginary.[22] The social imaginary transcends cinema and permeates other mediums. For example, think about how cinematic violence and domination appear in the televisual spectacle when people of color are framed as threats and must therefore be punished. Television is part of the public sphere, as Noriega tells us. The social imaginaries of nationalism, assimilation, and whiteness, ideas that were highly represented in cinema at the time, spilled into the domestic sphere via the televisual apparatus. So we can say that the social imaginary also appeared in television. As a result, Chicanas/os were interpellated by the state and the social imaginaries.[23] Althusser explains that in the matrix of capitalism, the subject (in this case the Chicana and Chicano) maintains a relationship, however troubled, with the state according to ideologies that reproduce the subject vis-à-vis economic modes and regimes of policing. These ideologies of the state are reproduced by institutions, enabling the subject to respond and identify with the ideologies of the state.[24] Chicanas and Chicanos resisted the ideologies that interpellated them by subverting their power, especially when film and television demanded that they see themselves as inferior in order to reproduce racial difference. That subversion included producing visual content that challenged authorities.

The most comprehensive Chicano film of the events during the Chicano Moratorium is *Requiem 29* by David García. A student in the newly inaugurated UCLA Ethno-Communications Program, García and his film played a foundational role in helping the Chicana/o community advance claims of inequality at the hands of policing and judicial institutions through visual evidence. David James explains that *Requiem 29*'s montage between handheld camera footage shot by the community and the static movement of the camera recording the inquest into Salazar's death communicated that "Chicanos are the victims of the police and the judicial apparatus alike, and so must secure their autonomy."[25]

As important to the history of the Chicano Movement as García's film is Herrón and Gronk's *The Black and White/Moratorium Mural*. Located on the wall of a two-floor apartment in Estrada Courts on the Olympic Boulevard side, Herrón and Gronk's mural is directed to the residents of the housing complex and to the public. The mural experiments with still photography and montage, giving the illusion that one is watching several screens simultaneously replay scenes of the moratorium. Although representing the moratorium in a graphic manner, the mural reclaims the event and gives it a complex dimension by showing how the community understood the chaos and ongoing trauma of that day. The interpretation of the events ranges from children organizing in the streets, to images of incarcerated people, to the lifeless body of Ruben Salazar lying at the Silver Dollar bar. *Requiem 29* does not provide footage of Salazar's body; but *Black and White* visualizes the reporter's lifeless body lying on the floor, creating a cathartic experience and hailing the viewer to be a witness. The mural overwhelms spectators with small "snapshots" of the community in a public space. Moreover, spectators are confronted with gazes from multiple visages, and with the violence depicted within. These images prompt spectators into action and reflection; they are also moving images in the sense of moving people to action.

The moving images can be seen as vignettes or episodic structures unfolding simultaneously. Many are presented in close-up shots, extreme close-ups, long shots, and establishing shots, invoking a cinematic form and, in particular, a documentary-like aesthetic. For instance, the long strip at the center of the mural shows armed authorities blocking an intersection. Viewing this section of the mural from left to right, our mind creates a moving image, especially because we recognize scenes of protest. Note also that many of the bodies in that strip face left, creating for the spectator a complex set of motions and directions. The last vignette of the mural appears to be an incomplete long-distance shot, where we make out the silhouette of demonstrators protecting their eyes and covering their mouth from the toxic tear gas that authorities launched. While the faces and eyes of the silhouetted protestors are not visible to us, the muralists use close-ups of eyes and faces of the community members to acknowledge the spectators by returning the gaze. These images of militarization, occupation, incarceration, and uprisings are recognizable in militant films and montage films. According to Benavidez, Gronk makes a direct cinematic reference to Marcel Carné's film *Les enfants du paradis* (1945), which was made during the Nazi occupation of France during World War II. The muralist explains that he borrowed the mime Baptiste from the film and transposed it to this mural to relate experiences of oppression: "it was the same thing; it's a feeling of occupation by the police in East Los Angeles."[26]

Benavidez argues that Gronk invokes the 1960s militant use of cameras and documentary films, such as Gillo Pontecorvo's *Battle of Algiers* (1965) and other countless cinema verité, guerilla, subversive, and direct cinemas, as catalysts for revolution.[27] To elaborate, I would suggest that this militant style of painting and cinematic influence related to the struggles of political cinema and the ways in which much of the decolonizing world used mobile cameras to shoot back against mainstream cinema and the systems of power that tried to suppress their right to liberation. The moving images also work on an affective level to mobilize the community into action. After all, early Soviet cinema used affective montage with rapid cuts to drive forward the apprehension of modernity and state control. When regarding the mural for the first time, the images assault us visually, emphasizing the drama of the Chicano Moratorium. These striking images catalyze spectators into action. For example, the images of militarized authorities, the smoke of the gas canisters, and the rage such as seen in the woman on the left side of the mural appeal to the emotions of spectators and call for solidarity against injustice.

Benavidez writes that *Black and White* exemplifies how artists rewrote histories "using the visual style of the very media that had presented distorted images to the public."[28] As Benavidez suggests, and as I argue, the mural shows us an alternative medium in which moving images tell stories about the community and the racism they experienced from a so-called subaltern point of view.

In the 1960s and 1970s, filmmakers in the Americas and across the globe aspired to transgress the boundaries established by the entertainment industry. Filmmakers and theorists Fernando Solanas and Octavio Getino's 1969 manifesto, "Toward a Third Cinema," called on subaltern groups to use the camera for militancy. Doing so would help dismantle cultural imperialism and transform cinema into a weapon of liberation. "Mass communications," write Solanas and Getino, "tend to complete the destruction of a national awareness and of a collective subjectivity on the way to enlightenment, a destruction which begins as soon as the child has access to these media, the education and culture of the ruling classes." Mass media colonized the mind and foreclosed the possibility of freeing oneself from the bondage of mental degeneracy.[29] David Botello's *Read Between the Lines* parallels Solanas and Getino's manifesto in that it represents the dangers of passive spectatorship and urgently calls for unbinding the self from the imperious restraints of entertainment.

Botello's mural explicitly cautions spectators about the perils of falling under the entertainment industry's hypnotic spectacle. The muralist visualizes the institutional inner workings of film and television as machinery of Americanization and assimilation. Jingoism, deprivation of knowledge, and consumer culture are among the themes represented in the mural as prime threats to the Chicana/o nuclear family. At the top of the mural, two cameras positioned in high angle overlook the family seated in the living room, while also aggressively pointing at spectators. Guisela Latorre argues that the mural "depicted a kind of panoptic space."[30] This panoptic and surveillance space invokes the legacies of state censorship of media, but it also implies the ways in which Brown people have been conditioned to police their behaviors in order to meet the forced acculturation into U.S. culture. In addition, these cameras remind us of the ways in which the community was under surveillance by the LAPD, much of which photographers of *La Raza* documented. Such intrusions into the domestic sphere and in public space pushed the community to question the function of mainstream images, raise skepticism about what they consumed, both ideologies and products, and what the best tactics would be to counteract these images.

Botello depicts an Orwellian and Foucauldian culture of surveillance where Chicana and Chicano bodies and culture are disciplined for operating outside the boundaries of U.S. nationalism and consumerism. On the left side of the mural, two investigators (represented as researchers), who could equally be Nielsen Media Research data analysts monitoring viewing and consumption habits, operate the surveillance apparatus, abstracting data from the half-clothed Chicano. The wires shackle the Chicano, constraining his freedom and impeding his mobility. The illegibility of the print in the contract refers to the ways in which the deceptive media tricked consumers.

The investigators dictate the activity of the enclosed space of the home through various interconnected instruments, such as the television in the living room drawing the spectators close and the stove in the background subjecting the woman to perform domesticity. In the center of the frame, a young boy mediates the possibility of a radical future if one breaks away from the harmful images of television, embodying the calls made in "El Plan." The child reads a book, *The History of Mexico*, as the Aztec god Quetzalcoatl descends upon him, enlightening him with cultural and historical lessons of Mexico not to be found on television and cinematic screens. The young boy is protected by light, showing that education can unbind people from mental oppression. As I mentioned earlier, scholars and writers were primarily concerned with the images inundating the Chicana/o community, and especially the damage they caused children. An article in *La Raza* touches on this issue:

> Our children do not want to identify with symbols that are looked upon as being foreign-looking, dirty-lazy, sneaky, funny, etc. So, in the past, many of our children have not identified as being "Mexican or Mexican-American" because of the negative connotations. And in not wanting to identify with their people, serious personality problems and inferiority problems have resulted to the point where many of our people have not felt good about themselves.[31]

The young boy offers an alternative, of what breaking away from the television screens might do for the movement and for Chicana/o political consciousness.

Guisela Latorre offers a compelling reading of this mural, writing that "while this male Chicano worker offers physical and psychological resistance to the forces and tools of assimilation, other members of the nuclear Chicano family . . . have been completely lured by the seductive images of the manipulative U.S. mass media." Moving images have arrested and immobilized political action.[32] The images on the television screen in the mural are counterproductive to the anti-Vietnam War protests that were taking place in the Chicana/o community, especially considering that Black and Brown people were dying at disproportionate rates in Southeast Asia. Furthermore, the image of patriotism represented in the mural undercuts the idea that all people in the United States are treated equally. Those constructed images risked blurring the lived experience of people of color at the time.

Holly Barnet-Sanchez and Tim Drescher write that *Read Between the Lines* represents classic Chicano Movement iconography in how Botello endows his work with symbols of protest.[33] Although the mural is most obviously a critique of film and television, it also includes references to the community's protest against Coors Brewing Company and homage to the United Farm Workers grape strike in Delano, California. The mural visualizes the risks of the loss of Chicana/o nationalism and anxieties of emasculation. It is important to read these masculinist impulses of Chicana/o visual culture through a critical contemporary lens in order to point out the limitations of the Chicano Movement and how ideas of liberation and cultural affirmation were rooted in masculinist rhetoric. Nevertheless, it is productive to revisit this mural and place it within the history of Chicano moving images and media activism operating in opposition to the entertainment industry.

Herrón and Gronk and Botello's critique of mainstream media during the Chicano Movement and the various ways in which the community participated in media activism shows that murals were an alternative medium in which artists experimented with form to create moving images. These moving images were more than visual artifacts: they were didactic and invited spectators to engage with these works in order to challenge one-dimensional representations of Brown people.

CONCLUSION

I conclude this essay with a reflection: where else might we happen on Chicana/o moving images? Chicano Movement posters and prints, cartoons, theater, and music fill our minds with scenes related to protests, resistance, and solidarity. We have acquired a visual language and reading skill that defies teleology in favor of an intersectional understanding of cosmic struggles in the past and present. In the contemporary moment, we must continue to write histories of visual culture during and after the Chicano Movement and emphasize that there are other visual cultural artifacts that need to be historically contextualized and studied. A *rasquachismo* framework proposed by Tomás Ybarra-Frausto could help us uncover visual material that functioned as moving images in the sense that they played with the perceptual powers of looking and inspired activism.[34] With the prominence of social media and other platforms through which images are disseminated, we might find fascinating ways to expand our understanding of moving images and resistance to misrepresentation.

NOTES

1. I open with these lines from Scott-Heron's poem/song to illustrate how communities of color in United States during the 1960s and 1970s called attention to mainstream media's apathetic coverage of community issues. Ideally, the reader would listen to the song as a point of departure before reading this essay.

2. Scholars such as Colin Gunckel have written on the importance of photography in the Chicano Movement. In fall 2017, the Autry Museum in Los Angeles unveiled an exhibition titled La Raza, part of the Getty's Pacific Standard Time: LA/LA. The La Raza exhibit contains an archive of unreleased photographs from *La Raza* newspaper and magazine out of East Los Angeles. These photographs contextualize the importance of Chicano photojournalism and the heterogeneity of quotidian life during El Movimiento.

3. Thomas M. Martínez and José Peralez, "Chicanos and the Motion Picture Industry," Image Stereotyping, 1970–undated, box 41, folder 10, Anthony Quinn Files, John F. Kennedy Memorial Library, California State University, Los Angeles, California.

4. Martínez and Peralez, "Chicanos and the Motion Picture Industry."

5. "Statement," Chicano Movement Leaders, 1969–1970, box 41, folder 4, Anthony Quinn Files, John F. Kennedy Memorial Library, California State University, Los Angeles, California.

6. "Statement," 2.

7. "El Mexicano Through the Eyes of the Tavacho," *La Raza* 1, no. 4 (1971): 26.

8. "Rated X: Racist Films," *La Raza* 1, no. 7 (1972): 57.

9. "Justicia o Muerte," *La Raza* 1, no. 8 (1972): 14.

10. Max Benavidez, *Gronk* (Los Angeles: UCLA Chicano Studies Research Center Press, 2007), 45.

11. *Please, Don't Bury Me Alive! / Por Favor, No Me Entierren Vivo!* (1976), www.chicanostudiesresearchcenter.com/publications/dvds.

12. In this volume, Jesse Esparza writes about uncovering a film left unattended from 1970 in Houston, Texas, concerning a protest against the war. This underscores the importance of searching for and writing the histories of both fiction and nonfiction film and video, as well as helping make the material available as primary historical documents.

13. Ben Walsh, "Police Monitor KMEX Newscasts," The Ruben Salazar Files, *Los Angeles Times Data Desk*, February 19, 2011, http://documents.latimes.com/salazar-kmex-transcripts/.

14. Walsh, "Police Monitor KMEX Newscasts."
15. "Statement."
16. "Statement."
17. National Youth Liberation Conference, "El Plan de Aztlán," April 1969, Denver, Colorado.
18. Chon Noriega, *Shot in America: Television, the State, and the Rise of Chicano Cinema* (Minneapolis: University of Minnesota Press, 2000), 23.
19. Noriega, *Shot in America*, 24.
20. Noriega, *Shot in America*, 25.
21. Colin Gunckel, "The Chicano/a Photographic: Art as Social Practice in the Chicano Movement," *American Quarterly* 67, no. 2 (2015): 377–412.
22. Noriega, *Shot in America*, 26.
23. See Louis Althusser, *On the Reproduction of Capitalism: Ideology and Ideological State Apparatuses*, trans. G. M. Goshgarian (New York: Verso, 2014).
24. Althusser, *On the Reproduction of Capitalism*.
25. David James, *The Most Typical Avant-Garde: History and Geography of Minor Cinemas in Los Angeles* (Berkeley: University of California Press, 2005), 310.
26. Benavidez, *Gronk*, 30.
27. Benavidez, *Gronk*, 29.
28. Benavidez, *Gronk*, 28.
29. Fernando Solanas and Octavio Getino, "Toward a Third Cinema," *Cinéaste* 4, no. 3 (1970): 3.
30. Guisela Latorre, *Walls of Empowerment: Chicana/o Indigenist Murals of California* (Austin: University of Texas Press, 2008), 181.
31. "El Mexicano Through the Eyes of the Gavacho," *La Raza* 1, no. 4 (1971): 30.
32. Latorre, *Walls of Empowerment*, 181.
33. Holly Barnet-Sanchez and Tim Drescher, *Give Me Life: Iconography and Identity in East LA Murals* (Albuquerque: University of New Mexico Press, 2016), 134.
34. See Tomás Ybarra-Frausto, *Rasquachismo: A Chicano Sensibility* (San Antonio, Tex.: School by the River Press, 2017).

10

"WE WERE IN A FOREIGN LAND"

The Chicano Movement in Fresno County

PATRICK FONTES

I tell people the 60s—people think it's drugs and free love—to me and to so many of us what it represented was us standing up for ourselves, we said, we're Chicanos, our people, Mexicanos deserve the best education, the best jobs and everything else. The 60s gave us the realization that we could make a change, that change was possible, but we had to be part of it.
—DR. LEA YBARRA

RESNO COUNTY, and the larger San Joaquin Valley, offers a unique Chicano experience compared to the histories of Mexican-origin communities elsewhere along the California coast, from San Diego to the San Francisco Bay Area. Unlike the coastal regions that were founded by Mexico through the Mission enterprise, the Fresno area did not have an identifiable Spanish or Mexican past. Although hacienda owners held land grants in the Valley region, the Mission system did not extend into the area, nor did Spain or Mexico found any cities within the Valley. When the great wave of Mexican immigrants ventured to El Norte during the Mexican Revolution to work the thousands of miles of crops, no identifiable Mexican architectural markers greeted those immigrants, unlike those who worked and settled along the coast. What Mexicans encountered in Fresno County was an area wholly founded by whites for whites—they indeed entered a foreign land.

The influence of Fresno State College must be seen in a larger geographical context than merely Fresno County. The first wave of Chicano students at FSC, the United Farm Workers presence where most of these Chicanos were born and grew up, the growers that Chávez and the UFW stood up to, and the deeply entrenched conservatism enmeshed with Valley grower culture—a culture that has roots in the Confederacy—all must be viewed as part of an intertwined history that gave birth to El Movimiento at Fresno State in the late 1960s. Indeed, it is my contention that FSC was ground zero for major issues taken up by young Chicanos across California and the Southwest. For one, while Chicanos at other universities such as San Francisco State also challenged a power structure founded on an Anglo-American standard, FSC Chicanos not only contended with structural racism that bound together conservative college and rural cultures, but fought against—in a few cases, literally—a white student body who were the offspring and products of that agricultural, conservative power foundation. At Fresno State, in classrooms, in the free speech area, the sons and daughters of growers at the center of the grape boycott who demonized the UFW sat beside, verbally confronted, and, a few times, physically attacked the sons and daughters who marched alongside Chávez—Chicanos fought back. In many respects, the Chicano students who entered FSC in the late 1960s paralleled their grandparents who were part of the great wave of immigration during the revolution. The students took up the cause unrealized since the revolution, that of economic equality, dignity, and freedom.

Three factors characterized the experiences of Chicanos at Fresno State during the late sixties and early seventies, granting them a unique outlook and dedication to the Movement compared to other parts of California. Firstly, starting at a young, grade-school age, Chicanos at FSC worked the fields with their parents, receiving hard life lessons picking grapes under the intense San Joaquin Valley summer sun. For most, working alongside their siblings and parents in dusty, pesticide-laden vineyards continued well into high school. Secondly, FSC Chicanos supported, and often worked directly with and for, the UFW. Since many of the growers whom the UFW challenged resided in the Valley, carloads of FSC students regularly attended boycotts, interspersing radical activity, arrests, and jail time with their college studies. Lastly, FSC Chicanos received radical education from professors and mentors that included the likes of Eleazar Risco and Luis Valdéz.[1] Risco brought to Fresno State several years' experience of activism, including serving as the founding editor of *La Raza* newspaper. Indeed, it was Risco's work in Los Angeles forming *La Raza* as a community publication with "young people, street people . . . , gangs, and students" that set the stage in 1969 for the creation of Fresno State's Chicano newspaper, *La Voz de Atzlan*. Risco recalled talking with Fresno State Chicanos about their unique experience as farm laborers turned college students. "I would have the students . . . talk about their experience working in the fields, and what I told them was, you already know who you are and what you're about. And that is the basis, the core of what learning is about." Indeed, gaining control of the campus press constituted one of the first major victories in 1969, though the year leading up to that victory was hard-fought.

On May 5, 1969, the following image graced the opening page of *La Pluma Morena*, the first Chicano student edition of the Fresno State College (FSC) newspaper the *Daily Collegian*: a company of Mexican revolutionaries stands defiant, shoulder-to-shoulder, and ready to plunge into attack with bayonets pointing forth. Their hardened, war-torn faces belie years of revolutionary struggle. Behind them stand an army of Chicano activists, also with rifles drawn, ready for war. On closer look, however, the bayonets are actually large inkwell pens—the revolutionaries transform into warriors of the printed word.

Topics addressed in *La Pluma Morena* by Chicano students and faculty represent the issues at stake in 1969.[2] The front-page article "Semana de la Raza Bronce y Cinco de Mayo," explains the historical origins of the holiday, as well as its significance for contemporary Chicanos. The author calls on FSC Chicanos to rally around the holiday as a source of identity and anchor to their Mexican past, yet also calls on all Americans, "regardless of national origin," to join in on the celebration.[3] In reaching out to all Americans, FSC Chicano professor J. C. Canales acknowledged the racial tensions and violent encounters over the previous year on campus, and sought to ease animosities by inviting white students also to observe Cinco de Mayo. Corky Gonzales's poem "I Am Joaquin" is printed on page 2, alongside "El Plan Espiritual de Aztlán."

On page 3, FSC professor Luis Valdéz in "The Tale of La Raza" views the farm laborer struggle in the San Joaquin Valley as a foundational tale of the Mexican American.[4] According to Valdéz, the fight of the farm laborer is the fight of the Chicano. Valdéz views the struggle of the farm laborer and UFW as more than a fight for better wages and economic equality; it is part of the larger revolution of "a New World race to reconcile conflicts of its 500-year history." To the author, the march from Delano to Sacramento reenacted centuries of migratory journeys, beginning with the original Mexica migration from Aztlán to what is now Mexico City. Arriving at the steps of the capitol building solidified Chicano identity, as "Huelga!" (strike) was shouted in unison. According to Valdéz, "huelga" is "a declaration, a challenge, a greeting, a feeling, a movement, it is the most significant word in our entire Mexican American history."[5] If César Chávez is now remembered and studied by academics principally as a union organizer, to Valdéz the UFW leader was primarily a representation of the Chicano struggle for liberation, the first Mexican American leader to rise up to lead his people out of oppression, one who looked like the people he led: "Here was César, burning with a patient fire, poor like us, talking quietly, moving people to talk about their problems. . . . César is our first real Mexican-American leader."[6] Writing from FSC, Valdéz looked out on the Central Valley of California and viewed the uprising and struggle of the farm laborer as a regional phenomenon, but also as the first Chicano uprising in the United States. After decades of oppression from Central Valley conservative interests, "after years of isolation in the barrios of great valley slum towns like Delano, after years of living in labor camps and ranches at the mercy and caprice of growers, the Mexican-American farmworker is developing his own ideas."[7] The cry of "Huelga!," according to Valdéz, the fight for better wages and working conditions, was the first articulation of the need for unity among Mexican Americans, and the first uprising in the United States since the Mexican Revolution. Taken together with the image of Mexican revolutionaries gracing the front page of the newspaper, the cry of "Huelga!" was the "first murmurings of revolution."[8]

On page 4 of *La Pluma Morena*, in "Why the Grape Boycott?," FSC student Ron Ortega views the UFW boycott as a fight for the recognition of the Mexican "as a man, and not a humble, inferior, servant." As in the image on the opening page, Ortega sees the farm laborer union members as revolutionary warriors led by César Chávez, a new revolutionary: "as Zapata before him, he leads an army of the people . . . poor, non-violent farm-working people who are struggling for self-determination." In the end, the author calls for FSC students to support the grape boycott. If all men are created equal and have equal economic opportunity, then FSC students have a moral obligation to support the boycott.

In an editorial column, FSC student and editor of *La Pluma Morena* John F. Ramírez explains the importance of the newspaper as a tool for "avoiding the possibility of a San Francisco State debacle here, but it was a reality there and no matter where, an understandable, yet license [*sic*], violently manifested, volcano of frustration can exist. This is no threat."[9] Indeed, Ramírez's editorial is directed at both conservative forces on campus and Chicano students. His forceful reference to the turmoil at San Francisco State offered a cautionary tale, yet no threat, to those on campus who still opposed Chicanos and their demands.[10] Indeed, that Central Valley residents were watching the events at San Francisco State College with a keen eye is evidenced by one Fresno man's letter to the *Fresno Bee*: "I am sick and tired of any part of small vocal groups forcing their will upon a vast majority as is exemplified in the current San Francisco State College anarchist movement."[11]

Ramírez also tackles the apathy that was part of a culture at the *Daily Collegian* and on campus, where political activism was virtually nonexistent and involvement in student government was severely lacking. According to Ramírez, if the white students running the *Daily Collegian* had allowed Chicanos to voice their issues in print, then there would not have been a need for a Chicano edition. If the *Collegian* showed more than a "mere token amount of sensitivity, commitment and fairness . . . the students have also shown their share of complacency, apathy, and little sense of urgency and are as blameworthy." In the end Ramírez issues a call for unity among white, Black, and Chicano students, promising readers that *La Pluma Morena* will serve to "unite and not incite, to seek cooperation and not revenge, and to end racism and not enhance it, for together is the only real way we can seek and build a better world."[12]

In all the pieces published in the inaugural Chicano edition, the authors thoughtfully wove together a Mexican past with roots in the Mexican Revolution, calling on the memory of Zapata a few times. The contemporary struggle of Chicano students is not a separate issue from the farmworker cause; they are enmeshed as a total life experience, as most of the FSC Chicano students were brought up in farm-laboring families. They witnessed firsthand the oppressive, poverty-stricken lifestyles their families endured, viewing at the same time the privileged lives of the growers and their families. Most often, the Chicano children who picked crops went to school with the growers' kids. In all, the particular struggles in the fields and on campus were seen as a larger fight for Mexicans in the Valley to rise out of poverty and gain the respect and economic, educational, and political voices and opportunities afforded to whites. The landmark victory of a Chicano edition of the *Daily Collegian* allowed Chicano students to at last bring these demands into print, for all to see. The fight was difficult up to that point, and as the 1970s rolled around, there would be many more challenges.

With the publication *La Pluma Morena*, Chicano students won a major victory at FSC in making their presence, concerns, and identity known on campus and to a wider Valley community. Long the voice of Fresno County conservatism, the FSC newspaper, the *Daily Collegian*, was once a week handed over to Chicano and Black students, who alternated on a biweekly basis. This essay details the tumultuous and sometimes violent two-year period of 1968–69 leading up to the hard-won victory of gaining complete control of the *Daily*

Collegian every other week. Several factors make the struggle at Fresno State College both unique and important in understanding the local Central Valley experience and its place in a larger California Movimiento portrait.

In the 1960s, Fresno State College was the only four-year college serving the San Joaquin Valley, from Bakersfield to Fresno.[13] Chicano students from every region of the Valley entered Fresno State in the late sixties, many as Educational Opportunity Program (EOP) participants. Overwhelmingly from outlying small rural communities, as first-generation college students and as the first wave of Chicanos at FSC, they entered an Anglo-dominated world. Eva Joaquín, a Chicana activist attending FSC at the time, remembers the initial feeling of entering a wholly new world, one entirely different from the rural town of Arvin in Kern County. "We were in a foreign land. Nothing at Fresno State connected to us. We couldn't identify. We didn't see our people." After she connected with other Chicanas/os who also at first felt an alienation, the nascent political activism and Chicano professors transformed her from a timid country girl who grew up in the fields to one dedicated to La Causa. "We were energized finally, that we were something, that we were going to make a difference. . . . [Eleazar] Risco really influenced, [Ricardo] Durán too, and I took a class from Luis Valdéz." Furthermore, as FSC professor Valdéz wrote, "this is a society largely hostile to our cultural values . . . no depth; no faith; no allowance for human contrariness; no soul, no mariachi, no chili sauce, no pulque, no mysticism, no chingaderas."[14]

For most of the FSC Chicano students, white control colored their lives from their earliest memories. Working as child laborers in fields alongside their parents, they were exposed to a racial and class dichotomy that had pervaded the Valley's social, economic, and political structure since the nineteenth century, one that posited poor, laboring Mexican-origin people at the bottom of the social and racial spectrum in opposition to white produce growers. As one Chicana activist, Gloria Hernández, remembered, "back then they used to prolong the school opening day so that the growers who were our principals and board of directors would get their crops picked. If we knew then what we know now."[15] Like for other Chicanas who worked in the fields, there came a time of awakening, when they realized there was an economic divide founded on a racial dichotomy:

> You could tell the difference. You could tell the cliques. You can tell when they would come back from vacation. Our hands were all green, and our knees were

green and black from picking the walnuts, and the oil would rub into you, or the tomatoes, it was awful. And they came back all sun tanned, looking good, you know? Then you start realizing the differences; you're working your ass off for their patron while they're in summer camp or whatever. So, you start getting angry. You're growing up and you start checking out the differences. That's the way it was, nobody fought it, nobody fought it, until the UFW [United Farm Workers] came to town. Then things happened. The line was drawn.[16]

Chicana activist and scholar Lea Ybarra also remembers working in the fields as a child:

In my 7, 8, 9 years of age we were out working in the fields picking cotton, the little we could pick. We picked grapes and blackberries, which were awful to pick. It was so hot. Then when I was 12 or 13 I began working in the packing houses in Sanger, packing peaches and nectarines. In all the years I worked in the fields and packing houses as a minor I never once saw an inspector come into the fields and say, "Children shouldn't be working in the fields." So, as far as I'm concerned they exploited us, the farmers and everyone else. No one cared we were kids working in the fields, they just wanted us to contribute.[17]

Under the leadership of César Chávez, the UFW challenged the Anglo-grower power structure that most FSC Chicanas/os had grown up under. Indeed, for FSC Chicano students, their first political awakenings and education in El Movimiento occurred while still in elementary and high school when the UFW came to their towns, and into their living rooms for house meetings, as their families took up La Causa.

In the fall of 1968 FSC extended its progressive Experimental College. Created during President Frederic W. Ness's tenure, the program was an answer to student uprisings and demands across the nation. The Experimental College sought to offer students unique classes with novel ways of learning and looking at the world—"a potpourri of courses as providing a liberalizing experience" for FSC students.[18] While it was a force for positive change, conservative groups on campus opposed the Experimental College from its inception. Chicano students entering in the fall of 1968 were offered a new course as part of the Experimental College: La Raza Studies. Black history courses were also part of the new offerings that fall, bringing the Experimental College courses to twenty in total. That La Raza studies was part of an experimental program is telling, revealing an uncertainty from the beginning, a tentativeness concerning the role of newly arrived Chicano students and their identity. For newly arrived Mexican American students, La Raza Studies would open avenues of place, time, and identity. Taught by Chicano professors such as Eleazar Risco and Luis Valdéz, students transformed from Mexican Americans into Chicanos with a purpose.[19] In 1967, Risco, after working alongside Valdéz as a union organizer for César Chávez, ventured to Los Angeles, where, along with a handful of others, he founded the *La Raza* newspaper.[20] The newspaper influenced the Chicano Moratorium against the war in Vietnam in August 1970. Born in Cuba, Risco fled during the Cuban Revolution, but not before being influenced by revolutionary ideals. Only one year after founding the *La Raza* newspaper, Risco returned to FSC, transforming young field-workers into political activists. Luis Valdéz also brought the energy he gained from his work in the UFW to the classroom at FSC, teaching students revolutionary methods and ideas through theater. Energized by courses and professors they could identify with, the politicization of the Chicano students was quickly under way. Several Chicano students soon set their nascent politicization in action.

On September 18, 1968, two weeks after fall classes started at FSC, Richard Nixon came to town on his presidential campaign tour. When Nixon stopped in Fresno, he was cheerfully welcomed at the airport by two hundred supporters as well as leading Fresno Republicans, including Fresno police chief Henry R. Morton and Sheriff Melvin A. Willmirth.[21] Leaving the airport, the first group he met with were farmers—farmers who were in opposition to César Chávez and the grape boycott.[22] Indeed, Nixon came to Fresno for his first major speech on farm policy because it was ground zero for the issue. More than five thousand supporters turned out to hear about Nixon's "Forgotten America" at the Convention Center in downtown Fresno.[23] A group of around fifty activists supporting the grape boycott also showed up to Nixon's speech.[24] As the GOP candidate arrived at the Convention Center, the demonstrators chanted "Huelga! Huelga!"[25] Once inside, the activists booed during California governor Ronald Reagan's introduction of Nixon. Reagan called the demonstrators "noisy barbarians," who "will not follow orderly procedures."[26]

During his speech, Nixon laid out his plan to deal with the crisis facing San Joaquin Valley farmers: César Chávez. Nixon declared that as president he would be an advocate for both farmers and farm laborers. Addressing the rural poor, he said their plight of high unemployment was "high on our priority list." He declared: "those who seek to divide the farmer and the farm worker do no service to either."[27] While Nixon spoke out against the boycott, the activists yelled loud boos. The activists did not act out in violence or threaten Nixon, Reagan, or any of their supporters. When the activists refused to quiet down, Morton called into the area additional police, sheriff's deputies, and highway patrolmen.[28] Soon after, Secret Service agents along with Fresno police physically confronted the demonstrators. Law enforcement seized and ripped apart the protestors' signs, and a scuffle ensued between the police and three protestors. Two female students, Lea Ybarra and Yolanda Huerta, "were pummeled, manhandled, and pushed to the ground."[29] One male protestor was slapped in the face "for no reason."[30] Fresno police then escorted the group out of the center.[31] Indeed, the demonstration was the first major anti-Nixon protest the candidate had encountered during his presidential campaign tour and "the noisiest and most hostile."[32] Even though the protestors did not perpetrate violence and were exercising their constitutional rights, Police Chief Morton "complimented the restraint of his officers," and said that had they acted otherwise, "somebody might have been hurt."[33]

Nixon then called on farmers to help alleviate the plight of farmworkers by taking the initiative in improving wages. He called for a cessation of the discriminatory practices of the Johnson administration toward poor rural schools, and said that "good, rural education must be provided to our poorer counties, with special emphasis on the problems of the migratory worker's child."[34] Yet, he offered no specific ways of achieving the goal, except for an appeal to the farmers' generosity. After his speech, Nixon participated in a panel discussion that included leading farm interests and Republican leaders, but no one who represented farm laborer interests.[35] Jack Ortega, regional director of the Mexican American Political Association (MAPA), stated that the panel "excluded the voice of the farm workers and the UFWOC, saying there was no room to seat them. How can anyone discuss farm worker problems without discussing them with those being affected? Mr. Nixon spoke only to the growers and the farmers."[36] In a display of solidarity with grape growers and defiance against the boycotters, Nixon stated, "I will continue to eat California grapes and drink grape products."[37]

Two days later Jack Ortega called for an investigation into the harsh treatment of the anti-Nixon protestors, in what Ortega called "the Neanderthal actions of certain police officers and Secret Service men."[38] Police Chief Morton defended the actions taken by the police. He stated he was looking into the matter, but added, "I'm sure Mr. Ortega won't be happy with the results of it."[39]

The hostility in Chief Morton's statement is transparent and demonstrates a prejudicial view of Ortega and MAPA.

What the incident at Nixon's rally reveals is twofold. First, it shows that a nascent activism was in effect at FSC among Chicano students, and that these students were directly connected with both MAPA and the UFW. Furthermore, these students not only engaged in political activism on campus and locally with the UFW, but protested national leadership. Their protest in Fresno was the first major protest Nixon had encountered anywhere in the nation, including Californian metropolitan areas. That theirs was the "noisiest and most hostile" of any protest Nixon had encountered is a testament to the passion created at FSC. In the conservative enclave of Fresno County, where growers still filled the highest echelons of power and respect, the passions of Chicano student activists were more than an irritation to the ears at a Republican rally; they represented an unraveling of a culture that was founded in Fresno after the Civil War, a type of New South, that placed brown-skinned peoples at the bottom of society, in a neatly fitted niche of farm labor—not one of education; not one where civil rights were exercised; not one where their discordant voices could drown out the powerful voices of Reagan and Nixon. Indeed, in a statement a few days after the event, Police Chief Morton revealed that an extensive background search had been conducted on the protestors, through photographs taken at the event. Although his team had tried to identify the Mexican Americans present, they were "unable to discover one bonafide grape picker in the group."[40] When three officers ripped the protest sign out of Lea Ybarra's hands, throwing her to the ground in the process, their aggression represented the interests of the grower class attempting to silence and put back into place their docile workers.[41] The Nixon debacle was the first notable rebellion of San Joaquin Valley Chicano youth in their quest to be heard.

A week later, on September 27, Police Chief Morton issued a six-page statement on how the Fresno police department would deal with activists in the future, in order to ensure that what happened at the Nixon rally would never occur again. That is, never again would radical protestors openly challenge Republican leaders in Fresno. The statement was sent to every radio station, TV station, and local newspaper. Through the use of photographs taken at the event, Morton's investigators were able to identify thirteen demonstrators, nine of whom were FSC Mexican American students. Although the identities of the FSC students were not revealed in the report—because of their age—they were now on Morton's radar. In the report, the students were listed as "Subject

No. 1, Subject No. 2," and so on, criminalizing the youth activists akin to an FBI wanted list. An example of Morton's nine-student list may be seen in Subject No. 5:

> Subject No. 5 is a Fresno State College student who has received a National Defense college loan and is a disrupting influence on campus. A check with the CIA revealed that this subject has had communist affiliations since 1963 and has been involved in strikes and demonstrations throughout the Valley. He was one of the persons in the group who kept the demonstrators in a high state of emotion.[42]

In all nine cases listed, the Fresno Police Department pulled and examined the file of each of the students at FSC; examined whether the students received any type of student aid; researched their political activities; and even checked if their family members participated in UFW protests throughout the Valley. Morton's report included in No. 6's description: "his mother was also demonstrating at the Nixon rally." The report also identified the student demonstrators as "troublemakers," and "social leeches who demonstrate against the system that helped them."[43]

That Morton included in the report whether the students received National Defense loans or were part of the federal work study program reveals that these students were viewed as outsiders, or quasi-citizens, tapping into a system that they were tied to only through tenuous cultural and economic moorings. Moreover, Morton and his team were doing more than attempting to keep students from overstepping propriety in public; they investigated the students in an indepth sophisticated manner, unveiling every aspect of their lives, viewing them as radical, communist threats.

When Police Chief Morton released his nine-page statement and list, an avalanche of criticism from students and faculty came down on the FSC administration. How, students and faculty asked, did Morton gain access to private student information? It was discovered that the financial aid office willingly gave student information to one of Morton's officers, James Stoeckel.[44] No warrants were issued, nor red tape or protocol gone through, for the police department to gain legal access to student documents. On September 26, Sergeant Edward Heizenrader phoned Alan Cano, assistant director of the financial aid office. Cano told the officer he would be willing to cooperate in providing the information he requested on the particular students.

Heizenrader sent Officer Stoeckel, who went to the financial aid office with photographs of the demonstrators at the rally. When Stoeckel arrived, both Alan Cano and Kenneth Lewis, the financial aid director, met him. Cano turned out to be a close friend of the officer. Cano said that the officer "assured us it was strictly an investigation and the identifications would be considered confidential. We just identified the students that we knew."[45] Fresno State College president Frederic Ness issued a statement of light condemnation concerning the release of private student information: "Although this was done in a personal, not official capacity, the results were obviously the same. This is regretted by all concerned."[46] Dr. Ace Griffiths, a professor of education and member of the Academic Senate Executive Committee, voiced concern at a meeting that the descriptions offered in the report might cause unjustified prejudices to arise. Not long after the publication of Morton's list, a group of Chicano students led by Lea Ybarra read a statement at an academic senate meeting, demanding the removal of financial aid director Kenneth Lewis. The Chicano students' statement charged the Financial Aid Office with "racism and harassment," "cruel neglect," and a lack of attention for the personal needs and "feelings" of students, especially those who were Black and Chicano. Ybarra and her group also demanded the creation of an FSC policy that barred sharing classified student information without the consent of students.[47]

During the conflict that ensued in the aftermath of the Nixon rally, FSC was four weeks into its fall 1968 semester. Conservative groups on campus began to voice concern and even outrage at what they saw as Chicanos being given and taking more of their share of student services. One angry white student, concerned over losing control of the campus, pondered, "I'm wondering who is in control of this campus; certain left wing students and faculty members?" The student attacked Professor Risco: "I wonder if Ness knows that a Marxist and Cuban-trained revolutionist is teaching at his school?"[48] He went on, complaining that the Educational Opportunity Program (EOP) and La Raza studies "give certain minorities books, teachers, courses, senate representation, rooms in 'our' College Union or why not give them the whole school?" This student's frustrations concerning Chicano students and faculty members would only grow and spread across campus. Although the anger exhibited by this white student was symptomatic of antagonistic feelings about Chicano students, there were also efforts toward inclusion and empathy. In the column "I, Too, Exist," Eric Gilliam examined what is must be like for a Chicano student on campus, negotiating through prejudice and being voiceless. Gilliam's description offers a telling window into how white students on campus viewed and treated Chicano students, and also a sincere examination into the free and open engagement of white students in a world that was created for them. He writes:

> Reflect, if you will, on what it must mean to be black, or brown, in a white man's world. A world of uplifted eyebrows, of curling lips, of knowing looks and icily polite condescension. A world of discomfort, of juiceless toleration, of prejudice so terribly subtle as to deny its articulation. And, always you will hear the plaintive cry of the white man: "Why can't you be more like us? Why can't you go through channels? When are your people going to go through the mainstream?" And so you would try; you would go to college; you would study hard, make good grades, star on the athletic teams. But you would hear many say college means more than that. College means participation, college means involvement, college means activity, college means a say-so in what goes on.
>
> But you would remain alone, silent because no one spoke for you, powerless because no one thought to include you in the councils of power, impotent because white students didn't realize—in their passion to be thought liberal and all-knowing—that they could not speak and act for you precisely the same reason old people cannot speak for young people. Here the issues are clearly defined—the right of all students to be given the representation they personally deserve, the right to say "I, too, exist."[49]

For Chicano students at FSC in 1968 the right to freely express their concerns in protest, speech, and the written word was not freely given; as seen in the Morton case, their free expression was an attainment fraught with struggle. Gilliam's viewpoint is telling: a white student on the side of power who sees Chicano students as powerless without the aid of white students. In his interpretation, unless white students include Chicanos in the power structure, unless they give Chicanos a platform for their voice, Chicanos will remain powerless and voiceless. Chicanas like Lea Ybarra were not going to wait for the white power structure to do this—they were going to seize it. Seizing a platform for Chicano concerns also meant facing head-on conservative groups at FSC. The Aggies, or agricultural students, at FSC were one of the conservative groups that Chicanos contended with on several occasions. Indeed, the Aggies were more than merely one group of conservative students; they represented traditional Valley mores; they represented a vast agricultural industry that viewed Mexicans as a much-needed labor force, yet as unfit for citizenship and certainly not fit to be educated alongside future farm leaders; they represented a college bulwark against the grape boycott. If Chicanos at FSC took on the mission to support César Chávez and the boycott, then the Aggies also felt a personal mission to speak and act out against those forces they believed would destroy their industry—Chicanos and their support of the UFW.

On November 13, 1968, Phil Sagaser, the agricultural senator to the Student Senate, introduced a resolution at the Senate meeting opposing the grape boycott.[50] In doing so, Sagaser acted as the unofficial voice of the Agricultural Department and spokesman for his fellow Aggies at FSC. The resolution was a symbolic show of solidarity with the growers who were at odds with the UFW, and also a direct challenge to a new growing force on campus—Chicano students, with demands.[51] Sagaser's resolution stated that the success of the boycott could lead to "similar boycotts into other product fields within agriculture," and called on "the Fresno State College Senate to go on record in opposition to the boycott of California's grapes and grape products."[52] The Student Senate accepted Sagaser's resolution in a 15–11 vote—with one abstention—condemning the boycott.

Moments after the Senate adopted the resolution, a group of twenty Chicano students led by Guillermo Martínez stormed into the meeting, chanting "Nosotros venceremos," "Viva la Raza," "Viva la Huelga," and "Down with the pigs."[53] The Senate was forced to adjourn when the demonstration carried on for fifteen minutes. As part of the group, Lea Ybarra said the resolution "ignores the troubles of the farm workers. . . . One of the problems is that not everybody gets an equal share and this is especially true as far as the farm boycott is concerned."[54] Another Chicano student, Steve Santos, voiced his opinion that "the farm worker is excluded from the basic right that all workers have to unionize . . . this is social injustice."[55] Aggies also voiced their thoughts on the matter. One freshman class senator said, "César Chávez organized the boycott after he was not able to organize the workers. The movement is an attempt to force unions on the farmer."[56] Steve Pavich, a sophomore agricultural student and son of a Valley grape grower said, "My father is a Delano grape grower and since the strike we have had one worker out of 100 go on strike."[57] Pavich added, "The strike is fictitious. It is not our fault the farm workers are at the bottom of the ladder. If they aren't happy, why do they keep working?"[58] In the end, College Union senator Bill Enns noted, "This matter should have never been brought here. What effect do we (the Student Senate) have?"[59] Indeed, although lacking real application, the adoption of the resolution condemning the boycott had tangible meaning on campus and throughout the Valley. The next day, Student Senate president Bruce Bronzan vetoed the resolution, saying, "I feel we didn't gain any mileage by taking a stand on it. . . . We didn't gain any political ground at this time if we come out in favor of the boycott. If we support the resolution to go against the boycott we are splitting our own campus."[60] Nevertheless, a Pandora's box had been opened, and there was no going back. The incident strengthened positions for and against the boycott among various groups, including the Aggies, the athletic department, Greek fraternities, and Chicana/os. One student reporter referred to the boycott on campus as "a festering sore."[61]

On November 14, the next day after the Student Senate passed the resolution, a group of sixty Chicano student protestors, including the Brown Berets, marched on campus carrying a banner that read "Justice or Revolution!" Shouting "Don't buy grapes," "Viva la Raza," "Viva la Huelga," and "Chicano power," the group first filled President Ness's outer office, then marched through campus past several campus buildings, and through hallways where classes were being conducted, marching finally through both floors of the library, all the while shouting slogans.[62] The march ended in a rally, where the protestors issued a statement that the Senate "has blindly refused to recognize the fact that the grape boycott involves much more than just an economic struggle; it is a long and hard fight for social justice by the farm worker."[63]

The Chicano statement included:

> Economics is what has left these people out of democracy. Their exclusion of the right to arbitrate the wrong has stripped them totally of any kind of method of participating and bargaining in society. The grape boycott is the only recourse the farm worker has. These people are only trying to determine their destiny. . . . When a college community not only refused to recognize the fact but covers it with a resolution based strictly on economics, then it has not only become insensitive but it has become inhuman.[64]

While Chicano students marched through Fresno State chanting slogans in favor of the boycott, Aggies rolled onto campus with a truckload of FSC-grown table grapes. One of the Aggies began to throw grapes at Chicano students as they walked past the truck. The grapes were then taken to a section between the Student Union and cafeteria where the marching Chicanos held a rally. There the Aggies began to pass out grapes to passerby students as a gesture of condemning the grape boycott and opposing the marching Chicano students. As Aggies passed out grapes, Chicano students from the march entered the area—they had been told by a Chicana that she was pelted with grapes by the Aggies from their truck. Arguments ensued; the Aggies pelted a few Chicano students during the verbal altercation; emotions ran high and nearly turned into violence. In the aftermath, crushed grapes and ripped-apart signs carried by the Chicanos littered the floor.[65]

If the resolution angered Chicano students, their demonstration and march across campus stirred the ire of conservatives on and off campus. As one FSC student said concerning the march: "It gave the protestors a chance to make their ideas heard and it made a lot of people mad, the marchers think this is great. I don't. Hooray for them (maybe), but now hear a voice from the other side."[66] The student went on: "This planned chaos was a direct transgression against the rights of others. The time has come when such rabble-rousing should be stopped by appropriate legal action."[67] He then went on to compare Chicano students to weeds that need to be plucked out, not just any weed, but marijuana plants growing across the pristine lawns of white Fresnans: "When no action is taken by those in authority to squelch disobedience the seeds of anarchy are sown."[68] Agricultural and horticultural metaphors and allusions are a common cultural literary device in the Valley's rhetoric, and it is not surprising that Chicanos were likened to a bad plant: "The young weed of strife has already germinated here at FSC and if it isn't soon uprooted the next step will be a whole lot of loco weed on our lawn."[69]

In late November 1968, FSC president Ness, under pressure from conservative forces—including old guard professors who stood as a wall against progressive programs like the EOP (Educational Opportunity Program) and the Experimental College—issued a statement defending his stance not to punish the Chicano demonstrators.[70] Ness called for rational dialogue on an "intellectual and not a physical level." He stated, "we must earnestly seek ways of meeting the reasonable grievances of those who may feel, rightly or wrongly, that no other ways are open to them except through disruptive action."[71]

During the spring semester in March 1969 Chicano students presented to President Ness a list of eleven demands. These demands included, among other things, EOP funding issues, that FSC take an official stand in favor of the grape boycott, that an immediate investigation be made into the Financial Aid Office (because of its assistance with Police Chief Morton's list), and that "Blacks and Chicanos shall have complete control of one edition of the Collegian every two weeks."[72] Although the EOP demands were reasonably met, Ness replied that FSC could not take an official stand on the grape boycott either for or against. He also denied their demand to take control of the *Daily Collegian*, stating that he did not believe that was the correct course of action, but he did support their inclusion in the newspaper. This was not acceptable to Chicano students, who clamored to be heard in their own version of the newspaper. Again, on April 10, Guillermo Martínez led a group of Black and Chicano students in presenting a proposal to the campus publications board for control of two issues per month of the *Daily Collegian* newspaper. Once again their demand was not met. Dr. Harold Walker, executive vice president of FSC, presented President Ness's official response to the Black and Chicano students. It was the same response Ness had issued a month earlier. Finally, on May 2, 1969, the FSC Board of Publications passed a resolution giving the Chicano and Black students control of one four-page issue per week of the school newspaper, the *Daily Collegian*, starting in the fall semester, 1969.[73] The intent of the board was to give Black and Chicano students control of one edition every week until the time came when their special "separatist" edition could be dissolved and minority student issues would be included in the regular edition.[74] Three days later on May 5, Cinco de Mayo, Chicanos published the first edition of *La Pluma Morena*, later to be called *La Voz*.[75] The old, tired, Porfirio Díaz–era holiday of Cinco de Mayo found fresh reason for celebration. John Ramírez, the editor of the first edition, stated: "There is no other way, because minority views are not respected. Preempting the *Collegian* will provide the most impact, and there will be no animosity of conflict that will come from a mixed publication." Ramírez added: "we feel that we should be heard as a voice independent of the *Collegian*."[76]

Control of the campus newspaper twice a month represented a major victory in the struggle for Chicano rights at FSC and the wider San Joaquin Valley. Yet many more battles into the 1970s would occur on campus, and sometimes violent clashes on campus and in the fields alongside Chávez and the UFW. As Lea Ybarra noted, "We were constantly fighting for our program. We were constantly fighting for existence." Ybarra also remembered Central Valley police brutality during the lettuce boycott in the early seventies: "And those same ugly red-faced faces I saw as a student in high school shouting against Black children trying to get into a school were the same faces I saw there. That same kind of anger—they had so much hatred towards us. You could see it in their faces—the sheriff's department."[77]

For many Chicanas/os present on campus, it was a life-transforming journey from being the sons and daughters of field-workers who grew up occupying a defined economic and cultural niche created by growers to becoming activists clamoring that their voices be heard. They raised their voices on campus, at GOP campaign rallies, were confronted by groups like the Aggies, and demanded changes from the FSC president. As one Chicano student present during the 1968–69 events noted: "We were energized finally, that we were something, that we were going to make a difference. And that we would go out and help our brothers and sisters. We made a pact that when we left Fresno State, we would go back into our communities."[78]

NOTES

1. Eleazar Risco brought to Fresno State a radicalism rooted in Cuban history and, specifically, the Cuban Revolution. Risco was born in Santiago de Cuba, a province historically rich in revolutionary movements and ideas. Risco recalled that his home region was "where most of the movements against the Spaniards developed, where the guerra against Bastista developed; the Moncada attacked by Castro and his people, the Moncada was about five blocks from my house." Santiago de Cuba's radical culture was the "environment in which I grew up." Risco added. "Those were ideas that were constantly being argued. . . . Some of the people that had been classmates of my uncles and aunts in college, they were involved in, you know, pretty radical stuff." Risco, transcript of an oral history conducted in 2016 by Patrick Fontes. Risco fled Cuba following the capture and assassination of revolutionary organizer Frank País in 1957. According to Risco, his name appeared on a list of radicals connected with Frank País and the revolution. Before the government called in Risco for questioning, Baptist Church leaders (Risco grew up within the Baptist Church in Cuba) granted him a two-year scholarship in the United States. After his two-year scholarship in Kansas, Risco ventured to California.
2. *La Pluma Morena* was the title of the first Chicano-run newspaper edition. This was the only instance where this title was used. Not long after, the title was changed to *Chicano Liberation*, then at last to *La Voz de Aztlan*.
3. *La Pluma Morena*, May 5, 1969.
4. *La Pluma Morena*, May 5, 1969, 3.
5. *La Pluma Morena*, May 5, 1969, 3.
6. *La Pluma Morena*, May 5, 1969, 3.
7. *La Pluma Morena*, May 5, 1969, 3.
8. *La Pluma Morena*, May 5, 1969, 3.
9. *La Pluma Morena*, May 5, 1969, 2.

10. From November 6, 1968, until March 21, 1969, San Francisco State experienced the longest student strike on a college campus in the United States. As tensions ran high between Black and white students, the administration, and police, violent conflict broke out on several occasions. "Strike Escalation: SF State, in Recess, Faces More Turmoil," *Fresno Bee*, November 9, 1968, 6; "Student, Police Violence Triggers SF State Closing," *Fresno Bee*, November 14, 1968, 1.

11. John A. Crawford, "Letters from the People: Says the Tail Wags Dog," *Fresno Bee*, November 20, 1968, 18.

12. Crawford, "Letters from the People," 18.

13. California State University, Bakersfield, was founded in 1965, and opened for classes in 1970. Fresno State was originally founded as Fresno Normal School in 1911, becoming Fresno State College in 1947, and finally California State University, Fresno, in 1972. Although Fresno State College was the only four-year college in the region, Fresno City College was established in Fresno in 1910 as California's first community college. Many Chicano students who would enter FSC in the late 1960s and 1970s were first students at Fresno City College.

14. *La Pluma Morena*, May 5, 1969, 3.

15. Gloria Hernandez, interview by author, May 5, 2017.

16. Hernandez, interview.

17. Lea Ybarra, interview, Chicano Legacy of Fresno County, April 23, 2017, http://chicanolegacy.com/dr-lea-ybarra/.

18. Kenneth A. Seib, *The Slow Death of Fresno State: A California Campus Under Reagan and Brown* (Palo Alto, Calif.: Ramparts Press, 1979), 19.

19. Carmen George, "This Champion for Migrants Opened Health Clinics, Started Chicano Studies at Fresno State," *Fresno Bee*, June 23, 2017; Caribbean Fragoza, "La Raza: The Community Newspaper That Became a Political Platform," KCET, April 4, 2018, https://www.kcet.org/shows/artbound/la-raza-the-community-newspaper-that-became-a-political-platform.

20. According to Risco, in an interview, he wrote most of the Plan de Delano while up late one night with Luis Valdéz.

21. "Nixon: Fresno Talk," *Fresno Bee Republican*, September 18, 1968, A1, A6.

22. "Nixon: Fresno Talk."

23. "Grape Boycotters Rough on Nixon," *Detroit Free Press*, September 19, 1968, 10.

24. "Farm Workers Heckle Nixon in Fresno Talk," *Daily Collegian*, September 19, 1968; "Grape Unit Heckles at Nixon Talk," *Pasadena Independent*, September 19, 1968, 1.

25. "Grape Boycotters Rough on Nixon," 10.

26. "Grape Boycotters Rough on Nixon," 10.

27. "Grape Boycotters Rough on Nixon," 10.

28. "Morton Says Police Will Act to Bar Unruly Political Protests," *Fresno Bee Republican*, September 27, 1968, 1B.

29. "Police Action at Nixon Fete Draws Ortega Ire," *Fresno Bee Republican*, September 20, 1968, 17A.

30. "Police Action at Nixon Fete."

31. "Nixon Backs Growers in Labor Dispute in California," *Palladium-Item*, September 19, 1968.

32. "Nixon Backs Growers"; "Nixon's Backers' Cheers Drown Out Hecklers' Jeers," *Fresno Bee Republican*, September 19, 1968, 1.

33. "Police," *Fresno Bee*, September 20, 1969, 20.

34. "Nixon: Fresno Talk," A1, A6.

35. "Nixon: Fresno Talk."

36. "Police Action at Nixon Fete."

37. "Police Action at Nixon Fete."

38. "Police Action at Nixon Fete."

39. "Police Action at Nixon Fete."

40. "Morton Says Police Will Act," 4B.

41. "Candidates' Triumphant Day," *Fresno Bee*, September 19, 1968, 8.

42. "9 FSC Students on Police Watch List," *Daily Collegian*, October 1, 1968, 1.

43. Eric Gilliam, "Inside Morton's Action," *Daily Collegian*, October 4, 1968, 2.

44. Gilliam, "Inside Morton's Action."

45. Dennis McCall, "Chief Morton's List Draws Criticism," *Daily Collegian*, October 3, 1968, 1.

46. McCall, "Chief Morton's List," 1.

47. "Chicanos Demand the Firing of Lewis," *Daily Collegian*, October 11, 1968, 1.

48. Russell Sivick, "YAF Replies," letter to the editor, *Daily Collegian*, October 8, 1968, 2.

49. Eric W. Gilliam, "I, Too, Exist," *Daily Collegian*, October 11, 1969, 3.

50. Phillis Martin, "Student Senate Opposes Boycott Chicanos Balk," *Daily Collegian*, November 14, 1968, 1. The FSC Student Senate was the only one in California to adopt a resolution in opposition to the grape boycott. For example, the student senates at UC Berkeley and San Francisco State took firm stands supporting the boycott.

51. On September 3, 1968, the Fresno County Board of Supervisors issued a counter boycott against any city or state that backed the boycott of California table grapes. "County Orders Table Grape Counterboycott," *Fresno Bee Republican*, September 3, 1968, 1.

52. "Student Senate," *Daily Collegian*, November 13, 1968, 3.

53. "Student Senate."

54. "Student Senate."

55. "Student Senate."

56. "Student Senate."

57. "Student Senate."

58. "Student Senate."

59. "Student Senate."

60. Dennis McCall, "Senate Opens Pandora's Box," *Daily Collegian*, November 15, 1968, 1.

61. Gerald Merrel, "Grape Boycott Issue Gives Rise to Demonstrations," *Daily Collegian*, November 15, 1968, 1.

62. "Student Senate"; Martin, "Student Senate Opposes."
63. McCall, "Senate Opens Pandora's Box," 2.
64. McCall, "Senate Opens Pandora's Box," 2.
65. Merrel, "Grape Boycott Issue."
66. Paul Sullivan Jr., "Impressions," *Daily Collegian*, November 19, 1968, 3.
67. Sullivan, "Impressions."
68. Sullivan, "Impressions."
69. Sullivan, "Impressions."
70. A group of professors had called for immediate disciplinary action against the Chicano marchers, including expulsion.
71. Frederic W. Ness, "President Ness's Statement," *Daily Collegian*, November 25, 1968, 2. Over the next few months, scuffles between the Chicano students and Aggies took place on campus, never with serious injuries to either party, although the early 1970s would witness an escalation in violence between the two groups.
72. "Ness Makes Reply to Student Demands," Daily Collegian, April 8, 1969, 1.
73. Chicano and Black students alternated, so that each group had complete control of the newspaper every other week. The Black-student-run edition was titled *UHURU*.
74. Pat Halpern, "Minority Demand Met," *Daily Collegian*, May 5, 1969, 1.
75. The first edition was titled *La Pluma Morena*, with several more titled *Chicano Liberation*, and at last *La Voz de Aztlan*, published on December 15, 1969.
76. Halpern, "Minority Demand Met," 1.
77. Ybarra, *interview*.
78. Eva and Joaquin Patino, interview by author, July 27, 2015.

AFTERWORD

MARIO T. GARCÍA AND ELLEN MCCRACKEN

THE CHICANO Movement is a seminal social movement in Chicano history and in American history. For Chicanos, and by extension other Latinos, it marked a political coming of age. The movement forced the U.S. body politic to recognize the Chicano and Latino populations of the country as major political players. They no longer could be ignored. Since the Chicano Movement, the political influence and power of the Chicano/Latino population has continued to increase. While the movement had tapered by the end of the 1970s, its spirit of struggle and of a more humane and democratic society has lived on. Inspired by the movement, contemporary Chicanos/ Latinos, for the most part, support a progressive agenda. This includes immigration rights, civil rights, voters' rights, health care for all, a good and relevant education for all, college for all, economic equality, women's rights, gay rights, transsexual rights, human rights, and nonintervention in the affairs of other nations. Chicanos/Latinos represent one of the most progressive ethnic groups in the country. This is the legacy of the Chicano Movement. Chicanos are also a growing population and will continue to influence the political, economic, and cultural present as well as future of the United States.

The history of the Chicano Movement also reminds us that Chicano history is important not only because of the movement, but because people of Mexican and Latino descent in this country have always been major contributors to American history. Chicano history, for example, is not a new history or the result of a new ethnic group. Mexican Americans have been a vital part of what becomes American history since the 1500s in areas such as the Southwest and California that would become parts of the United States. As workers, Chicanos and other Latinos, both U.S.-born and immigrants, have historically produced much of the economic richness of the country. Chicanos/Latinos have given their blood, sweat, and tears for this country—the United States. They have spilled their blood in defense of the United States. Chicanos/Latinos are as American as any other ethnic group. They have been American history from day one.

The profound history of the movement, so well expressed in the essays in *Rewriting the Chicano Movement*, further reminds us of the challenge of integrating Chicano history into our curricula at all levels. This book, the history of the Chicano Movement, and Chicano history in general should not be relegated to Chicano Studies departments. They need to be part of the curriculum at the university level in both the humanities and social sciences. They should be integrated in general U.S. history courses as well as in courses dealing with American ethnicity, race, immigration, labor, gender, and civil rights, to mention only some areas. The excuse can no longer be that there are not sufficient scholarly publications, because that simply is not true. The number of publications in Chicano history and in other areas of Chicano studies has been nothing short of phenomenal, with new texts appearing each year, each month. As we advance into the twenty-first century, when this country will become composed primarily of people of color, we will need a fully integrated American history to be taught. This includes Chicano and Latino history. But this integration cannot be only at the university level. It also has to be in the K–12 curriculum, especially since in many locations in the country the majority of students are Chicanos and Latinos. They need to learn this history. As Sal Castro often said, "a kid who doesn't know about his history and culture and be proud of it will fail." We cannot allow this. We call on teachers and administrators, many of them Chicanos and Latinos, to move to integrate this history into curricula at all levels to reflect the Chicano/Latino experience. This cannot be left to chance; it has to be mandated and enforced.

The history of the Chicano Movement can likewise serve as an inspiration for new social movements today. These can be inspired by the movement as well as learn much about commitment, dedication, resilience, and strategies from it. Today we need not so much a new Chicano Movement, but movements from all ethnic groups to protect, defend, and expand American democracy. During the last few years under the Trump administration the very future of our democracy has been endangered. But it is not only Trump. It is a system that makes the rich and powerful more rich and powerful and relegates the rest to uncertain futures. We cannot allow such a system to continue and American democracy be further endangered and possibly destroyed. Good Americans of all ethnic backgrounds can join with the spirit of the Chicano Movement and say "Basta!"—Enough! We need to regain our democracy, but it has to be a people's democracy in the way that the Chicano Movement proposed. A democracy of and for the people and not the elites, corporate tycoons, and their political agents. We call for the spirit and the ethos of the Chicano Movement to be revitalized and spread throughout the country. We can do it! ¡Sí se puede!

This edited volume emerged from the Sal Castro memorial conferences held biannually in Santa Barbara since 2012. The conference is dedicated to the memory and spirit of Sal Castro, a great American and a great Chicano who had the courage to demand the school system provide a good and equitable education for Chicano students. That spirit has encouraged us in putting together this book. In one form or another, the contributors to this volume and other scholars who research and write Chicano history will work to perpetuate Sal's place in history and meet his challenge for all of us to be "change makers."

As we write these words in April of 2020, we are living through the darkness of one of the worst pandemics in history. But we write these words with confidence that we will all surmount this crisis and that we as a people throughout the world will go forward and make a better world especially for our children and grandchildren like baby Luca, our grandson. Be well and be safe.

CONTRIBUTORS

Holly Barnet-Sanchez is emerita associate professor of modern Latin American and Chicano/a and Latino/a art history at the University of New Mexico. The author of several publications focusing on Chicano/a murals and graphic arts, her most recent co-authored book is *Give Me Life: Iconography and Identity in East L.A. Murals*.

Tim Drescher is an independent scholar specializing in community murals and political posters. His publications include *San Francisco Bay Area Murals: Communities Create Their Muses, 1904–1997*. He is the co-author of *Give Me Life: Iconography and Identity in East L.A. Murals*.

Jesús Jesse Esparza is an assistant professor of history at Texas Southern University. His area of expertise is the history of Latinos in the United States, with an emphasis on civil rights. His current book project is "Raza Schools: Latino Educational Autonomy and Activism in Texas, 1920–1980."

Patrick Fontes received his PhD in American history from Stanford University. His research interests include Chicano history, U.S. immigration history, twentieth-century youth subcultures, and Central California history. He teaches at Clovis Community College in Fresno, California.

Mario T. García is distinguished professor of Chicano studies and history at the University of California, Santa Barbara. He is the author of over twenty books on Chicano history, including *The Making of a Mexican American Mayor: Raymond L. Telles of El Paso and the Origins of Latino Political Power.*

Tiffany Jasmin González earned her PhD in history from Texas A&M University, College Station, and earned an accolade from the American Association of University Women for her dissertation, "Representation for a Change: Women in Government and the Chicana/o Movement in Texas." Tiffany holds the Bonquois Postdoctoral Fellow in Women's History at the Newcomb Institute of Tulane University.

Ellen McCracken is professor of Spanish and Portuguese at the University of California, Santa Barbara. She is the author of several books on Chicano literature, including *New Latina Narrative: The Feminine Space of Postmodern Ethnicity.* She is the co-author of *Roque's Corner: The Life and Times of Roque García and His Santa Fe.*

Juan Pablo Mercado received his PhD from UCLA and teaches Chicana/o history at Chabot College and San José State University. His research focuses on the uses and function of public art.

Andrea Muñoz received her BA in Chicana and Chicano studies at the University of California, Santa Barbara. She is a Teach for America member and after her teaching commitment will attend graduate school.

Michael Anthony Turcios is completing his PhD in cinema and media studies in the School of Cinematic Arts at USC. He specializes in the visual and literary culture of subaltern groups from the Global South. His dissertation is "Art of Displacement: Decolonial Visual and Literary Culture in the East Los Angeles Barrios and the Banlieues of Paris, France."

Omar Valerio-Jiménez is an associate professor of history at the University of Texas at San Antonio. He is the author of *River of Hope: Forging Identity and Nation in the Río Grande Borderlands.* His current book project is "Remembering Conquest: Mexican Americans, Memory, and Citizenship."

INDEX

Note: Photographs and other illustrations are shown by page numbers in italics; *n* denotes an endnote number.